THE ROMANCE OF WORDS

THE ROMANCE OF WORDS

BY ERNEST WEEKLEY, M.A.

PROFESSOR OF FRENCH AND HEAD OF THE MODERN LANGUAGE
DEPARTMENT AT UNIVERSITY COLLEGE, NOTTINGHAM; SOMETIME
SCHOLAR OF TRINITY COLLEGE, CAMBRIDGE; AUTHOR OF "THE
ROMANCE OF NAMES," "SURNAMES"

"Vous savez le latin, sans doute?"—
"Oui, mais faites comme si je ne le savais pas."
(MOLIÈRE, *Le Bourgeois Gentilhomme*, ii. 6.)

LONDON
JOHN MURRAY, ALBEMARLE STREET, W.

9999057403

First Edition	.	.	.	.	.	.	March 1912
Reprinted	.	.	.	.	.	.	June 1912
Second Edition, Revised and Enlarged	.	November 1913
Third Edition	.	.	.	.	.	.	May 1917
Fourth Edition	.	.	.	.	.	January 1922
Reprinted	.	.	.	.	.	.	February 1925
Reprinted	.	.	.	.	.	January 1927

PREFACE

A LONG and somewhat varied experience in language teaching has convinced me that there are still, in spite of the march of science, many people who are capable of getting intellectual pleasure from word-history. I hope that to such people this little book, the amusement of occasional leisure, will not be unwelcome. It differs, I believe, from any other popular book on language in that it deals essentially with the origins of words, and makes no attempt to enforce a moral. My aim has been to select especially the unexpected in etymology, "things not generally known," such as the fact that *Tammany* was an Indian chief, that *assegai* occurs in Chaucer, that *jilt* is identical with *Juliet*, that *brazil* wood is not named from *Brazil*, that to *curry favour* means to comb down a horse of a particular colour, and so forth. The treatment is made as simple as possible, a bowing acquaintance with Latin and French being all that is assumed, though words from many other languages are necessarily included. In the case of each word I have traced the history just so far back as it is likely to be of interest to the reader who is not a philological specialist.

I have endeavoured to state each proposition in its simplest terms, without enumerating all the reservations and indirect factors which belong to the history of almost every word.

The chapter headings only indicate in a general way the division of the subject matter, the arrangement of

which has been determined rather by the natural association which exists between words. The quotations are,
with few exceptions, drawn from my own reading. They
come from very varied sources, but archaic words are
exemplified, when possible, from authors easily accessible, generally Shakespeare or Milton, or, for revived
archaisms, Scott. In illustrating obsolete meanings I
have made much use of the earliest dictionaries[1]
available.

It seemed undesirable to load a small work of this
kind with references. The writer on word-lore must of
necessity build on what has already been done, happy if
he can add a few bricks to the edifice. But philologists
will recognise that this book is not, in the etymological
sense, a mere compilation,[2] and that a considerable
portion of the information it contains is here printed for
the first time in a form accessible to the general reader.[3]
Chapter VII., on Semantics, is, so far as I know, the
first attempt at a simple treatment of a science which
is now admitted to an equality with phonetics, and
which to most people is much more interesting.

Throughout I have used the *New English Dictionary*,
in the etymological part of which I have for some years
had a humble share, for purposes of verification. Without the materials furnished by the historical method of
that great national work, which is now complete from
A to R, this book would not have been attempted.
For words in S to Z, I have referred chiefly to
Professor Skeat's *Etymological Dictionary* (4th ed.,
Oxford, 1910).

---

[1] For a list of these see p. xii.

[2] *Compilatio*, " pillage, polling, robbing " (Cooper).

[3] Among words on which the reader will find either entirely new
information or a modification of generally accepted views are *akimbo, anlace,
branks, caulk, cockney, felon* (a whitlow), *foil, kestrel, lugger, mulligrubs,
mystery* (a craft), *oriel, patch, petronel, salet, sentry, sullen, tret,* etc.

It is not many years since what passed for etymology in this country was merely a congeries of wild guesses and manufactured anecdotes. The persistence with which these crop up in the daily paper and the class-room must be my excuse for "slaying the slain" in Chapter XIII. Some readers may regret the disappearance of these fables, but a little study will convince them that in the life of words, as in that of men, truth is stranger than fiction.

ERNEST WEEKLEY.

NOTTINGHAM, *January* 1912.

PREFACE TO THE SECOND EDITION

ON its first publication this little book was very kindly treated by both reviewers and readers. The only criticism of any importance was directed against its conciseness. There seemed to be a consensus of expert opinion that, the book being intended for the non-specialist, the compression was a little too severe, and likely sometimes to lead to misunderstanding. I have tried to remedy this defect in the present edition, both by giving fuller explanations and by supplying further quotations in illustration of the less common words and uses. No absolutely new matter is introduced, but a number of fresh words have been added as examples of points already noticed. The general arrangement of the book remains unchanged, except that a few paragraphs have been shifted to what seemed more natural positions.

Friendly correspondents in all parts of the world, to many of whom I must apologise for my failure to answer their letters, have sent me information of interest and value. In some cases I have been able to make use of such information for this edition. Many readers have called my attention to local and American survivals of words and meanings described as obsolete. This is a subject on which a great deal could be written, but it lies outside the plan of this book, which does not aspire to do more than furnish some instruction or entertainment to those who are interested in the curiosities of etymology.

ERNEST WEEKLEY.

PREFACE TO THE THIRD EDITION

IT is just five years since this little book was first submitted to the toleration of word-lovers, a class much more numerous than the author had suspected. The second edition, revised and slightly enlarged, appeared in 1913. Since then the text has once more been subjected to a searching revision, and it is hoped that the book now contains no statement which is not in accord with common sense and the present state of philological knowledge. Only those who have experience of such work know how easy it is to stray unconsciously from the exact truth in publishing the results of etymological research. Moreover, new light is constantly being thrown on old problems, and theories long triumphant have occasionally to yield to fresh evidence. To take an example from this volume, the traditional derivation of *trousers* from French *trousse* is now shown by the *New English Dictionary* to be chronologically improbable. That great and cautious work unhesitatingly describes *hatchment* as a corruption of *achievement*, but Professor Derocquigny, of Lille, has shown (*Modern Language Review*, January 1913) that this etymology is "preposterous," *hachement* being a good old French word which in 16th century English was ignorantly confused with *achievement*. Apart from these two etymologies,[1] the only essential alterations have been made in the chapter on Surnames (p. 170), further research in medieval records having convinced the author that most of what has been written about "corrupted" surnames is nonsense, and that no nickname is too fantastic to be genuine.[2] Two slight contemplated alterations have not been carried out. The adjective applied (p. 156) to a contemporary ruler seemed to need reconsideration, but the author was baffled by the *embarras du choix*. A word mentioned on p. 48 might gracefully have been omitted, but it is likely that the illustrious man alluded to would, if the page should ever accidentally meet his eye, only chuckle at the thought of time's revenges.

In the interval since the last edition of the *Romance of Words* the greatest *Romance of Deeds* in our story has been written in the blood of our noblest and best.

---

[1] In spite of the fact that the *New English Dictionary* now finds *shark* applied to the fish some years before the first record of *shark*, a sharper, parasite, I adhere to my belief that the latter is the earlier sense. The new example quoted, from a Tudor "broadside," is more suggestive of a sailor's apt nickname than of zoological nomenclature—"There is no proper name for it that I knowe, but that sertayne men of Captayne Haukinses doth call it a *sharke*" (1569).

[2] See the author's *Surnames* (John Murray, 1916), especially pp. 177-83.

Only a sense of proportion withholds the author from dedicating this new edition to the glorious memory of his many old pupils dead on the field of honour. Nothing in the modest success of the book has given him so much pleasure as the fact, to which his correspondence bears witness, that his little contribution to word-lore has helped to amuse the convalescence of more than one stricken fighting-man.

ERNEST WEEKLEY.

NOTTINGHAM, *March* 1917.

PREFACE TO THE FOURTH EDITION

IN preparing a new edition of this little book, ten years after its first appearance, I have corrected a few slight inaccuracies which had been overlooked in earlier revisions, and modified or expanded some statements which were not quite consonant with the present state of etymological knowledge.   In word-lore, as in other sciences, it is seldom safe to lay down the law without a little conscientious "hedging." The only two considerable alterations have to do with the word *snickersnee*, the history of which is now clearly traced, and the name *Bendigo*. It is rather strange that no reader or reviewer has ever put me right on the subject of this Nottingham worthy, for the facts are plainly stated in the *Dictionary of National Biography*.

ERNEST WEEKLEY.

NOTTINGHAM, *January* 1922.

CONTENTS

xi

The following dictionaries are quoted without further reference :—

Palsgrave, French and English (1530).
Cooper, Latin and English (1573).
Percyvall, Spanish and English (1591).
Florio, Italian and English (1598).
Cotgrave, French and English (1611).
Torriano, Italian and English (1659).
Hexham, Dutch and English (1660).
Ludwig, German and English (1716).

THE ROMANCE OF WORDS

CHAPTER I

OUR VOCABULARY

THE bulk of our literary language is Latin, and consists of words either borrowed directly or taken from "learned" French forms. The every-day vocabulary of the less educated is of Old English, commonly called Anglo-Saxon, origin; and from the same source comes what we may call the machinery of the language, *i.e.*, its inflexions, numerals, pronouns, prepositions, and conjunctions. Along with Anglo-Saxon, we find a considerable number of words from the related Norse languages, this element being naturally strongest in the dialects of the north and east of England. The third great element of our working vocabulary is furnished by Old French, *i.e.*, the language naturally developed from the spoken Latin of the Roman soldiers and colonists, generally called Vulgar Latin. To its composite character English owes its unequalled richness in expression. For most ideas we have three separate terms, or groups of terms, which, often starting from the same metaphor, serve to express different shades of meaning. Thus a deed done with malice *prepense* (an Old French compound from Lat. *pensare*, to weigh), is *deliberate* or *pondered*, both Latin words which mean literally

A

"weighed"; but the four words convey four distinct shades of meaning. The Gk. *sympathy* is Lat. *compassion*, rendered in English by *fellow-feeling*.

Sometimes a native word has been completely supplanted by a loan word, *e.g.*, Anglo-Sax. *here*, army (*cf.* Ger. *Heer*), gave way to Old Fr. (*h*)*ost* (p. 158). This in its turn was replaced by *army*, Fr. *armée*, which, like its Spanish doublet *armada*, is really a feminine past participle with some word for host, band, etc., understood. *Here* has survived in *Hereford*, *harbour* (p. 164), *harbinger* (p. 90), etc., and in the verb *harry* (*cf.* Ger. *verheeren*, to harry).

Or a native word may persist in some special sense, *e.g.*, *weed*, a general term for garment in Shakespeare—

> "And there the snake throws her enamel'd skin,
> *Weed* wide enough to wrap a fairy in"
> (*Midsummer Night's Dream*, ii. 2.)

survives in "widow's *weeds*." *Chare*, a turn of work—

> "the maid that milks
> And does the meanest *chares*."
> (*Antony and Cleopatra*, iv. 15.)

has given us *charwoman*, and persists as American *chore*—

> "Sharlee was . . . concluding the post-prandial *chores*."
> (H. S. HARRISON, *Queed*, Ch. 17.)

Sake, cognate with Ger. *Sache*, thing, cause, and originally meaning a contention at law, has been replaced by *cause*, except in phrases beginning with the preposition *for*. See also *bead* (p. 74). *Unkempt*, uncombed, and *uncouth*, unknown, are fossil remains of obsolete verb forms.

In addition to these main constituents of our language, we have borrowed words, sometimes in

considerable numbers, sometimes singly and accidentally, from almost every tongue known to mankind, and
every year sees new words added to our vocabulary.
The following chapters deal especially with words
borrowed from Old French and from the other
Romance languages, their origins and journeyings,
and the various accidents that have befallen them in
English. It is in such words as these that the romance
of language is best exemplified, because we can usually
trace their history from Latin to modern English, while
the earlier history of Anglo-Saxon words is a matter
for the philologist.

Words borrowed directly from Latin or Greek lack
this intermediate experience, though the study of their
original meanings is full of surprises. This, however,
is merely a question of opening a Latin or Greek
dictionary, if we have not time for the moment's
reflexion which would serve the same purpose. Thus,
to take a dozen examples at random, to *abominate* [1] is to
turn shuddering from the evil *omen*, a *generous* man is a
man of " race " (*genus*), an *innuendo* can be conveyed
" by nodding," to *insult* is to " jump on," a *legend* is
something " to be read," a *manual* is a " hand-book," an
obligation is essentially " binding," to *relent* is to " go
slow," *rivals* are people living by the same " stream " [2]
(*rivus*), a *salary* is an allowance for " salt " (*sal*), a
supercilious man is fond of lifting his " eyebrows "
(*supercilium*), and a *trivial* matter is so commonplace
that it can be picked up at the meeting of " three ways "
(*trivium*). *Dexterity* implies skill with the " right " hand
(*dexter*), while *sinister* preserves the superstition of the
ill-omened " left."

---

[1] *Abominable* is regularly spelt *abhominable* in late Old French and
Mid. English, as though meaning " inhuman," Lat. *homo, homin-*, a man.

[2] This etymology is doubted by some authorities.

It may be remarked here that the number of Latin words used in their unaltered form in every-day English is larger than is generally realised. Besides such phrases as *bona-fide, post-mortem, viva-voce*, or such abbreviations as A.M., *ante meridiem*, D.V., *Deo volente*, and L. s. d., for *libræ, solidi, denarii*, we have, without including scientific terms, many Latin nouns, e.g., *animal, genius, index, odium, omen, premium, radius, scintilla, stimulus, tribunal*, and adjectives, e.g., *complex, lucifer, miser, pauper, maximum, senior*, and the ungrammatical *bonus*. The Lat. *veto*, I forbid, has been worked hard of late. The stage has given us *exit*, he goes out, and the Universities *exeat*, let him go out, while law language contains a number of Latin verb forms, e.g., *affidavit* (late Latin), he has testified, *caveat*, let him beware, *cognovit*, he has recognised—

"You gave them a *cognovit* for the amount of your costs after the trial, I'm told."

(*Pickwick*, Ch. 46.)

due to the initial words of certain documents. Similarly *item*, also, is the first word in each paragraph of an inventory. With this we may compare the *purview* of a statute, from the Old Fr. *pourveu* (*pourvu*), provided, with which it used to begin. A *tenet* is what one "holds." *Fiat* means "let it be done." When Mr Weller lamented—

"Oh, Sammy, Sammy, vy worn't there a *alleybi*?"

(*Pickwick*, Ch. 34.)

it is safe to say that he was not consciously using the Latin adverb *alibi*, elsewhere, nor is the printer who puts in a *viz.* always aware that this is an old abbreviation for *videlicet*, i.e., *videre licet*, it is permissible to see. A *nostrum* is "our" unfailing remedy, and *tandem*, at length, instead of side by side, is a university joke.

Sometimes we have inflected forms of Latin words. A *rebus*[1] is a word or phrase represented "by things." *Requiem*, accusative of *requies*, rest, is the first word of the introit used in the mass for the dead—

"*Requiem* æternam dona eis, Domine,"

while *dirge* is the Latin imperative *dirige*, from the antiphon in the same service—

"*Dirige*, Domine meus, in conspectu tuo viam meam."

The spelling *dirige* was once common—

"Also I byqwethe to eche of the paryshe prystys beying at my *dyryge* and masse xiid."
                    (Will of John Perfay, of Bury St. Edmunds, 1509.)

Query was formerly written *quære*, seek, and *plaudit* is for *plaudite*, clap your hands, the appeal of the Roman actors to the audience at the conclusion of the play—

"Nunc, spectatores, Iovis summi causa clare *plaudite*."
                    (PLAUTUS, *Amphitruo*.)

Debenture is for *debentur*, there are owing. *Dominie* is the Latin vocative *domine*, formerly used by schoolboys in addressing their master, while *pandy*, a stroke on the hand with a cane, is from *pande palmam*, hold out your hand. *Parse* is the Lat. *pars*, occurring in the question *Quæ pars orationis?* What part of speech? *Omnibus*, for all, is a dative plural. *Limbo* is the ablative of Lat. *limbus*, an edge, hem, in the phrase "in *limbo* patrum," where *limbus* is used for the abode of the Old Testament saints on the verge of Hades. It is already jocular in Shakespeare—

"I have some of 'em in *limbo* patrum, and there they are like to dance these three days."
                    (*Henry VIII.*, v. 3.)

---

[1] But the word comes to us from French. In the 16th century such puzzles were called *rébus de Picardie*, because of their popularity in that province.

Folio, quarto, etc., are ablatives, from the phrases *in folio, in quarto,* etc., still used in French. *Premises,* earlier *premisses,* is a slightly disguised Lat. *præmissas,* the aforesaid, lit. sent before, used in deeds to avoid repeating the full description of a property. It is thus the same word as logical *premisses,* or assumptions. *Quorum* is from a legal formula giving a list of persons "of whom" a certain number must be present. A *teetotum* is so called because it has, or once had, on one of its sides, a *T* standing for *totum,* all. It was also called simply a *totum.* The other three sides also bore letters to indicate what share, if any, of the stake they represented. Cotgrave has *totum* (*toton*), "a kind of game with a whirle-bone." In spite of the interesting anecdote about the temperance orator with an impediment in his speech, it was probably *teetotum* that suggested *teetotaller.*

We have also a few words straight from Greek, e.g., *analysis, aroma, atlas,* the world-sustaining demigod whose picture used to decorate map-books, *colon, comma, dogma, epitome, miasma, nausea,* Gk. ναυσία, lit. sea-sickness, *nectar,* whence the fruit called a *nectarine*—

> " *Nectarine* fruits which the compliant boughs
> Yielded them, sidelong as they sat recline."
> (*Paradise Lost,* iv. 332.)

pathos, python, pyx, synopsis, etc. ; but most of our Greek words have passed through French *via* Latin, or are newly manufactured scientific terms, often most unscientifically constructed.

Gamut contains the Gk. *gamma* and the Latin conjunction *ut.* Guy d'Arezzo, who flourished in the 11th century, is said to have introduced the method of indicating the notes by the letters *a* to *g.* For the note below *a* he used the Gk. *gamma.* To him is attributed also the series of monosyllables by which the notes are also indicated. They are supposed to be taken from a Latin hymn to St John—

> *Ut* queant laxis *re*sonare fibris
> *Mi*ra gestorum *fa*muli tuorum
> *Sol*ve polluti *la*bii reatum
> Sancte *I*ohannes.

Do is sometimes substituted for *ut* in French, and always in modern English.

In considering the Old French element in English, one has to bear in mind a few elementary philological facts. Nearly all French nouns and adjectives are derived from the accusative. I give, for simplicity, the nominative, adding the stem in the case of imparisyllabic words. The foundation of French is Vulgar Latin, which differs considerably from that we study at school. I only give Vulgar Latin forms where it cannot be avoided. For instance, in dealing with *culverin* (p. 38), I connect Fr. *couleuvre*, adder, with Lat. *cólŭber*, a snake. Every Romance philologist knows that it must represent Vulgar Lat. * *colóbra* ; but this form, which, being conjectural, is marked with an asterisk, had better be forgotten by the general reader.

Our modern English words often preserve a French form which no longer exists, or they are taken from dialects, especially those of Normandy and Picardy, which differ greatly from that of Paris. The word *caudle* illustrates both these points. It is the same word as modern Fr. *chaudeau*, "a *caudle ;* or, warme broth" (Cotgrave), but it preserves the Old French [1] -*el* for -*eau*, and the Picard *c*- for *ch*-. An uncomfortable bridle which used to be employed to silence scolds was

---

[1] For simplicity the term Old French is used here to include all words not in modern use. Where a modern form exists it is given in parentheses.

called the *branks*. It is a Scottish word, originally applied to a bridle improvised from a halter with a wooden "cheek" each side to prevent it from slipping—

> "And then its shanks,
> They were as thin, as sharp and sma'
> As cheeks o' *branks*."
> (BURNS, *Death and Doctor Hornbook*, vii. 4.)

These cheeks correspond to the two parallel levers called the "branches" of a bridle, and *brank* is the Norman *branque*, branch. All the meanings of *patch* answer to those of Fr. *pièce*. It comes from the Old French dialect form *peche*, as *match* comes from *mèche*, and *cratch*, a manger, from *crèche*, of German origin, and ultimately the same word as *crib*. *Cratch* is now replaced, except in dialect, by *manger*, Fr. *mangeoire*, from *manger*, to eat, but it was the regular word in Mid. English—

> "Sche childide her firste born sone, and wlappide him in clothis, and puttide in a *cracche*."
>
> (WYCLIF, *Luke*, ii. 7.)

Pew is from Old Fr. *puy*, a stage, eminence, Lat. *podium*, which survives in *Puy de Dôme*, the mountain in Auvergne on which Pascal made his experiments with the barometer. *Dupuy* is a common family name in France, but the *Depews* of the West Indies have kept the older pronunciation.

Many Old French words which live on in England are obsolete in France. *Chime* is Old Fr. *chimbe* from Greco-Lat. *cymbalum*. Minsheu (1617) derived *dismal* from Lat. *dies mali*, evil days. This, says Trench, "is exactly one of those plausible etymologies which one learns after a while to reject with contempt." But Minsheu is substantially right, if we substitute Old Fr. *dis mal*, which is found as early as 1256. Old Fr.

di, a day, also survives in the names of the days of the week, *lundi*, etc. In *remainder* and *remnant* we have the infinitive and present participle of an obsolete Old French verb derived from Lat. *remanēre*. *Manor* and *power* are also Old French infinitives, the first now only used as a noun (*manoir*), the second represented by *pouvoir*. *Misnomer* is the Anglo-French infinitive, "to misname."

In some cases we have preserved meanings now obsolete in French. *Trump*, in cards, is Fr. *triomphe*, "the card game called ruffe, or *trump*; also, the ruffe, or *trump* at it" (Cotgrave), but the modern French word for trump is *atout*, to all. *Rappee* is for obsolete Fr. (tabac) *râpé*, pulverised, rasped. Fr. *talon*, heel, from Vulgar Lat. * *talo, talon-*, for *talus*, was applied by falconers to the heel claw of the hawk. This meaning, obsolete in French, has persisted in English. The *mizen* mast is the rearmost of three, but the Fr. *mât de misaine* is the fore-mast, and both come from Ital. *mezzana*, middle, "also the poop or *mizensail*[1] in a ship" (Torriano).

As in the case of Latin, we have some inflected French forms in English. *Lampoon* is from the archaic Fr. *lampon*, "a drunken song" (Miège, *French Dict.*, 1688). This is coined from the imperative *lampons*, let us drink, regularly used as a refrain in seditious and satirical songs. For the formation we may compare

[1] The name was thus applied to a sail before it was given to a mast. Although the Italian word means "middle," it is perhaps, in this particular sense, a popular corruption of an Arabic word of quite different meaning. The discussion of so difficult a problem is rather out of place in a book intended for the general reader, but I cannot refrain from giving a most interesting note which I owe to Mr W. B. Whall, Master Mariner, the author of *Shakespeare's Sea Terms Explained*—"The sail was (until c. 1780) lateen, *i.e.*, triangular, like the sail of a galley. The Saracens, or Moors, were the great galley sailors of the Mediterranean, and *mizen* comes from Arab., *miezên*, balance. The *mizen* is, even now, a sail that 'balances,' and the reef in a mizen is still called the 'balance' reef."

American *vamose*, to skedaddle, from Span. *vamos*, let us go. The military *revelly* is the French imperative *réveillez*, wake up, but in the French army it is called the *diane*. The *gist* of a matter is the point in which its importance really "lies." *Ci-gît*, for Old Fr. *ci-gist*, Lat. *jacet*, here lies, is seen on old tombstones. *Tennis*, says Minsheu, is so called from Fr. *tenez*, hold, "which word the Frenchmen, the onely tennis-players, use to speake when they strike the ball." This etymology, for a long time regarded as a wild guess, has been shewn by recent research to be most probably correct. The game is of French origin, and it was played by French knights in Italy a century before we find it alluded to by Gower (c. 1400). Erasmus tells us that the server called out *accipe*, to which his opponent replied *mitte*, and as French, and not Latin, was certainly the language of the earliest tennis-players, we may infer that the spectators named the game from the foreign word with which each service began. In French the game is called *paume*, palm of the hand; cf. *fives*, also a slang name for the hand. The archaic *assoil*—

"And the holy man he *assoil'd* us, and sadly we sail'd away."
(TENNYSON, *Voyage of Maeldune*, xi. 12.)

is the present subjunctive of the Old Fr. *asoldre* (*absoudre*), to absolve, used in the stereotyped phrase *Dieus asoile*, may God absolve.

A linguistic invasion such as that of English by Old French is almost unparalleled. We have instances of the expulsion of one tongue by another, *e.g.*, of the Celtic dialects of Gaul by Latin and of those of Britain by Anglo-Saxon. But a real blending of two languages can only occur when a large section of the population is bilingual for centuries. This, as we know, was the case in England. The Norman dialect, already familiar through inevitable intercourse, was transplanted to England in 1066. It developed further on its own lines into Anglo-Norman, and then, mixed with other French dialects, for not all the invaders were Normans, and political events brought various French provinces into relation with England, it produced Anglo-French, a somewhat barbarous tongue which was the official language till 1362, and with which our legal jargon is saturated. We find in Anglo - French many words which are unrecorded in continental Old French, among them one which we like to think of as essentially English, viz., *dueté*, duty, an abstract formed from the past participle of Fr. *devoir*. This verb has also given us *endeavour*, due to the phrase *se mettre en devoir*—

" Je me suis *en debvoir* mis pour moderer sa cholere tyrannicque." [1]
(*Rabelais*, i. 29.)

No dictionary can keep up with the growth of a language. The *New English Dictionary* had done the letter *C* before the *cinematograph* arrived, but got it in under *K*. Words of this kind are manufactured in such numbers that the lexicographer is inclined to wait and see whether they will catch on. In such cases it is hard to prophesy. The population of this country may be divided into those people who have been operated for *appendicitis* and those who are going to be. Yet this word was considered too rare and obscure for insertion in the first volume of the *New English Dictionary* (1888), the greatest word-book that has ever been projected. *Sabotage* looks, unfortunately, as if it had come to stay. It is a derivative of *saboter*, to scamp work, from *sabot*, a wooden shoe, used contemptuously of an

---

[1] " I have *endeavoured* to moderate his tyrannical choler " (Urquhart's Translation, 1653).

inferior article. The great French dictionaries do not know it in its latest sense of malicious damage done by strikers, and the *New English Dictionary*, which finished *Sa-* in the year 1912, just missed it. *Hooligan* is not recorded by the *New English Dictionary*. The original *Hooligans* were a spirited Irish family of that name whose proceedings enlivened the drab monotony of life in Southwark towards the end of the 19th century. The word is younger than the Australian *larrikin*, of doubtful origin (see p. 190), but older than Fr. *apache*. The adoption of the Red Indian name *Apache* for a modern Parisian bravo is a curious parallel to the 18th-century use of *Mohock* (Mohawk) for an aristocratic London ruffler.

Heckle is first recorded in its political sense for 1880. The *New English Dictionary* quotes it from *Punch* in connection with the Fourth Party. In Scottish, however, it is old in this sense, so that it is an example of a dialect word that has risen late in life. Its southern form *hatchell* is common in Mid. English in its proper sense of "teasing" hemp or flax, and the metaphor is exactly the same. *Tease*, earlier *toose*, means to pluck or pull to pieces, hence the name *teasel* for the thistle used by wool-carders. The older form is seen in the derivative *tousle*, the family name *Tozer*, and the dog's name *Towser*. *Feckless*, a common Scottish word, was hardly literary English before Carlyle. It is now quite familiar—

"Thriftless, shiftless, *feckless*."
(Mr LLOYD GEORGE, 1st Nov. 1911.)

There is a certain appropriateness in the fact that almost the first writer to use it was James I. It is for *effectless*. I never heard of a *week-end* till I paid a visit to Lancashire in 1883. It has long since invaded the whole island. An old *geezer* has a modern sound, but it is the medieval *guiser, guisard,* mummer, which has persisted in dialect and re-entered the language.

The fortunes of a word are sometimes determined by accident. *Glamour* (see p. 145) was popularised by Scott, who found it in old ballad literature. *Grail,* the holy dish at the Last Supper, would be much less familiar but for Tennyson. *Mascot,* from a Provençal word meaning sorcerer, dates from Audran's operetta *La Mascotte* (1880). *Jingo* first appears in conjurors' jargon of the 17th century. It has been conjectured to represent Basque *jinko,* God, picked up by sailors. If this is the case, it is probably the only pure Basque word in English. The Ingoldsby derivation from St Gengulphus—

"Sometimes styled 'The Living *Jingo,*' from the great tenaciousness of vitality exhibited by his severed members,"

is of course a joke. In 1878, when war with Russia seemed imminent, a music-hall singer, the Great Macdermott, delighted large audiences with—

"We don't want to fight, but, by *Jingo,* if we do,
We've got the ships, we've got the men, we've got the money too."

Hence the name *jingo* applied to that ultra-patriotic section of the population which, in war-time, attends to the shouting.[1] Fr. *chauvin,* a jingo, is the name of a real Napoleonic veteran introduced into Scribe's play *Le Soldat Laboureur.* *Barracking* is known to us only through the visits of English cricket teams to Australia. It is said to come from a native Australian word meaning derision. The American *caucus* was first applied (1878) by Lord Beaconsfield to the Birmingham Six Hundred. In 18th-century American it means

[1] The credit of first using the word in the political sense is claimed both for George Jacob Holyoake and Professor Minto.

meeting or discussion. It is probably connected with a North American Indian (Algonkin) word meaning counsellor, an etymology supported by that of *pow-wow*, a palaver or confab, which is the Algonkin for a medicine-man. With these words may be mentioned *Tammany*, now used of a famous political body, but, in the 18th century, of a society named after the "tutelar saint" of Pennsylvania. The original Tammany was an Indian chief with whom William Penn negotiated for grants of land about the end of the 17th century. *Littoral* first became familiar in connection with Italy's ill-starred Abyssinian adventure, and *hinterland* marked the appearance of Germany as a colonial power—

"'Let us glance a moment,' said Mr Queed, 'at Man, as we see him first emerging from the dark *hinterlands* of history.'"
(H. S. HARRISON, *Queed*, Ch. 17.)

Sometimes the blunder of a great writer has enriched the language. Scott's *bartisan*—

"Its varying circle did combine
Bulwark, and *bartisan*, and line
And bastion, tower ..." (*Marmion*, vi. 2.)

is a mistake for *bratticing*, timber-work, a word of obscure origin of which several corruptions are found in early Scottish. It is rather a favourite with writers of "sword and feather" novels. Other sham antiques are *slug-horn*, Chatterton's absurd perversion of the Gaelic *slogan*, war-cry, copied by Browning—

"Dauntless the *slug-horn* to my lips I set,
And blew 'Childe Roland to the Dark Tower came.'"

and Scott's extraordinary misuse of *warison*, security, a doublet of *garrison*, as though it meant "war sound"—

"Or straight they sound their *warison*,
And storm and spoil thy garrison." (*Lay*, iv. 31.)

Scott also gave currency to *niddering*, a coward—

> "Faithless, mansworn,[1] and *niddering*."
>
> *(Ivanhoe*, Ch. 42.)

which has been copied by Lytton and Kingsley, and elaborated into *nidderling* by Mr Crockett. It is a misprint in an early edition of William of Malmesbury for *niding* or *nithing*, cognate with Ger. *Neid*, envy. This word, says Camden, is mightier than *Abracadabra*,[2] since—

> "It hath levied armies and subdued rebellious enemies. For when there was a dangerous rebellion against King William Rufus, and Rochester Castle, then the most important and strongest fort of this realm, was stoutly kept against him, after that he had but proclaimed that his subjects should repair thither to his camp, upon no other penalty, but that whosoever should refuse to come should be reputed a *niding*, they swarmed to him immediately from all sides in such numbers that he had in a few days an infinite army, and the rebels therewith were so terrified that they forthwith yielded." (*Remains concerning Britain.*)

Derring-do is used several times by Spenser, who explains it as "manhood and chevalrie." It is due to his misunderstanding of a passage in Lidgate, in which it is an imitation of Chaucer, complicated by a misprint. Scott took it from Spenser—

> "'Singular,' he again muttered to himself, 'if there be two who can do a deed of such *derring-do*.'" (*Ivanhoe*, Ch. 29.)

and from him it passed to Bulwer Lytton and later writers.

---

[1] From Anglo-Sax. *mān*, deceit, cognate with the first syllable of Ger. *Meineid*, perjury.

[2] This word, which looks like an unsuccessful palindrome, belongs to the language of medieval magic. It seems to be artificially elaborated from ἀβραξάς, a word of Persian origin used by a sect of Greek gnostics. Its letters make up the magic number 365, supposed to represent the number of spirits subject to the supreme being.

Such words as these, the illegitimate offspring of genius, are to be distinguished from the " ghost-words " which dimly haunt the dictionaries without ever having lived (see p. 201). Speaking generally, we may say that no word is ever created *de novo*. The names invented for commercial purposes are not exceptions to this law. *Bovril* is compounded of Lat. *bos*, ox, and *vril*,[1] the mysterious power which plays so important a part in Lytton's *Coming Race*, while *Tono-Bungay* suggests *tonic*. The only exception to this is *gas*, the arbitrary coinage of the Belgian chemist Van Helmont in the 17th century. But even this is hardly a new creation, because we have Van Helmont's own statement that the word *chaos* was vaguely present to his mind. *Chortle* has, however, secured a limited currency, and is admitted by the *New English Dictionary*—

> " O frabjous day ! Callooh ! callay !
> He *chortled* in his joy."
> > (*Through the Looking-Glass.*)

and, though an accurate account of the *boojum* is lacking, most people know it to be a dangerous variety of *snark*.

---

[1] In coining *vril* Lytton probably had in mind Lat. *vis*, *vires*, power, or the adjective *virilis*.

CHAPTER II

WANDERINGS OF WORDS

In assigning to a word a foreign origin, it is necessary to show how contact between the two languages has taken place, or the particular reasons which have brought about the borrowing. A Chinese word cannot suddenly make its appearance in Anglo-Saxon, though it may quite well do so in modern English. No nautical terms have reached us from the coast of Bohemia (*Winter's Tale*, iii. 3), nor is the vocabulary of the wine trade enriched by Icelandic words. Although we have words from all the languages of Europe, our direct borrowings from some of them have been small. The majority of High German words in English have passed through Old French, and we have taken little from modern German. On the other hand, commerce has introduced a great many words from the old Low German dialects of the North Sea and the Baltic.

The Dutch[1] element in English supplies a useful object lesson on the way in which the borrowing of words naturally takes place. As a great naval power, the Dutch have contributed to our nautical vocabulary a number of words, many of which are easily recognised as near relations; such are *boom* (beam), *skipper*

---

[1] This includes Flemish, spoken in a large part of Belgium and in the North East of France.

B

(shipper), *orlop* (over leap), the name given to a deck
which "over-runs" the ship's hold.   *Yacht*, properly a
"hunting" ship, is cognate with Ger. *Jagd*, hunting, but
has no English kin.   Hexham has *jaght*, "zee-roovers
schip, pinace, or pirats ship."   The modern Dutch
spelling is *jacht*.   We should expect to find art terms
from the country of Hobbema, Rubens, Vandyke, etc.
See *easel* (p. 39), *etch* (p. 133), *lay-figure* (p. 166), *sketch*
(p. 22).   *Landscape*, earlier *landskip*, has the suffix which
in English would be -*ship*.   In the 16th century Camden
speaks of "a *landskip*, as they call it."   The Low
Countries were for two centuries the cock-pit of Europe,
and many military terms were brought back to England
by Dugald Dalgetty and the armies which "swore
terribly in Flanders."   Such are *cashier* (p. 157), *forlorn
hope* (p. 129), *tattoo* (p. 162).   Other interesting military
words are *leaguer* (lair), recently re-introduced from
South Africa as *laager*, and *furlough*.   The latter word,
formerly pronounced to rime with *cough*, is from Du.
verlof (for leave) ; *cf.* archaic Ger. *Verlaub*, now replaced
by *Urlaub*.   *Knapsack*,[1] a food sack, comes from colloquial
Du. *knap*, food, or what the Notts colliers call *snap*.
We also find it called a *snapsack*.   Both *knap* and *snap*
contain the idea of "crunching"—

"I would she (Report) were as lying a gossip in that as ever
knapped ginger." (*Merchant of Venice*, iii. 1.)

Roster (roaster) is the Dutch for gridiron, the allusion
being to the parallel lines of the list or plan ; for a
somewhat similar metaphor cf. *cancel* (p. 88).   The
pleasant fiction that—

"The children of Holland take pleasure in making
What the children of England take pleasure in breaking,"

confirms the derivation of *toy* from Du. *tuig*, implement,

[1] *Haversack*, oat-sack, comes through French from German.

thing, stuff, etc., a word, like its German cognate *Zeug*, with an infinity of meanings. We now limit *toy* to the special sense represented by Du. *speel-tuig*, play-thing.

Our vocabulary dealing with war and fortification is chiefly French, but most of the French terms come from Italian. Addison wrote an article in No. 165 of the *Spectator* ridiculing the Frenchified character of the military language of his time, and, in the 16th century, Henri Estienne, patriot, printer, and philologist, lamented that future historians would believe, from the vocabulary employed, that France had learnt the art of war from Italy. As a matter of fact she did. The earliest writers on the new tactics necessitated by villainous saltpetre were Italians trained in condottiere warfare. They were followed by the great French theorists and engineers of the 16th and 17th centuries, who naturally adopted a large number of Italian terms which thus passed later into English.

A considerable number of Spanish and Portuguese words have reached us in a very roundabout way (see pp. 23-7). This is not surprising when we consider how in the 15th and 16th centuries the world was dotted with settlements due to the Portuguese and Spanish adventurers who had a hundred years' start of our own.

There are very few Celtic words either in English or French. In each country the result of conquest was, from the point of view of language, complete. A few words from the Celtic languages have percolated into English in comparatively recent times, but many terms which we associate with the picturesque Highlanders are not Gaelic at all.[1] *Tartan* comes through French from the *Tartars* (see p. 47); *kilt* is a Scandinavian

---

[1] This applies also to some of the clan names, e.g., *Macpherson*, son of the parson, *Macnab*, son of the abbot.

verb, "to tuck up," and *dirk*,[1] of unknown origin, first
appears about 1600. For *trews* see p. 117.

A very interesting part of our vocabulary, the
canting, or rogues', language, dates mostly from the 17th
and 18th centuries, and includes contributions from most
of the European languages, together with a large Romany
element. The early dictionary makers paid great attention to this aspect of the language. Elisha Coles, who
published a fairly complete English dictionary in 1676,
says in his preface, "'Tis no disparagement to understand
the canting terms: it may chance to save your throat from
being cut, or (at least), your pocket from being pick'd."

Words often go long journeys. *Boss* is in English
a comparatively modern Americanism. But, like many
American words, it belongs to the language of the Dutch
settlers who founded New Amsterdam (New York). It
is Du. *baas*, master, which has thus crossed the Atlantic
twice on its way from Holland to England. A number
of Dutch words became familiar to us about the year
1900 in consequence of the South African war. One
of them, *slim*, 'cute, seems to have been definitely
adopted. It is cognate with Ger. *schlimm*, bad, and
Eng. *slim*, slender, and the latter word has for centuries
been used in the Eastern counties in the very sense
in which it has now been re-introduced.

Apricot is a much travelled word. It comes to us
from Fr. *abricot*, while the Shakespearean *apricock*—

> "Feed him with *apricocks* and dewberries."
>   (*Midsummer Night's Dream*, iii. 1.)

represents the Spanish or Portuguese form. Ger.
Aprikose comes, *via* Dutch, from the French plural.

---

[1] My own conviction is that it is identical with Dan. *dirik*, *dirk*, a pick-
lock. See *Dietrich* (p. 42). An implement used for opening an enemy may
well have been named in this way. *Cf.* Du. *opsteeker* (up sticker), "a pick-
lock, a great knife, or a dagger" (Sewel, 1727).

The word was adopted into the Romance languages from Arab. *al-barquq*, where *al* is the definite article (*cf.* examples on p. 115), while *barquq* comes, through medieval Greek, from Vulgar Lat. *præcoquum*, for *præcox*, early-ripe. Thus the word first crossed the Adriatic, passed on to Asia Minor or the North coast of Africa, and then travelling along the Mediterranean re-entered Southern Europe.

Many other Arabic trade words have a similar history. *Carat* comes to us, through French, from Italian *carato*, "a waight or degree called a *caract*" (Florio). The Italian word is from Arabic, but the Arabic form is a corruption of Gk. κεράτιον, fruit of the locust tree, lit. little horn, also used of a small weight. The verb to *garble*, now used only of confusing or falsifying,[1] meant originally to sort or sift, especially spices—

"*Garbler* of spices is an officer of great antiquity in the city of London, who may enter into any shop, warehouse, etc., to view and search drugs, spices, etc., and to *garble* the same and make them clean." (Cowel's *Interpreter*.)

It represents Span. *garbellar*, from *garbello*, a sieve. This comes from Arab. *ghirbāl*, a sieve, borrowed from Lat. *cribellum*, diminutive of *cribrum*. *Quintal*, an old word for hundred-weight, looks as if it had something to do with five. Fr. and Span. *quintal* are from Arab. *qintar*, hundred-weight, which is Lat. *centenarium* (whence directly Ger. *Zentner*, hundred-weight). The French word passed into Dutch, and gave, with a diminutive ending, *kindekijn*, now replaced by *kinnetje*, a firkin.[2] We have adopted it as *kilderkin*, but have

---

[1] "It was a wholly *garbled* version of what never took place" (Mr Birrell, in the House, 26th Oct. 1911). The bull appears to be a laudable concession to Irish national feeling.

[2] Formerly *ferdekin*, a derivative of Du. *vierde*, fourth; cf. *farthing*, a little fourth.

doubled its capacity. With these examples of words that have passed through Arabic may be mentioned *talisman*, not a very old word in Europe, from Arab. *tilsam*, magic picture, ultimately from Gk. τελεῖν, to initiate into mysteries, lit. to accomplish, and *effendi*, a Turkish corruption of Gk. αὐθέντης, a master, whence Lat. *authentic*.

Hussar seems to be a late Latin word which passed into Greece and then entered Central Europe *via* the Balkans. It comes into 16th-century German from Hungar. *huszar*, freebooter. This is from a Serbian word which means also pirate. It represents medieval Gk. κουρσάριος, a transliteration of Vulgar Lat. *cursarius*, from *currere*, to run, which occurs also with the sense of pirate in medieval Latin. *Hussar* is thus a doublet of *corsair*. The immediate source of *sketch* is Du. *schets*, "draught of any picture" (Hexham), from Ital. *schizzo*, "an ingrosement or first rough draught of anything" (Florio), whence also Fr. *esquisse* and Ger. *Skizze*. The Italian word represents Greco-Lat. *schedium*, an extempore effort.

Assassin and *slave* are of historic interest. *Assassin*, though not very old in English, dates from the Crusades. Its oldest European form is Ital. *assassino*, and it was adopted into French in the 16th century. Henri Estienne, whose fiery patriotism entered even into philological questions, reproaches his countrymen for using foreign terms. They should only adopt, he says, Italian words which express Italian qualities hitherto unknown to the French, such as *assassin, charlatan, poltron !* *Assassin* is really a plural, from the *hachaschin*, eaters of the drug *haschish*, who executed the decrees of the Old Man of the Mountains. It was one of these who stabbed Edward Longshanks at Acre. The first *slaves* were captive *Slavonians*. We

find the word in most of the European languages.
The fact that none of the Western tribes of the race
called themselves *Slavs* or *Slavonians* shows that
the word could not have entered Europe *via* Germany,
where the Slavs were called Wends. It must have
come from the Byzantine empire *via* Italy.

Some Spanish words have also come to us by the
indirect route. The *cocoa* which is grateful and com-
forting was formerly spelt *cacao*, as in French and
German. It is a Mexican word. The *cocoa* of *cocoa-nut*
is for *coco*, a Spanish baby-word for an ugly face or
bogie-man. The black marks at one end of the nut
give it, especially before the removal of the fibrous
husk, some resemblance to a ferocious face. Stevens
(1706) explains *coco* as "the word us'd to fright children;
as we say the Bulbeggar."

Mustang seems to represent two words, *mestengo
y mostrenco*, "a straier" (Percyvall). The first appears
to be connected with *mesta*, "a monthly fair among
herdsmen; also, the laws to be observed by all that
keep or deal in cattle" (Stevens), and the second with
mostrar, to show, the finder being expected to advertise
a stray. The original *mustangs* were of course
descended from the strayed horses of the Spanish
conquistadors. *Ranch*, Span. *rancho*, a row (of huts), is
a doublet of *rank*, from Fr. *rang*, Old Fr. *reng*, Old
High Ger. *hring*, a ring. Thus what is now usually
straight was once circular, the ground idea of ar*range*-
ment surviving. Another doublet is Fr. *harangue*, due
to the French inability to pronounce *hr-* (see p. 55), a
speech delivered in the ring. *Cf.* also Ital. *aringo*, "a
riding or carreering place, a liste for horses, or feates
of armes: a declamation, an oration, a noise, a common
loud speech" (Florio), in which the "ring" idea is also
prominent.

Other "cow-boy" words of Spanish origin are the less familiar *cinch*, girth of a horse, Span. *cincha*, from Lat. *cingula*, also used metaphorically—

"The state of the elements enabled Mother Nature 'to get a *cinch*' on an honourable æstheticism." (Snaith, *Mrs Fitz*, Ch. 1.)

and the formidable riding-whip called a *quirt*, Span. *cuerda*, cord—

"Whooping and swearing as they plied the *quirt*."
(Masefield, *Rosas.*)

Stories of Californian life often mention Span. *reata*, a tethering rope, from the verb *reatar*, to bind together, Lat. *re-aptare*. Combined with the definite article (*la reata*) it has given *lariat*, a familiar word in literature of the Buffalo Bill character. *Lasso*, Span. *lazo*, Lat. *laqueus*, snare, is a doublet of Eng. *lace*.

When, in the *Song of Hiawatha*—

"Gitche Manito, the mighty,
Smoked the *calumet*, the Peace-pipe,
As a signal to the nations,"

he was using an implement with a French name. *Calumet* is an Old Norman word for *chalumeau*, reed, pipe, a diminutive from Lat. *calamus*. It was naturally applied by early French voyagers to the "long reed for a pipe-stem." Eng. *shawm* is the same word without the diminutive ending. Another Old French word, once common in English, but now found only in dialect, is *felon*, a whitlow. It is used more than once by Mr Hardy—

"I've been visiting to Bath because I had a *felon* on my thumb." (*Far from the Madding Crowd*, Ch. 33.)

This is still an every-day word in Canada and the United States. It is a metaphorical use of *felon*, a fell villain. A whitlow was called in Latin *furunculus*, "a little theefe; a sore in the bodie called a *fellon*" (Cooper), whence Fr. *furoncle*, or *froncle*, "the hot and hard bumpe, or swelling, tearmed, a *fellon*" (Cotgrave). Another Latin name for it was *tagax*, "a *felon* on a man's finger" (Cooper), lit. thievish. One of its Spanish names is *padrastro*, lit. step-father. I am told that an "agnail" was formerly called a "step-mother" in Yorkshire. This is a good example of the semantic method in etymology (see pp. 99-104).

Some of the above instances show how near to home we can often track a word which at first sight appears to belong to another continent. This is still more strikingly exemplified in the case of Portuguese words, which have an almost uncanny way of pretending to be African or Indian. Some readers will, I think, be surprised to hear that *assegai* occurs in Chaucer, though in a form not easily recognisable. It is a Berber word which passed through Spanish and Portuguese into French and English. We find Fr. *archegaie* in the 14th century, *azagaie* in Rabelais, and the modern form *zagaie* in Cotgrave, who describes it as "a fashion of slender, long, and long-headed pike, used by the Moorish horsemen." In Mid. English *l'archegaie* was corrupted by folk-etymology (see p. 115) into *lancegay*, *launcegay*, the form used by Chaucer—

> " He worth upon his stede gray,
> And in his hond a *launcegay*,
> A long swerd by his syde."
>
> (*Sir Thopas*, l. 40.)

The use of this weapon was prohibited by statute in 1406, hence the early disappearance of the word.

Another "Zulu" word which has travelled a long way is *kraal*. This is a contracted Dutch form from

Port. *curral,* a sheepfold (*cf.* Span. *corral,* a pen, enclosure). Both *assegai* and *kraal* were taken to South East Africa by the Portuguese and then adopted by the Boers and Kafirs.[1]   *Sjambok* occurs in 17th-century accounts of India in the form *chawbuck.* It is a Persian word, spelt *chabouk* by Moore, in *Lalla Rookh.* It was adopted by the Portuguese as *chabuco,* "in the Portuguese India, a whip or scourge"[2] (Vieyra, *Port. Dict.,* 1794). *Fetish,* an African idol, first occurs in the records of the early navigators, collected and published by Hakluyt and Purchas. It is the Port. *feitiço,* Lat. *factitius,* artificial, applied by the Portuguese explorers to the graven images of the heathen. The corresponding Old Fr. *faitis* is rather a complimentary adjective, and everyone remembers the lady in Chaucer who spoke French fairly and *fetousli.* *Palaver,* also a travellers' word from the African coast, is Port. *palavra,* word, speech, Greco-Lat. *parabola.* It is thus a doublet of *parole* and *parable,* and is related to *parley.* *Ayah,* an Indian nurse, is Port. *aia,* nurse, of unknown origin. *Caste* is Port. *casta,* pure, and a doublet of *chaste.* *Tank,* an Anglo-Indian word of which the meaning has narrowed in this country, is Port. *tanque,* a pool or cistern, Lat. *stagnum,* whence Old Fr. *estang* (*étang*) and provincial Eng. *stank,* a dam, or a pond banked round. *Cobra* is the Portuguese for snake, cognate with Fr. *couleuvre,* Lat. *coluber* (see p. 7). We use it as an abbreviation for *cobra de capello,* hooded snake, the second part of which is identical with Fr. *chapeau* and cognate with *cape, chapel* (p. 152), *chaplet,* a garland,

----

[1] *Kafir* (Arab.) means infidel.

[2] Eng. *chawbuck* is used in connection with the punishment we call the *bastinado.* This is a corruption of Span. *bastonada,* "a stroke with a club or staff" (Stevens, 1706). On the other hand, we extend the meaning of *drub,* the Arabic word for *bastinado,* to a beating of any kind.

and *chaperon*, a "protecting" hood. From still further afield than India comes *joss*, a Chinese god, a corruption of Port. *deos*, Lat. *deus*. Even *mandarin* comes from Portuguese, and not Chinese, but it is an Eastern word, ultimately of Sanskrit origin.

The word *gorilla* is perhaps African, but more than two thousand years separate its first appearance from its present use. In the 5th or 6th century, B.C., a Carthaginian navigator named Hanno sailed beyond the Pillars of Hercules along the west coast of Africa. He probably followed very much the same route as Sir Richard Dalyngridge and Saxon Hugh when they voyaged with Witta the Viking. He wrote in Punic a record of his adventures, which was received with the incredulity usually accorded to travellers' tales. Among the wonders he encountered were some hairy savages called *gorillas*. His work was translated into Greek and later on into several European languages, so that the word became familiar to naturalists. In 1847 it was applied to the giant ape, which had recently been described by explorers.

The origin of the word *silk* is a curious problem. It is usually explained as from Greco-Lat. *sericum*, a name derived from an Eastern people called the *Seres*, presumably the Chinese. It appears in Anglo-Saxon as *seolc*. Now, at that early period, words of Latin origin came to us by the overland route and left traces of their passage. But all the Romance languages use for silk a name derived from Lat. *sæta*, bristle, and this name has penetrated even into German (*Seide*) and Dutch (*zijde*). The derivatives of *sericum* stand for another material, *serge*. Nor can it be assumed that the *r* of the Latin word would have become in English always *l* and never *r*. There are races which cannot sound the letter *r*, but we are not one of them. As the word *silk* is found also in Old Norse, Swedish, Danish, and Old Slavonian, the natural inference is that it must have reached us along the north of Europe, and, if derived from *sericum*, it must, in the course of its travels, have passed through a dialect which had no *r*.

CHAPTER III

WORDS OF POPULAR MANUFACTURE

IN a sense, all nomenclature, apart from purely scientific language, is popular. But real meanings are often so rapidly obscured that words become mere labels, and cease to call up the image or the poetic idea with which they were first associated. To take a simple instance, how many people realise that the *daisy* is the "day's eye"?—

> "Wele by reson men it calle may
> The *dayeseye* or ellis the 'eye of day.'"
> (CHAUCER, *Legend of Good Women*, Prol., l. 184.)

In studying that part of our vocabulary which especially illustrates the tendencies shown in popular name-giving, one is struck by the keen observation and imaginative power shown by our far-off ancestors, and the lack of these qualities in later ages.

Perhaps in no part of the language does this appear so clearly as in the names of plants and flowers. The most primitive way of naming a flower is from some observed resemblance, and it is curious to notice the parallelism of this process in various languages. Thus our *crowfoot*, *crane's bill*, *larkspur*, *monkshood*, *snap-dragon*, are in German *Hahnenfuss* (cock's foot), *Storch-schnabel* (stork's bill), *Rittersporn* (knight's spur), *Eisenhut*

29

(iron hat), *Löwenmaul* (lion's mouth).   I have purposely chosen instances in which the correspondence is not absolute, because examples like *Löwenzahn* (lion's tooth), *dandelion* (Fr. *dent de lion*) may be suspected of being mere translations.   I give the names in most general use, but the provincial variants are numerous, though usually of the same type.   The French names of the flowers mentioned are still more like the English. The more learned words which sometimes replace the above are, though now felt as mere symbols, of similar origin, e.g., *geranium* and *pelargonium*, used for the cultivated *crane's bill*, are derived from the Greek for crane and stork respectively.   So also in *chelidonium*, whence our *celandine* or *swallow-wort*, we have the Greek for swallow.

In the English names of plants we observe various tendencies of the popular imagination.   We have the crudeness of *cowslip* for earlier *cowslop*, cow-dung, and many old names of unquotable coarseness, the quaintness of *Sweet William, lords and ladies, bachelors' buttons, dead men's fingers*, and the exquisite poetry of *forget-me-not, heart's ease, love in a mist, traveller's joy*.   There is also a special group named from medicinal properties, such as *feverfew*, a doublet of *febrifuge*, and *tansy*, Fr. *tanaisie*, from Greco-Lat. *athanasia*, immortality.   We may compare the learned *saxifrage*, stone-breaker, of which the Spanish doublet is *sassafras*.   The German name is *Steinbrech*.

There must have been a time when a simple instinct for poetry was possessed by all nations, as it still is by uncivilised races and children.   Among European nations this instinct appears to be dead for ever.   We can name neither a mountain nor a flower. Our Mount Costigan, Mount Perry, Mount William cut a sorry figure beside the peaks of the Bernese Oberland, the Monk, the Maiden, the Storm Pike, the Dark Eagle Pike.[1]   Occasionally a race which is accidentally brought into closer contact with nature may have a happy inspiration, such as the *Drakensberg* (dragon's mountain) or *Weenen*[2] (weeping) of the old *voortrekkers*.   But the Cliff of the Falling Flowers, the name of a precipice over which the Korean queens cast themselves to escape dishonour, represents an imaginative realm which is closed to us.[3]   The botanist who describes a new flower hastens to join the company of Messrs *Dahl*, *Fuchs*, *Lobel*, *Magnol* and *Wistar*, while fresh varieties are used to immortalise a florist and his family.

The names of fruits, perhaps because they lend themselves less easily to imaginative treatment, are even duller than modern names of flowers.   The only English names are the *apple* and the *berry*.   New fruits either retained their foreign names (*cherry*, *peach*, *pear*, *quince*) or were violently converted into *apples* or *berries*, usually the former.   This practice is common to the European languages, the *apple* being regarded as the typical fruit.   Thus the orange is usually called in North Germany *Apfelsine*, apple of China, with which we may compare our "China orange."   In South Germany it was called *Pomeranze* (now used especially of the Seville orange), from Ital. *pomo*, apple, *arancia*, orange.   Fr. *orange* is folk-etymology (*or*, gold) for **arange*, from Arab. *narandj*, whence Span. *naranja*. *Melon* is simply the Greek for "apple," and has also given us *marmalade*, which comes, through French, from Port. *marmelada*, quince jam, a derivative of Greco-Lat.

---

[1] But *Finsteraarhorn* is perhaps from the river *Aar*, not from *Aar*, eagle.

[2] A place where a number of settlers were massacred by the Zulus.

[3] " Two mountains near Dublin, which we, keeping in the grocery line, have called the Great and the Little Sugarloaf, are named in Irish the Golden Spears."—(Trench, *On the Study of Words*.)

melimelum, quince, lit. honey-apple. *Pine-apple* meant
"fir-cone" as late as the 17th century, as Fr. *pomme de
pin* still does.[1] The fruit was named from its shape,
which closely resembles that of a fir-cone. *Pomegranate*
means "apple with seeds." We also find the apricot,
lemon (*pomcitron*), peach, and quince all described as
apples.

At least one fruit, the *greengage*, is named from a
person, Sir William Gage, a gentleman of Suffolk, who
popularised its cultivation early in the 18th century.
It happens that the French name of the fruit, *reine-
claude* (pronounced *glaude*), is also personal, from the
wife of Francis I.

Animal nomenclature shows some strange vagaries.
The resemblance of the *hippopotamus*, lit. river-horse,
to the horse, hardly extends beyond their common
possession of four legs.[2] The lion would hardly recognise
himself in the *ant-lion* or the *sea-lion*, still less in the
chameleon, lit. earth-lion, the first element of which
occurs also in *camomile*, earth-apple. The *guinea-pig* is
not a pig, nor does it come from Guinea (see p. 51).
Porcupine means "spiny pig." It has an extraordinary
number of early variants, and Shakespeare wrote it *por-
pentine*. One Mid. English form was *porkpoint*. The
French name has hesitated between *spine* and *spike*. The
modern form is *porc-épic*, but Palsgrave has "*porkepyn* a
beest, *porc espin*." *Porpoise* is from Old Fr. *porpeis*, for
porc peis (Lat. *porcus piscis*), pig-fish. The modern French
name is *marsouin*, from Ger. *Meerschwein*, sea-pig; *cf.*

---

[1] The French name for the fruit is *ananas*, a Brazilian word. A vege-
tarian friend of the writer, misled by the superficial likeness of this word to
banana, once petrified a Belgian waiter by ordering half a dozen for his lunch.

[2] A reader calls my attention to the fact that, when the hippopotamus
is almost completely submerged, the pointed ears, prominent eyes, and large
nostrils are grotesquely suggestive of a horse's head. This I have recently
verified at the Zoo.

the name *sea-hog*, formerly used in English. Old Fr. *peis* survives also in *grampus*, Anglo-Fr. *grampais* for *grand peis*, big fish, but the usual Old French word is *craspeis* or *graspeis*, fat fish.

The *caterpillar* seems to have suggested in turn a cat and a dog. Our word is corrupted by folk-etymology from Old Fr. *chatepeleuse*, "a corne-devouring mite, or weevell" (Cotgrave). This probably means "woolly cat," just as a common species is popularly called *woolly bear*, but it was understood as being connected with the French verb *peler*, "to *pill*, pare, barke, unrinde, unskin" (Cotgrave). The modern French name for the cater-pillar is *chenille*, a derivative of *chien*, dog. It has also been applied to a fabric of a woolly nature; *cf.* the botanical *catkin*, which is in French *chaton*, kitten.

Some animals bear nicknames. *Dotterel* means "dotard," and *dodo* is from the Port. *doudo*, mad. *Ferret* is from Fr. *furet*, a diminutive from Lat. *fur*, thief. *Shark* was used of a sharper or greedy parasite before it was applied to the fish. This, in the records of the Elizabethan voyagers, is more often called by its Spanish name *tiburon*, whence Cape Tiburon, in Haiti. The origin of *shark* is unknown, but it appears to be identical with *shirk*, for which we find earlier *sherk*. We find Ital. *scrocco* (whence Fr. *escroc*), Ger. *Schurke*, Du. *schurk*, rascal, all rendered "shark" in early dictionaries, but the relationship of these words is not clear. The *palmer*, *i.e.* pilgrim, worm is so called from his wandering habits. *Ortolan*, the name given by Tudor cooks to the garden bunting, means "gardener" (Lat. *hortus*, garden). It comes to us through French from Ital. *ortolano*, "a gardener, an orchard keeper. Also a kinde of daintie birde in Italie, some take it to be the linnet" (Florio). We may compare Fr. *bouvreuil*, bull-finch, a diminutive of *bouvier*, ox-herd. This is

C

called in German *Dompfaffe*, a contemptuous name for a cathedral canon. Fr. *moineau*, sparrow, is a diminutive of *moine*, monk. The wagtail is called in French *lavandière*, laundress, from the up and down motion of its tail suggesting the washerwoman's beetle, and *bergeronnette*, little shepherdess, from its habit of following the sheep. *Adjutant*, the nickname of the solemn Indian stork, is clearly due to Mr Atkins, and the *secretary* bird is so named because some of his head feathers suggest a quill pen behind an ear.

The converse process of people being nicknamed from animals is also common and the metaphor is usually pretty obvious. An interesting case is *shrew*, a libel on a very inoffensive little animal, the *shrew-mouse*, Anglo-Sax. *scrēawa*. Cooper describes *mus araneus* as " a kinde of mise called a *shrew*, which if he go over a beastes backe he shall be lame in the chyne ; if he byte it swelleth to the heart and the beast dyeth." This "information" is derived from Pliny, but the superstition is found in Greek. The epithet was, up to Shakespeare's time, applied indifferently to both sexes. From *shrew* is derived *shrewd*, earlier *shrewed*,[1] the meaning of which has become much milder than when Henry VIII. said to Cranmer—

> " The common voice I see is verified
> Of thee which says, ' Do my lord of Canterbury
> A *shrewd* turn, and he's your friend for ever.' "
>
> *(Henry VIII., v. 2.)*

The title *Dauphin*, lit. dolphin, commemorates the absorption into the French monarchy, in 1349, of the lordship of Dauphiné, the cognisance of which was three dolphins.

The application of animals' names to diseases is a

---

[1] For the rather illogical formation, cf. *dogged* from *dog*.

familiar phenomenon, e.g., *cancer* (and *canker*), crab, and *lupus*, wolf. To this class belongs *mulligrubs*, for which we find in the 17th century also *mouldy grubs*. Its oldest meaning is stomach-ache, still given in Hotten's Slang Dictionary (1864). *Mully* is still used in dialect for mouldy, earthy, and *grub* was once the regular word for worm. The Latin name for the same discomfort was *verminatio*, from *vermis*, a worm. For the later transition of meaning we may compare *megrims*, from Fr. *migraine*, head-ache, Greco-Lat. *hemicrania*, lit. half-skull, because supposed to affect one side only of the head.

A good many names of plants and animals have a religious origin. *Hollyhock* is for *holy hock*, from Anglo-Sax. *hoc*, mallow : for the pronunciation cf. *holiday*. *Halibut* means *holy butt*, the latter word being an old name for flat fish ; for this form of *holy* cf. *halidom*. *Lady* in names of flowers such as *lady's bedstraw*, *lady's garter*, *lady's slipper*, is for Our Lady. So also in *ladybird*, called in French *bête à bon Dieu* and in German *Marienkäfer*, Mary's beetle. Here may be mentioned *samphire*, from Old Fr. *herbe de Saint Pierre*, " sampire, crestmarin " (Cotgrave). The *filbert*, earlier *philibert*, is named from St Philibert, the nut being ripe by St Philibert's day (22nd Aug.). We may compare Ger. *Lambertsnuss*, filbert, originally " Lombard nut," but popularly associated with St Lambert's day (17th Sept.).

The application of baptismal names to animals is a very general practice, though the reason for the selection of the particular name is not always clear. The most famous of such names is *Renard* the Fox. The Old French for fox is *goupil*, a derivative of Lat. *vulpes*, fox. The hero of the great beast epic of the Middle Ages is *Renard le goupil*, and the fact that *renard* has now completely supplanted *goupil* shows how popular the Renard

legends must have been. *Renard* is from Old High
Ger. *regin-hart*, strong in counsel; *cf.* our names
Reginald and *Reynold*, and Scot. *Ronald*, of Norse origin.
From the same source come *Chantecler*, lit. sing-clear,
the cock, and *Partlet*, the hen, while *Bruin*, the bear, lit.
"brown," is from the Dutch version of the epic.   In the
Low German version, *Reinke de Vos*, the ape's name is
Moneke, a diminutive corresponding to Ital. *monicchio*,
"a pugge, a *munkie*, an ape" (Florio), the earlier history
of which is much disputed. The cat was called *Tibert*
or *Theobald*—

> MERCUTIO. "*Tybalt*, you rat-catcher, will you walk?"
> TYBALT. "What wouldst thou have with me?"
> MERCUTIO. "Good king of cats, nothing but one of your
>   nine lives."
>
> *(Romeo and Juliet*, iii. 1.)

The fact that the donkey was at one time regularly
called *Cuddy* made *Cuthbert* for a long period unpopular
as a baptismal name.   He is now often called *Neddy*.
The hare was called *Wat* (*Walter*) in Tudor times.   In
the *Roman de Renard* he is *Couard*, whence *coward*, a
derivative of Old Fr. *coue* (*queue*), tail, from Lat. *cauda*.
The idea is that of the tail between the legs, so that the
name is etymologically not very appropriate to the
hare. *Parrot*, for earlier *perrot*, means "little Peter."
The extension *Poll parrot* is thus a kind of herma-
phrodite.   Fr. *pierrot* is still used for the sparrow.
The family name *Perrot* is sometimes a nickname, "the
chatterer," but can also mean literally "little Peter,"
just as *Emmot* means "little Emma," and *Marriot*
"little Mary." *Petrel* is of cognate origin, with an
allusion to St Peter's walking upon the sea; *cf.* its
German name, *Sankt Peters Vogel*. Sailors call the
petrel *Mother Carey's chicken*, probably a nautical cor-

ruption of some old Spanish or Italian name. But, in spite of ingenious guesses, this lady's genealogy remains as obscure as that of Davy Jones or the Jolly Roger.

Robin has practically replaced *red-breast*. The *martin* is in French *martinet,* and the name may have been given in allusion to the southward flight of this swallow about Martinmas; but the king-fisher, not a migrant bird, is called *martin-pêcheur,* formerly also *martinet pêcheur* or *oiseau de Saint-Martin,* so that *martin* may be due to some other association. Sometimes the double name survives. We no longer say *Philip sparrow,* but *Jack ass, Jack daw, Jenny wren, Tom tit* (see p. 123), and the inclusive *Dicky bird,* are still familiar. With these we may compare *Hob* (*i.e.* Robert) *goblin. Madge owl,* or simply *Madge,* was once common. For *Mag pie* we find also various diminutives—

> "Augurs, and understood relations, have
> By *magot-pies*, and choughs, and rooks, brought forth
> The secret'st man of blood."
>
> (*Macbeth*, iii. 4.)

Cotgrave has *pie,* "a pye, pyannat, *meggatapie.*" In Old French it was also called *jaquette,* "a proper name for a woman; also, a piannat, or *megatapie*" (Cotgrave).

The connection of this word, Fr. *pie,* Lat. *pica,* with the comestible *pie* is uncertain, but it seems likely that the magpie's habit of collecting miscellaneous trifles caused its name to be given to a dish of uncertain constituents. It is a curious coincidence that the obsolete *chuet* or *chewet* meant both a round pie and a jackdaw.[1] It is uncertain in which of the two senses Prince Hal

---

[1] Connection has even been suggested between *haggis* and Fr. *agasse,* "a pie, piannet, or *magatapie*" (Cotgrave). *Haggis,* now regarded as Scottish, was once a common word in English. Palsgrave has *haggas,* a podyng, " caliette (caillette) de mouton," *i.e.,* sheep's stomach.

applies the name to Falstaff (1 *Henry IV.*, v. 1).   It comes from Fr. *chouette*, screech-owl, which formerly meant also "a chough, daw, jack-daw" (Cotgrave).

A *piebald* horse is one *balled* like a magpie. *Ball* is a Celtic word for a white mark, especially on the forehead; hence the tavern sign of the *Baldfaced Stag*.   Our adjective *bald* is thus a past participle.

Things are often named from animals.   *Crane, kite, donkey-engine, monkey-wrench, pig-iron*, etc., are simple cases.   The *crane* picture is so striking that we are not surprised to find it literally reproduced in many other languages.   The toy called a *kite* is in French *cerf volant*, flying stag, a name also applied to the stag-beetle, and in Ger. *Drachen*, dragon.   It is natural that terrifying names should have been given to early fire-arms. Many of these, e.g., *basilisk, serpent, falconet, saker* (from Fr. *sacre*, a kind of hawk), are obsolete—

> "The cannon, blunderbuss, and *saker*,
> He was th' inventor of and maker."
>
> (*Hudibras*, i. 2.)

More familiar is *culverin*, Fr. *couleuvrine*, a derivative of *couleuvre*, adder, Lat. *coluber*—

> "And thou hast talk'd
> Of sallies and retires, of trenches, tents,
> Of palisadoes, frontiers, parapets,
> Of basilisks, of cannon, *culverin*."
>
> (1 *Henry IV.*, ii. 3.)

One name for a hand-gun was *dragon*, whence our *dragoon*, originally applied to a kind of mounted infantry or carbineers.   *Musket*, like *saker* (v.s.), was the name of a hawk.   Mistress Ford uses it playfully to her page—

> "How now, my eyas[1]-*musket*, what news with you?"
>
> (*Merry Wives*, iii. 3.)

[1] For *eyas* see p. 114

But the hawk was so nicknamed from its small size. Fr. *mousquet*, now replaced in the hawk sense by *émouchet*, is from Ital. *moschetto*, a diminutive from Lat. *musca*, fly. Thus *mosquito* (Spanish) and *musket* are doublets.

Porcelain comes, through French, from Ital. *porcellana*, "a kinde of fine earth called *porcelane*, whereof they make fine china dishes, called *porcellan* dishes" (Florio). This is, however, a transferred meaning, *porcellana* being the name of a particularly glossy shell called the "Venus shell." It is a derivative of Lat. *porcus*, pig. *Easel* comes, with many other painters' terms, from Holland. It is Du. *ezel*, ass, which, like Ger. *Esel*, comes from Lat. *asinus*. For its metaphorical application we may compare Fr. *chevalet*, easel, lit. "little horse," and Eng. "clothes-*horse*."

Objects often bear the names of individuals. Such are *albert* chain, *brougham*, *victoria*, *wellington* boot. Some elderly people can remember ladies wearing a red blouse called a *garibaldi*.[1] Sometimes an inventor is immortalised, e.g., *mackintosh* and *shrapnel*, both due to 19th-century inventors. The more recent *maxim* is named from one who, according to the late Lord Salisbury, has saved many of his fellow-men from dying of old age. Other benefactors are commemorated in *derringer*, first recorded in Bret Harte, and *bowie*, which occurs in Dickens' *American Notes*. *Sandwich* and *spencer* are coupled in an old rime—

> "Two noble earls, whom, if I quote,
>   Some folks might call me sinner ;
> The one invented half a coat,
>   The other half a dinner."

[1] To the same period belongs the colour *magenta*, from the victory of the French over the Austrians at Magenta in 1859.

An Earl Spencer (1782-1845) made a short overcoat fashionable for some time. An Earl of Sandwich (1718-1792) invented a form of light refreshment which enabled him to take a meal without leaving the gaming table. It does not appear that *Billy Cock* is to be classed with the above, or with *Chesterfield, Chippendale & Co.* The *New English Dictionary* quotes (from 1721) a description of the Oxford "blood" in his "*bully-cocked* hat," worn aggressively on one side. *Pinchbeck* was a London watchmaker (*fl. c.* 1700), and *doily* is from *Doyley*, a linen-draper of the same period. Etienne de *Silhouette* was French finance minister in 1759, but the application of his name to a black profile portrait is variously explained. *Negus* was first brewed in Queen Anne's reign by Colonel Francis Negus.

The first *orrery* was constructed by the Earl of Orrery (*c.* 1700). *Galvani* and *Volta* were Italian scientists of the 18th century. *Mesmer* was a German physician of the same period. *Nicotine* is named from Jean Nicot, French ambassador at Lisbon, who sent some tobacco plants to Catherine de Médicis in 1560. He also compiled the first Old French dictionary. The gallows-shaped contrivance called a *derrick* perpetuates the name of a famous hangman who officiated in London about 1600. It is a Dutch name, identical with *Dietrich, Theodoric*, and *Dirk* (Hatteraick). Conversely the Fr. *potence*, gallows, meant originally a bracket or support, Lat. *potentia*, power. The origin of *darbies*, handcuffs, is unknown, but the line—

"To bind such babes in father *Derbies* bands,"
(Gascoigne, *The Steel Glass*, 1576.)

suggests connection with some eminent gaoler or thief-taker.

Occasionally a verb is formed from a proper name.

On the model of *tantalise*, from the punishment of
Tantalus, we have *bowdlerise*, from *Bowdler*, who
published an expurgated "family Shakespeare" in
1818; cf. *macadamise*. *Burke* and *boycott* commemorate
a scoundrel and a victim. The latter word, from the
treatment of Captain Boycott of Co. Mayo in 1880,
seems to have supplied a want, for Fr. *boycotter* and
Ger. *boycottieren* have become every-day words. Burke
was hanged at Edinburgh in 1829 for murdering
people by suffocation in order to dispose of their
bodies to medical schools. We now use the verb only
of "stifling" discussion, but in the Ingoldsby Legends
it still has the original sense—

"But, when beat on his knees,
That confounded De Guise
Came behind with the 'fogle' that caused all this breeze,
Whipp'd it tight round his neck, and, when backward he'd jerk'd
        him,
The rest of the rascals jump'd on him and *Burk'd* him."

(*The Tragedy.*)

Jarvey, the slang name for a hackney coachman,
especially in Ireland, was in the 18th century *Jervis* or
Jarvis, but history is silent as to this modern *Jehu*.
A *pasquinade* was originally an anonymous lampoon
affixed to a statue of a gladiator which still stands
in Rome. The statue is said to have been nicknamed
from a scandal-loving cobbler named Pasquino. Florio
has *pasquino*, "a statue in Rome on whom all libels,
railings, detractions, and satirical invectives are
fathered." *Pamphlet* is an extended use of Old Fr.
Pamphilet, the name of a Latin poem by one *Pamphilus*
which was popular in the Middle Ages. The suffix *-et*
was often used in this way, *e.g.*, the translation of
Æsop's fables by Marie de France was called *Ysopet*,
and Cato's moral maxims had the title *Catonet*, or Parvus

Cato.   Modern Fr. *pamphlet*, borrowed back from English, has always the sense of polemical writing.   In Eng. *libel*, lit. "little book," we see a similar restriction of meaning.   A three-quarter portrait of fixed dimensions is called a *kitcat*—

> "It is not easy to see why he should have chosen to produce a replica, or rather a *kitcat.*"   (*Journal of Education*, Oct. 1911.)

The name comes from the portraits of members of the *Kitcat* Club, painted by Kneller.   *Kit Kat*, Christopher Kat, was a pastrycook at whose shop the club used to dine.

Implements and domestic objects sometimes bear christian names.   We may mention spinning-*jenny*, and the innumerable meanings of *jack*.   *Davit*, earlier *daviot*, is a diminutive of David.   Fr. *davier*, formerly *daviet*, is used of several mechanical contrivances, including a pick-lock.   A kind of davit is called in German *Jütte*, a diminutive of Judith.   The implement by which the burglar earns his daily bread is now called a *jemmy*, but in the 17th century we also find *bess* and *betty*.   The French name is *rossignol*, nightingale.   The German burglar calls it *Dietrich*, *Peterchen*, or *Klaus*, and the contracted forms of the first name, *dyrk* and *dirk*, have passed into Swedish and Danish with the same meaning.   In Italian a pick-lock is called *grimaldello*, a diminutive of the name Grimaldo.

A kitchen wench was once called a *malkin*—

> "The kitchen *malkin* pins
> Her richest lockram [1] 'bout her reechy neck,
> Clamb'ring the walls to eye him."
>
> (*Coriolanus*, ii. 1.)

This is a diminutive of Matilda or Mary, possibly of

---

[1] For *lockram*, see p. 48.

both. *Grimalkin*, applied to a fiend in the shape of a cat, is perhaps for *gray malkin*—

> "I come, *Graymalkin*." (*Macbeth*, i. 1.)

The name *malkin* was transferred from the maid to the mop. Cotgrave has *escouillon* (*écouvillon*), " a wispe, or dish-clowt; a *maukin*, or drag, to cleanse, or sweepe an oven." *Écouvillon* is a derivative of Lat. *scopa*, broom. Now another French word, which means both "kitchen servant" and "dish-clout," is *souillon*, from *souiller*, to soil. What share each of these words has in Eng. *scullion* is hard to say. The only thing certain is that *scullion* is not originally related to *scullery*, Old Fr. *escuelerie*, a collective from Old Fr. *escuelle* (*écuelle*), dish, Lat. *scutella*.

A *doll* was formerly called a *baby* or *puppet*. It is the abbreviation of *Dorothy*, for we find it called a *doroty* in Scottish. We may compare Fr. *marionnette*, a double diminutive of Mary, explained by Cotgrave as "little Marian or Mal; also, a puppet." *Little Mary*, in another sense, has been recently, but perhaps definitely, adopted into our language. Another old name for doll is *mammet*. Capulet uses it contemptuously to his daughter—

> "And then to have a wretched puling fool,
> A whining *mammet*, in her fortune's tender,
> To answer : ' I'll not wed,'—' I cannot love.'"
> (*Romeo and Juliet*, iii. 5.)

Its earlier form is *maumet*, meaning "idol," and it is a contraction of Mahomet.

The derivation of *jug* is not capable of proof, but a 17th-century etymologist regards it as identical with the female name *Jug*,[1] for Joan or Jane. This is

---

[1] *Jehannette*, "*Jug*, or Jinny" (Cotgrave). For strange perversions of baptismal names see Chap. XII. It is possible that the rather uncommon family name *Juggins* is of the same origin.

supported by the fact that *jack* was used in a similar sense—

> "That there's wrath and despair in the jolly black-*jack*,
> And the seven deadly sins in a flagon of sack."
>
> (*Lady of the Lake*, vi. 5.)

We may also compare *toby jug* and *demi-john*. The latter word is in French *dame-jeanne*, but both forms are possibly due to folk-etymology. A coat of mail was called in English a *jack* and in French *jaque*, "a *jack*, or coat of maile" (Cotgrave); hence the diminutive *jacket*. The German miners gave to an ore which they considered useless the name *kobalt*, from *kobold*, a goblin, gnome. This has given Eng. *cobalt*. Much later is the similarly formed *nickel*, a diminutive of Nicholas. It comes to us from Sweden, but appears earliest in the German compound *Kupfernickel*, copper nickel. Apparently *nickel* here means something like goblin; cf. *Old Nick* and, probably, the *dickens*—

> "I cannot tell what the *dickens* his name is my husband had him of.—What do you call your knight's name, sirrah?"
>
> (*Merry Wives*, iii. 2.)

Pantaloons come, *via* France, from Venice. A great many Venetians bore the name of *Pantaleone*, one of their favourite saints. Hence the application of the name to the characteristic Venetian hose. The "lean and slippered pantaloon" was originally one of the stock characters of the old Italian comedy. Torriano has *pantalone*, "a *pantalone*, a covetous and yet amorous old dotard, properly applyed in comedies unto a Venetian." *Knickerbockers* take their name from Diedrich *Knickerbocker*, the pseudonym under which Washington Irving wrote his History of Old New York, in which the early Dutch inhabitants are depicted in baggy knee-breeches. Certain christian names are curiously associated with stupidity. In modern English we speak of a *silly Johnny*, while the Germans say *ein dummer Peter*, or *Michel*, and French uses *Colas* (*Nicolas*), *Nicodème* and *Claude*, the reason for the selection of the name not always being known. English has, or had, in the sense of "fool," the words *ninny, nickum, noddy, zany*. *Ninny* is for *Innocent*, "Innocent, *Ninny*, a proper name for a man" (Cotgrave). With this we may compare French *benêt* (*i.e.* Benedict), "a simple, plaine, doltish fellow; a noddy peake, a ninny hammer, a peagoose, a coxe, a silly companion" (Cotgrave). *Nickum* and *noddy* are probably for Nicodemus or Nicholas, both of which are used in French for a fool—

> "'But there's another chance for you,' said Mr Boffin, smiling still. 'Do you like the name of Nicodemus? Think it over. *Nick* or *Noddy*.'" (*Our Mutual Friend*, Ch. 5.)

Noddy-peak, ninny-hammer, nickumpoop, now *nincompoop*, seem to be arbitrary elaborations. *Zany*, formerly a conjuror's assistant, is *zanni* (see p. 143), an Italian diminutive of *Giovanni*, John. With the degeneration of *Innocent* and *Benedict* we may compare Fr. *crétin*, idiot, an Alpine patois form of *chrétien*, Christian, and Eng. *silly*, which once meant blessed, a sense preserved by its German cognate *selig*. *Dunce* is a libel on the disciples of the great medieval schoolman John Duns Scotus, born at Duns in Berwickshire.

Dandy is Scottish for Andrew, *e.g.*, Dandie Dinmont (*Guy Mannering*). *Dago*, now usually applied to Italians, was used by the Elizabethans, in its original form *Diego*, of the Spaniards. The derivation of *guy* and *bobby* (peeler) is well known. *Jockey* is a diminutive of the north country *Jock*, for *Jack*. The history of *jackanapes* is obscure. The earliest record of the name is in a satirical song on the unpopular William de la Pole,

Duke of Suffolk, who was beheaded at sea in 1450. He is called *Jack Napes*, the allusion being apparently to his badge, an ape's clog and chain. But there also seems to be association with Naples ; cf. *fustian-anapes* for Naples fustian. A poem of the 15th century mentions among our imports from Italy—

> "Apes and japes and marmusettes tayled."

Jilt was once a stronger epithet than at present. It is for earlier *jillet*, which is a diminutive of *Jill*, the companion of Jack. *Jill*, again, is short for *Gillian*, i.e. *Juliana*, so that *jilt* is a doublet of Shakespeare's sweetest heroine. *Termagant*, like *shrew* (p. 34), was formerly used of both sexes, *e.g.*, by Sir John Falstaff—

> "'Twas time to counterfeit, or that hot *termagant* Scot (Douglas) had paid me scot and lot too." (1 *Henry IV.*, v. 4.)

In its oldest sense of a Saracen god it regularly occurs with *Mahound* (Mahomet)—

> "Marsilies fait porter un livre avant :
>   La lei i fut Mahum e *Tervagan*."[1]
>   (*Chanson de Roland*, l. 610.)

Ariosto has *Trivigante*. Being introduced into the medieval drama, the name became synonymous with a stage fury—

> "I would have such a fellow whipped for o'erdoing *Termagant*."
>   (*Hamlet*, iii. 2.)

The origin of the word is unknown, but its sense development is strangely different from that of Mahomet (p. 43).

[1] "Marsil has a book brought forward : the law of Mahomet and Termagant was in it."

CHAPTER IV

WORDS AND PLACES

A very large number of wares are named from the places from which they come. This is especially common in the case of woven fabrics, and the origin is often obvious, e.g., *arras, cashmere* (by folk-etymology, *kerseymere*), *damask, holland.* The following are perhaps not all so evident—*frieze* from *Friesland*[1]; *fustian*, Old Fr. *fustaine* (*futaine*), from *Fustat*, a suburb of Cairo; *muslin*, Fr. *mousseline*, from *Mosul* in Kurdistan; *shalloon* from *Châlons*-sur-Marne; *lawn* from *Laon*; *jean*, formerly *jane*, from *Genoa* (French *Gênes*[2]); *cambric* from *Kamerijk*, the Dutch name of Cambrai (*cf.* the obsolete *dornick*, from the Dutch name of *Tournay*); *tartan* from the *Tartars* (properly *Tatars*), used vaguely for Orientals; *sarcenet* from the Saracens; *sendal*, ultimately from *India* (*cf.* Greco-Lat. *sindon*, Indian cloth); *tabby*, Old Fr. *atabis*, from the name of a suburb of Bagdad, formerly used of a kind of silk, but now of a cat marked something like the material in question.

[1] Whence also *cheval de frise*, a contrivance used by the Frieslanders against cavalry. The German name is *die spanischen Reiter*, explained by Ludwig as "a bar with iron-spikes; *cheval de frise*, a warlick instrument, to keep off the horse."

[2] The form *jeans* appears to be usual in America—"His hands were thrust carelessly into the side pockets of a gray *jeans* coat."

(Meredith Nicholson, *War of the Carolinas*, Ch. 15.)

Brittany used to be famous for hempen fabrics, and the villages of *Locrenan* and *Daoulas* gave their names to *lockram* (see quotation from *Coriolanus*, p. 42) and *dowlas*—

> *Hostess.* You owe me money, Sir John ; and now you pick a quarrel to beguile me of it : I bought you a dozen of shirts to your back.
>
> *Falstaff.* Dowlas, filthy *dowlas;* I have given them away to bakers' wives, and they have made bolters of them.
>
> (1 *Henry IV.*, iii. 3.)

Duffel is a place near Antwerp—

> "And let it be of *duffil* gray,
>   As warm a cloak as man can sell."
>
> (WORDSWORTH, *Alice Fell.*)

and *Worstead* is in Norfolk. Of other commodities *majolica* comes from *Majorca*, called in Spanish *Mallorca*, and in medieval Latin *Majolica* ; *bronze* from *Brundusium* (Brindisi), *delf* from *Delft*, the *magnet* from *Magnesia*, the *shallot*, Fr. *échalote*, in Old French also *escalogne*, whence archaic Eng. *scallion*, from *Ascalon;* the *sardine* from *Sardinia*. A *milliner*, formerly *milaner*, dealt in goods from *Milan*. *Cravat* dates from the Thirty Years' War, in which the *Croats*, earlier *Cravats*, played a part. *Ermine* is in medieval Latin *mus Armenius*, Armenian mouse, but the name perhaps comes, through Fr. *hermine*, from Old High Ger. *harmo*, weasel. *Buncombe*, more usually *bunkum*, is the name of a county in North Carolina. To make a speech "for Buncombe" means, in American politics, to show your constituents that you are doing your best for your £400 a year or its American equivalent. Cf. *Billingsgate* and *Limehouse*.

The adjective *spruce* was formerly *pruce* and meant Prussia. Todd quotes from Holinshed—

> "Sir Edward Howard then admirall, and with him Sir Thomas Parre in doubletts of crimsin velvett, etc., were apparelled after the fashion of Prussia or *Spruce.*"

Of similar origin are *spruce-leather*, *spruce-beer*, and the *spruce-fir*, of which Evelyn says—

"Those from Prussia (which we call *spruce*) and Norway are the best."

Among coins the *bezant* comes from *Byzantium*, the *florin* from *Florence*, and Shylock's *ducat*, chiefly a Venetian coin, from the *ducato* d'Apuglia, the Duchy of Apulia, where it was first coined in the 12th century. The *dollar* is the Low Ger. *daler*, for Ger. *Taler*, originally called a *Joachimstaler*, from the silver-mine of Joachimstal, "Joachim's dale," in Bohemia. Cotgrave registers a curious Old French perversion *jocondale*, "a *daller*, a piece of money worth about 3s. sterl." Some fruits may also be mentioned, *e.g.*, the *damson* from *Damascus*, through Old Fr. *damaisine*, "a damascene or *damsen* plum" (Cotgrave); the *currant* from *Corinth*, and the *peach*, Fr. *pêche*, from Vulgar Lat. *pessica*, for *Persica*.

A *polony* was originally a *Bolonian* sausage, from *Bologna*. *Parchment*, Fr. *parchemin*, is the adjective *pergamenus*, from *Pergamus*, in Asia Minor. *Spaniel* is the Old Fr. *espagneul* (*épagneul*), lit. Spanish. We have the adjective *Moorish* in *morris*, or *morrice*, *pike*—

"He that sets up his rest to do more exploits with his mace than a *morris pike*." (*Comedy of Errors*, iv. 3.)

In *morris dance*, Fr. *danse mauresque*, the same adjective is used with something of the vagueness to be noticed in connection with India and Turkey (p. 52). Shakespeare uses the Spanish form—

> "I have seen him
> Caper upright, like to a wild *morisco*,
> Shaking the bloody darts as he his bells."
>
> (2 *Henry VI.*, iii. 1.)

Other "local" dances are the *polka*, which means Polish woman, *mazurka*, woman of Mazuria, and the obsolete *polonaise*, lit. Polish, *cracovienne*, from Cracow, and *varsovienne*, from Warsaw. The *tarantella*, like the *tarantula* spider, takes its name from Taranto, in Italy. The tune of the dance is said to have been originally employed as a cure for the lethargy caused by the bite of the spider. Florio has *tarantola*, "a serpent called an eft or an evet. Some take it to be a flye whose sting is perillous and deadly, and nothing but divers sounds of musicke can cure the patient."

The town of *Troyes* has given its name to *troy* weight. The armourers of *Bilbao*, in Spain, made swords of such perfect temper that they could be bent point to hilt. Hence Falstaff describes himself in the buck-basket as—

"Compassed, like a good *bilbo*, in the circumference of a peck, hilt to point, heel to head." (*Merry Wives*, iii. 5.)

The *Andrea Ferrara*, or Scottish broadsword, carried by Fergus M'Ivor, bears, according to some authorities, the name of an armourer of Ferrara, in Italy. According to others, *Andrea dei Ferrari* was a sword-maker at Belluno. I have heard it affirmed by a Scottish drill-sergeant that the real name of this genius was *Andrew Ferrars*,[1] and that he belonged to the same nationality as other great men.

An *argosy*, formerly also *ragusye*, was named from

---

[1] A Scotch reviewer (*Glasgow Herald*, 13th April 1912) corrects me here—"His name was certainly not Ferrars, but Ferrier. He was probably an Arbroath man." Some readers may remember that, after General *Todleben's* brilliant defence of Sebastopol (1854-5), *Punch* discovered a respectable ancestry for him also. In some lines commencing—

"I ken him weel, the chield was born in Fife,
　　The bairn of Andrew Drummond and his wife,"

it was shown that the apparently foreign name had been conferred on the gifted child because of the agility with which he used to "*toddle ben* the hoose."

the Adriatic port of *Ragusa*, and a *lateen* sail is a *Latin*, *i.e.* Mediterranean, sail; *gamboge* is the Fr. *Cambodge* Cambodia, and *indigo* is from Span. *indico*, Indian. Of wines, *malmsey*, chiefly remembered in connection with George of Clarence, and *malvoisie* are doublets, from *Monemvasia* in the Morea. *Port* is named from *Oporto*, i.e. *o porto*, the harbour (cf. *le Havre*), and *sherry* (see p. 116) from *Xeres*, Lat. *Cæsaris* (urbs); cf. *Saragossa*, from *Cæsarea Augusta*.

But it is possible to be mistaken in connecting countries with products. *Brazil* wood is not named from the country, but *vice-versâ*. It was known as a dye-wood as early as the 12th century, and the name is found in many of the European languages. The Portuguese navigators found large quantities of it in South America and named the country accordingly. They christened an island *Madeira*, timber, Lat. *materia*, for a similar reason. The *canary* comes from the Canary Islands, but its name is good Latin. The largest of these islands, *Canaria*, was so called by the Romans from the dogs found there. The *guinea*-fowl and *guinea* gold came first from the west coast of Africa, but the *guinea-pig* is a native of Brazil. The name probably came from the *Guinea-men*, or slave-ships, which regularly followed a triangular course. They sailed outward to the west coast of Africa with English goods. These they exchanged for slaves, whom they transported to the West Indies, the horrible "middle passage," and finally they sailed homeward with New World produce, including, no doubt, *guinea-pigs* brought home by sailors. The turkey is also called *guinea-fowl* in the 17th century, probably to be explained in the same way. The German name for guinea-pig, *Meerschweinchen*, seems to mean little pig from over the sea.

Guinea was a vague geographical expression in the
17th century, but not so vague as India or Turkey.
Indian ink comes from China (Fr. *encre de Chine*), and
Indian corn from America. The names given to the
turkey are extraordinary. We are not surprised that,
as an American bird, it should be naturally connected
with India; *cf.* West Indies, Red Indian, etc. *Turk*
was in the 16th and 17th centuries a vague term for
non-Christians—

"Jews, *Turks*, infidels, and hereticks." (Collect for Good Friday.)

and we find also *Turkey wheat* for maize. The following
names for the turkey, given in a *Nomenclator* in eight
languages, published in Germany in 1602, do not exhaust
the list:—

German.—*Indianisch* oder *Kalekuttisch*[1] oder *Welsch*[2] Hun.
Dutch.—*Calcoensche* oft *Turckische* Henne.
French.—Geline ou poulle d'*Inde*, ou d'*Africque*.
Italian.—Gallina d'*India*.
Spanish.—Pavon (peacock) de las *Indias*.
English.—Cok off Inde !

No doubt the turkey was confused with other birds, for
we find Fr. *geline d'Inde* before the discovery of America.
D'Inde has become *dinde*, whence a new masculine
dindon has been formed.

The early etymologists were fond of identifying
foreign wares with place-names. They connected *diaper*
with Ypres, *gingham* with Guingamp (in Brittany),
drugget with Drogheda, and the *sedan* chair with Sedan.
Such guesses are almost always wrong. The origin of
diaper is doubtful, that of *drugget* quite unknown, and
gingham is Malay. As far as we know at present, the
sedan came from Italy in the 16th century, and it is
there, among derivatives of Lat. *sedere*, to sit, that its

[1] Calicut, not Calcutta.   [2] See *walnut* (p. 151).

origin must be sought, unless indeed the original *Sedan* was some mute, inglorious *Hansom*.[1]

[1] As the *hansom* has now become of archæological interest only, it may be recorded here that it took its name from that of its inventor—" The *Hansom's* patent (cab) is especially constructed for getting quickly over the ground" (Pulleyn's *Etymological Compendium*, 1853). *Sic transit !*

CHAPTER V

PHONETIC ACCIDENTS

THE history of a word has to be studied from the double point of view of sound and sense, or, to use more technical terms, phonetics and semantics. In the logical order of things it seems natural to deal first with the less interesting aspect, phonetics, the physical processes by which sounds are gradually transformed. Speaking generally, it may be said that phonetic changes are governed by the law of least resistance, a sound which presents difficulty being gradually and unconsciously modified by a whole community or race. With the general principles of phonetics I do not propose to deal, but a few simple examples will serve to illustrate the one great law on which this science is based.

The population of this country is educationally divided by the letter *h* into three classes, which we may describe as the confident, the anxious, and the indifferent. The same division existed in imperial Rome, where educated people sounded the aspirate, which completely disappeared from the every-day language of the lower classes, the so-called Vulgar Latin, from which the Romance languages are descended, so far as their working vocabulary is concerned. The anxious class was also represented. A Latin epigrammatist[1] remarks that since Arrius, prophetic name, has visited the Ionic islands, they will probably be henceforth known as the *Hionic* islands. To the disappearance of the *h* from Vulgar Latin is due the fact that the Romance languages have no aspirate. French still writes the initial *h* in some words by etymological reaction, e.g., *homme* for Old Fr. *ome*, and also at one time really had an aspirate in the case of words of Germanic origin, e.g., *la honte*, shame. But this *h* is no longer sounded, although it still, by tradition, prevents elision and *liaison*, mistakes in which are regarded much in the same way as a misplaced aspirate in English. The "educated" *h* of modern English is largely an artificial restoration; *cf.* the modern *hotel*-keeper with the older word *ostler* (see p. 164), or the family name *Armitage* with the restored *hermitage*.

We have dropped the *k* sound in initial *kn*, as in *knave*, still sounded in Ger. *Knabe*, boy. French gets over the difficulty by inserting a vowel between the two consonants, e.g., *canif* is a Germanic word cognate with Eng. *knife*. This is a common device in French when a word of Germanic origin begins with two consonants. *Cf.* Fr. *dérive*, drift, Eng. *drive* ; Fr. *varech*, sea-weed, Eng. *wrack*. *Harangue*, formerly *harengue*, is Old High Ger. *hring*, Eng. *ring*, the allusion being to the circle formed by the audience. Fr. *chenapan*, rogue, is Ger. *Schnapphahn*, robber, lit. fowl-stealer. The *shallop* that "flitteth silken-sail'd, skimming down to Camelot," is Fr. *chaloupe*, probably identical with Du. *sloep*, sloop.

The general dislike that French has for a double

---

[1] " Nec sibi postilla metuebant talia verba,
    Cum subito adfertur nuntius horribilis,
    Ionios fluctus, postquam illuc Arrius isset,
    Iam non *Ionios* esse, sed *Hionios*."

                                                                     (*Catullus*, 84.)

consonant sound at the beginning of a word appears also
in the transformation of all Latin words which began
with *sc*, *sp*, *st*, e.g., *scola* > *escole* (*école*), *spongia* > *esponge*
(*éponge*), *stabulum* > *estable* (*étable*). English words
derived from French generally show the older form,
but without the initial vowel, *school*, *sponge*, *stable*.

The above are very simple examples of sound change.
There are certain less regular changes, which appear to
work in a more arbitrary fashion and bring about more
picturesque results. Three of the most important of
these are assimilation, dissimilation, and metathesis.

Assimilation is the tendency of a sound to imitate
its neighbour. The tree called the *lime* was formerly
the *line*, and earlier still the *lind*. We see the older
form in *linden* and in such place-names as *Lyndhurst*,
lime wood. *Line* often occurred in such compounds as
line-bark, *line-bast*, *line-wood*, where the second com-
ponent began with a lip consonant. The *n* became
also a lip consonant because it was easier to pronounce,
and by the 17th century we generally find *lime* instead
of *line*. We have a similar change in *Lombard* for
Ger. *lang-bart*, long-beard, or, according to some, long-
axe. For *Liverpool* we find also *Litherpool* in early
records. If the reader attempts to pronounce both
names rapidly, he will be able to form his own opinion
as to whether it is more natural for *Liverpool* to become
Litherpool or *vice-versa*, a vexed question with philologists. Fr. *vélin*, a derivative of Old Fr. *veel* (*veau*),
calf, and *venin*, Lat. *venenum*, have given Eng. *vellum*
and *venom*, the final consonant being in each case
assimilated[1] to the initial labial. So also *mushroom*, Fr.
mousseron, from *mousse*, moss.

---

[1] Apart from assimilation, there is a tendency in English to substitute
-*m* for -*n*, e.g. *grogram* for *grogran* (see p. 68). In the family name *Hansom*,
for *Hanson*, we have dissimilation of *n* (see p. 57).

Vulgar Lat. *circare* (from *circa*, around) gave Old Fr. *cerchier*, Eng. *search*. In modern Fr. *chercher* the initial consonant has been influenced by the medial *ch*. The *m* of the curious word *ampersand*, variously spelt, is due to the neighbouring *p*. It is applied to the sign &. I thought it obsolete till I came across it on successive days in two contemporary writers—

"One of my mother's chief cares was to teach me my letters, which I learnt from big A to *Ampersand* in the old hornbook at Lantrig." (QUILLER COUCH, *Dead Man's Rock*, Ch. 2.)

"Tommy knew all about the work. Knew every letter in it from A to *Emperzan*." (PETT RIDGE, *In the Wars*.)

Children used to repeat the alphabet thus — "A per se A, B per se B," and so on to "*and per se and*." The symbol & is an abbreviation of Lat. *et*, written &.

Dissimilation is the opposite process. The archaic word *pomander*—

"I have sold all my trumpery ; not a counterfeit stone, not a riband, glass, *pomander*, brooch, . . . to keep my pack from fasting." (*Winter's Tale*, iv. 3.)

was formerly spelt *pomeamber*. It comes from Old Fr. *pome ambre*, apple of amber, a ball of perfume once carried by the delicate. In this case one of the two lip consonants has been dissimilated. A like change has occurred in Fr. *nappe*, cloth, from Lat. *mappa*, whence our *napkin*, *apron* (p. 113), and the family name *Napier*.

The sounds most frequently affected by dissimilation are those represented by the letters *l*, *n*, and *r*. Fr. *gonfalon* is for older *gonfanon*. Chaucer uses the older form, Milton the newer—

"Ten thousand thousand ensigns high advanc'd,
 Standards and *gonfalons*, 'twixt van and rear,
 Stream in the air."

(*Paradise Lost*, v. 589.)

Gonfanon is of Germanic origin. It means literally "battle-flag," and the second element is cognate with English *fane* or *vane* (Ger. *Fahne*). Eng. *pilgrim* and Fr. *pèlerin*, from Lat. *peregrinus*, illustrate the change from *r* to *l*, while the word *frail*, an osier basket for figs, is due to a change from *l* to *r*, which goes back to Roman times. A grammarian of imperial Rome named Probus compiled, about the 3rd or 4th century, A.D., a list of cautions as to mispronunciation. In this list we find "*flagellum*, non *fragellum*." In the sense of switch, twig, *fragellum* gave Old Fr. *freel*, basket made of twigs, whence Eng. *frail;* while the correct *flagellum* gave Old Fr. *fleel* (*fléau*), whence Eng. *flail.* A Vulgar Lat. **mora*, mulberry, from Lat. *morus*, mulberry tree, has given Fr. *mûre*. The *r* of *berry* has brought about dissimilation in Eng. *mulberry* and Ger. *Maulbeere.* *Colonel* has the spelling of Fr. *colonel*, but its pronunciation points rather to the dissimilated Spanish form *coronel* which is common in Elizabethan English. Cotgrave has *colonel*, "a *colonell*, or *coronell;* the commander of a regiment."

The female name *Annabel* is a dissimilation of *Amabel*, whence *Mabel*. By confusion with the popular medieval name *Orable*, Lat. *orabilis*, *Annabel* has become *Arabel* or *Arabella*. Our *level* is Old Fr. *livel*, Vulgar Lat. **libellum*, for *libella*, a plummet, diminutive of *libra*, scales. Old Fr. *livel* became by dissimilation *nivel*, now *niveau*. Many conjectures have been made as to the etymology of *oriel*. It is from Old Fr. *oriol*, a recess, or sanctum, which first occurs in an Anglo-Norman poem of the 12th century on Becket. This is from a Late Latin diminutive *aulæolum*, a small chapel or shrine, which was dissimilated into *auræolum*.

Sometimes dissimilation leads to the disappearance of a consonant, *e.g.*, Eng. *feeble*, Fr. *faible*, represents

Lat. *flebilis*, lamentable, from *flere*, to weep. *Fugleman* was once *flugelman*, from Ger. *Flügelmann*, wing man, *i.e.*, a tall soldier on the wing who exaggerated the movements of musketry drill for the guidance of the rest.

Metathesis is the transposition of two sounds. A simple case is our *trouble*, Fr. *troubler*, from Lat. *turbulare*. *Maggot* is for Mid. Eng. *maddok*, a diminutive of Anglo-Sax. *maþa*; *cf.* Ger. *Made*, maggot. *Kittle*, in the phrase "kittle cattle," is identical with *tickle*; *cf.* Ger. *kitzeln*, to tickle. One theory for the origin of *tankard* is that it stands for **cantar*, from Lat. *cantharus*, with which it corresponds exactly in meaning; e.g., *cantharus*, "a pot, a jugge, a *tankerd*" (Cooper); *cantharo*, "a *tankard* or jug that houldeth much" (Florio); *canthare*, "a great jugge, or *tankard*" (Cotgrave). The metathesis may be due to association with the name Tankard (Tancred).

Wattle and *wallet* are used indifferently in Mid. English for a little bag. Shakespeare no doubt had in mind the *wattles* of a cock or turkey when he made Gonzalo speak of mountaineers—

> "Dew-lapp'd like bulls, whose throats had hanging at them
> *Wallets* of flesh."   (*Tempest*, iii. 3.)

Fr. *moustique* is for earlier *mousquite*, from Span. *mosquito*, a diminutive from Lat. *musca*, a fly. *Tinsel* is Fr. *étincelle*, spark, earlier *estincele*, which supposes a Lat. **stincilla* for *scintilla*. The old word *anlace*, dagger, common in Mid. English and revived by Byron and Scott—

> "His harp in silken scarf was slung,
> And by his side an *anlace* hung."
> (*Rokeby*, v. 15.)

has provoked many guesses. Its oldest form, *anelas*, is a metathesis of the common Old Fr. *alenas*, dagger. This is formed from *alêne*, of Germanic origin, cognate with *awl;* cf. *cutlass,* Fr. *coutelas* (p. 126). *Beverage* is from Old Fr. *bevrage,* or *beuvrage,* now *breuvage,* Vulgar Lat. **biberaticum,* from *bibere,* to drink. Here, as in the case of *level* (p. 58), and *search* (p. 57), English preserves the older form. In *Martello* tower, from a fort taken by the British (1794) in *Mortella, i.e.,* Myrtle, Bay, Corsica, we have vowel metathesis.

It goes without saying that such linguistic phenomena are often observed in the case of children and uneducated people. Not long ago the writer was urged by a gardener to embellish his garden with a *ruskit* arch. When metathesis extends beyond one word we have what is known as a *Spoonerism,* the original type of which is said to be—

> "*Kinquerings congs* their titles take."

We have seen (p. 57) that the letters *l, n, r* are particularly subject to dissimilation and metathesis. But we sometimes find them alternating without apparent reason. Thus *banister* is a modern form for the correct *baluster.*[1] This was not at first applied to the rail, but to the bulging colonets on which it rests. Fr. *balustre* comes, through Italian, from Greco-Lat. *balaustium,* a pomegranate flower, the shape of which resembles the supports of a balustrade. Cotgrave explains *balustres* as "*ballisters;* little, round and short pillars, ranked on the outside of cloisters, terraces, galleries, etc." *Glamour* is a doublet of *grammar* (see p. 145), and *flounce* was formerly *frounce,* from Fr *froncer,* now only used of "knitting" the brows—

> "Till civil-suited morn appear,
> Not trickt and *frounc't* as she was wont
> With the Attic boy to hunt."
>
> (*Penseroso,* l. 123.)

---

[1] *Cf.* the similar change in the family name *Banister* (p. 179).

Fr. *flibustier*, whence our *filibuster*, was earlier *fribustier*, a corruption of Du. *vrijbuiter*, whence directly the Eng. *freebooter*.[1]

All words tend in popular usage to undergo a certain amount of shrinkage. The reduction of Lat. *digitale*, from *digitus*, finger, to Fr. *dé*, thimble (little thumb) is a striking example. The strong tonic accent of English, which is usually on the first, or root, syllable, brings about a kind of telescoping which makes us very unintelligible to foreigners. This is seen in the pronunciation of names such as *Cholmondeley* and *Marjoribanks*. *Bethlehem* hospital, for lunatics, becomes *bedlam;* Mary *Magdalene*, taken as a type of tearful repentance, gives us *maudlin*, now generally used of the lachrymose stage of intoxication. *Sacristan* is contracted into *sexton*. Fr. *paralysie* becomes *palsy*, and *hydropisie* becomes *dropsy*. The fuller form of the word usually persists in the literary language, or is artificially introduced at a later period, so that we get such doublets as *proctor* and *procurator*.

In the case of French words which have a prefix this prefix is very frequently dropped in English, e.g., *raiment* for *arrayment;* while suffixes, or final syllables, often disappear, *e.g.*, treasure *trove*, for Old Fr. *trové* (*trouvé*), or become assimilated to some familiar English ending, e.g., *parish*, Fr. *paroisse*, *skirmish*, Fr. *escarmouche;* *cartridge*, Fr. *cartouche*, *partridge*, Fr. *perdrix*. A good example of such shrinkage is the word *vamp*, part of a shoe, Old Fr. *avant-pie* (*pied*), which became Mid. Eng. *vampey*, and then lost its final syllable. We may

---

[1] It may be noted here that a *buccaneer* was not originally a pirate, but a man whose business was the smoking of beef in the West Indies. The name comes from a native word *boucan*, adopted into French, and explained by Cotgrave as a "woodden-gridiron whereon the cannibals broile pieces of men, and other flesh."

compare *vambrace*, armour for the forearm, Fr. *avant-bras*, *vanguard*, Fr. *avant-garde*, often reduced to *van*—

> " Go, charge Agrippa
> Plant those that have revolted in the *van;*
> That Antony may seem to spend his fury
> Upon himself."
>
> (*Antony and Cleopatra*, iv. 6.)

and the obsolete *vaunt-courier*, forerunner—

> "You sulphurous and thought-executing fires,
> *Vaunt-couriers* of oak-cleaving thunderbolts."
>
> (*Lear*, iii. 2.)

When the initial vowel is *a-*, its loss may have been helped by confusion with the indefinite article. Thus for *anatomy* we find *atomy*, for a skeleton or scarecrow figure, applied by Mistress Quickly to the constable (2 *Henry IV.*, v. 4). *Peal* is for *appeal*, call ; *mend* for *amend*, *lone* for *alone*, i.e., *all one*. *Peach*, used by Falstaff—

> " If I be ta'en, I'll *peach* for this."
>
> (1 *Henry IV.*, ii. 2.)

is for older *appeach*, related to *impeach*. *Size*, in all its senses, is for *assize*, Fr. *assise*, with a general meaning of allowance or assessment, from Fr. *asseoir*, to put, lay. *Sizars* at Cambridge are properly students in receipt of certain allowances called *sizings*. With painters' *size* we may compare Ital. *assisa*, " *size* that painters use" (Florio). We use the form *assize* in speaking of the " sitting" of the judges, but those most familiar with this tribunal speak of being tried at the *'sizes*. The obsolete word *cate*, on which Petruchio plays—

> " For dainties are all *cates*—and therefore, Kate,
> Take this of me, Kate of my consolation."
>
> (*Taming of the Shrew*, ii. 1.)

is for earlier *acate*, an Old French dialect form corresponding to modern Fr. *achat*, purchase. The man entrusted with purchasing was called an *acatour* or *catour* (whence the name *Cator*), later *cater*, now extended to *caterer*, like *fruiterer* for *fruiter*, *poulterer* for *poulter* and *upholsterer* for *upholdster* or *upholder*.[1]

Limbeck has been squeezed out by the orthodox *alembic*—

> "Memory the warder of the brain,
> Shall be a fume, and the receipt of reason
> A *limbeck* only."
>
> (*Macbeth*, i. 7.)

and *prentice* has given way to *apprentice*. *Tire* and *attire* both survive, and *maze* persists by the side of *amaze* with the special sense which I have heard a Notts collier express by *puzzle-garden* (*cf.* Ger. *Irrgarten*). *Binnacle* is a corruption, perhaps due to association with *bin*, of earlier *bittacle*, from Lat. *habitaculum*, a little dwelling. It may have come to us through Fr. *habitacle* or Port. *bitacola*, "the *bittacle*, a frame of timber in the steerage, where the compass is placed on board a ship" (Vieyra, *Port. Dict.*, 1794). As King of Scotland, King George has a household official known as the *limner*, or painter. For *limner*[2] we find in the 15th century *lumner* and *luminour*, which is aphetic for *alluminour*, or *enlumineur*. Cotgrave, s.v. *enlumineur de livres*, says, "we call one that coloureth, or painteth upon, paper, or parchment, an *alluminer*."

But confusion with the article is not necessary in order to bring about aphesis. It occurs regularly in

---

[1] *Upholsterer* has become specialised in sense; cf. *undertaker* (of funerals), and *stationer*, properly a tradesman with a *station* or stall. *Costermonger* illustrates the converse process. It meant originally a dealer in *costards*, i.e. apples. The French costermonger has the more appropriate name of *marchand des quatre saisons*.

[2] English *i* sometimes occurs as an attempt at the French and Celtic *u*; cf. *brisk* from *brusque*, *periwig* (p. 69), and *whisky* (p. 68).

the case of words beginning with *esc, esp, est*, borrowed from Old French (see p. 56). Thus we have *squire* from *escuyer* (*écuyer*), *skew* from Old Fr. *eschuer*, to dodge, "eschew," ultimately cognate with Eng. *shy, spice* from *espice* (*épice*), *sprite* from *esprit, stage* from *estage* (*étage*), etc. In some cases we have the fuller form also, e.g., *esquire, eschew*; cf. *sample* and *example*. *Fender*, whether before a fireplace or slung outside a ship, is for *defender*; *fence* is always for *defence*, either in the sense of a barrier or in allusion to the noble art of self-defence.[1] The *tender* of a ship or of a locomotive is the *attender*, and *taint* is aphetic for *attaint*, Fr. *atteinte*, touch—

> "I will not poison thee with my *attaint*."
> (*Lucrece*, l. 1072.)

Puzzle was in Mid. Eng. *opposaile*, *i.e.*, something put before one. We still speak of "a poser."

Spital, for *hospital*, survives in *Spitalfields*, and *Spittlegate* at Grantham and elsewhere. *Crew* is for *accrewe* (Holinshed). It meant properly a reinforcement, lit. on-growth, from Fr. *accroître*, to accrue. In *recruit*, we have a later instance of the same idea. Fr. *recrue*, recruit, from *recroître*, to grow again, is still feminine, like many other military terms which were originally abstract or collective. Cotgrave has *recreuë*, "a supplie, or filling up of a defective company of souldiers, etc." We have *possum* for *opossum*, and *coon* for *racoon*, and this for *arrahacoune*, which I find in a 16th-century

---

[1] Our ancestors appear to have been essentially pacific. With *fence*, for *defence*, we may compare Ger. *schirmen*, to fence, from *Schirm*, screen (cf. *Regenschirm*, umbrella), which, passing through Italian and French, has given us *skirmish, scrimmage, scaramouch* (see p. 142), and Shakespearean *scrimer*, fencer (*Hamlet*, iv. 7). So also Ger. *Gewehr*, weapon, is cognate with Eng. *weir*, and means defence—

> "Cet animal est très méchant;
> Quand on l'attaque, il se défend."

record of travel; *cf.* American *skeeter* for *mosquito*. In these two cases we perhaps have also the deliberate intention to shorten (see p. 66), as also in the obsolete Australian *tench*, for the aphetic *'tentiary*, i.e., *penitentiary*. With this we may compare *'tec* for *detective*.

Drawing-room is for *withdrawing room*, and only the final *t* of *saint* is left in *Tooley St.*, famed for its three tailors, formerly *Saint Olave Street*, and *tawdry*. This latter word is well known to be derived from *Saint Audrey's* fair. It was not originally depreciatory—

"Come, you promised me a *tawdry* lace, and a pair of sweet gloves." (*Winter's Tale*, iv. 3.)

and the full form is recorded by Palsgrave, who has *Seynt Andries* (read *Audrie's*) *lace*, "cordon." The verb *vie* comes from Old Fr. *envier*, to challenge, Lat. *invitare*, whence the phrase *à l'envi l'un de l'autre*, "in emulation one of the other" (Cotgrave); cf. *gin* (trap), Fr. *engin*, Lat. *ingenium*. The prefix *dis* or *des* is lost in *Spencer* (see p. 165), *spite*, *splay*, *sport*, *stain*, etc.

In *drat*, formerly *'od rot*, *zounds* for *God's wounds*, *'sdeath*, *odsbodikins*, etc., there is probably a deliberate avoidance of profanity. The same intention appears in *Gogs*—

"'Ay, by *gogs-wouns*!' quoth he; and swore so loud,
That, all amaz'd, the priest let fall the book."
(*Taming of the Shrew*, iii. 2.)

Cf. Fr. *parbleu* for *par Dieu*, and Ger. *Potz* for *Gottes*.

This English tendency to aphesis is satirised in a French song of the 14th century, intentionally written in bad French. Thus, in the line—

"Or sont il vint le tans que Glais voura vauchier."[1]

Glais is for *Anglais* and *vauchier* is for *chevauchier*

[1] "Now the time has come when the English will wish to ride."

E

(*chevaucher*), to ride on a foray. The literary language runs counter to this instinct, though Shakespeare wrote *haviour* for *behaviour* and *longing* for *belonging*, while such forms as *billiments* for *habiliments* and *sparagus* for *asparagus* are regular up to the 18th century. Children keep up the national practice when they say *member* for *remember* and *zamine* for *examine*. It is quite certain that *baccy* and *tater* would be recognised literary forms if America had been discovered two centuries sooner or printing invented two centuries later.

Many words are shortened, not by natural and gradual shrinkage, but by deliberate laziness. The national distaste for many syllables appears in *wire* for *telegram*, the Artful Dodger's *wipe* for the clumsy *pocket handkerchief*, *soccer* for *association*, and such portmanteau words as *squarson*, an individual who is at once *squire* and *parson*, or *Bakerloo* for *Baker St. and Waterloo*.

The simplest way of reducing a word is to take the first syllable and make it a symbol for the rest. Of comparatively modern formation are *pub* and *Zoo*, with which we may compare *Bart's*, for Saint Bartholomew's, *Cri*, *Pav*, "half a *mo'*," *bike*, and even *paj*, for *pageant*.

This method of shortening words was very popular in the 17th century, from which period date *cit*(izen), *mob*(ile vulgus), the fickle crowd, and *pun*(digrion). We often find the fuller *mobile* used for *mob*. The origin of *pundigrion* is uncertain. It may be an illiterate attempt at Ital. *puntiglio*, which, like Fr. *pointe*, was used of a verbal quibble or fine distinction. Most of these clipped forms are easily identified, e.g., *cab*(riolet), *gent*(leman), *hack*(ney), *vet*(erinary surgeon). *Cad* is for Scot. *caddie*, errand boy, now familiar in connection with golf, and *caddie* is from Fr. *cadet*, younger. The word had not always the very strong meaning we now

associate with it. Among *Sketches by Boz* is one
entitled—

"The last Cab driver and the first Omnibus *Cad*,"

where *cad* means conductor. On *tick*, for on *ticket*, is
found in the 17th century. We may compare the more
modern *biz* and *spec*. *Brig* is for *brigantine*, Ital.
brigantino, "a kinde of pinnasse or small barke called a
brigantine" (Florio). The original meaning is pirate
ship; cf. *brigand*. *Wag* has improved in meaning. It
is for older *waghalter*. Cotgrave has *baboin* (*babouin*),
"a trifling, busie, or crafty knave; a crackrope, *waghalter*, etc." The older sense survives in the phrase "to
play the *wag*," *i.e.* truant. For the "rope" figure we may
compare Scot. *hempie*, a minx, and obsolete Ital.
cavestrolo, a diminutive from Lat. *capistrum*, halter,
explained by Florio as "a *wag*, a haltersacke." Modern
Ital. *capestro* is used in the same sense. *Crack-rope* is
shortened to *crack*. Justice Shallow remembered
Falstaff breaking Skogan's head—

"When he was a *crack*, not thus high."
(2 *Henry IV.*, iii. 2.)

Chap is for *chapman*, once in general use for a
merchant and still a common family name. It is
cognate with *cheap*, *chaffer*, and Ger. *kaufen*, to buy, and
probably comes from Lat. *caupo*, tavern keeper. We
have the Dutch form in *horse-coper*, and also in the
word *coopering*, the illicit sale of spirits by Dutch boats
to North Sea fishermen.[1] *Merchant* was used by the
Elizabethans in the same way as our *chap*. Thus the
Countess of Auvergne calls Talbot a "riddling *merchant*"

[1] *Cf.* also Dan *Kjöbenhavn* (Copenhagen), the merchants' haven, the
numerous Swedish place-names ending in *-köping*, e.g. *Jönköping*, and our
own *Chippings*, or market-towns.

(1 *Henry VI.*, ii. 3). We may also compare Scot. *callant*, lad, from the Picard form of Fr. *chaland*, customer—

> "He had seen many a braw callant, far less than Guse Gibbie, fight brawly under Montrose." (*Old Mortality*, Ch. 1.)

and our own expression "a rum *customer*," reduced in America to "a rum *cuss.*" *Hock*, for *Hochheimer*, wine from Hochheim, occurs as early as Beaumont and Fletcher; and *rum*, spirit, is for earlier *rumbullion*, of obscure origin. *Gin* is for *geneva*, a corruption of Fr. *genièvre*, Lat. *juniperus*, with the berries of which it is flavoured. The history of *grog* is more complicated. The stuff called *grogram*, earlier *grograyne*, is from Fr. *gros grain*, coarse grain. Admiral Vernon (18th century) was called by the sailors "Old Grog" from his habit of wearing grogram breeches. When he issued orders that the regular allowance of rum was henceforth to be diluted with water, the sailors promptly baptized the mixture with his nickname.

Sometimes the two first syllables survive. We have *navvy* for *navigator*, *brandy* for *brandywine*, from Du. *brandewyn*, lit. burnt wine, and *whisky* for *usquebaugh*, Gaelic *uisge-beatha*, water of life (cf. *eau-de-vie*), so that the literal meaning of *whisky* is very innocent. It has a doublet in the river-name *Usk*. Before the 18th century *usquebaugh* is the regular form. In the following passage the Irish variety is referred to—

> "The prime is *usquebaugh*, which cannot be made anywhere in that perfection ; and whereas we drink it here in *aqua vitæ* measures, it goes down there by beer-glassfuls, being more natural to the nation." (HOWELL, 1634.)

Canter is for *Canterbury* gallop, the pace of pilgrims

riding to the shrine of St Thomas. John Dennis, known as Dennis the Critic, says of Pope—

"Boileau's Pegasus has all his paces. The Pegasus of Pope, like a Kentish post-horse, is always on the *Canterbury*."

(On the Preliminaries to the Dunciad.)

In *bugle*, for *bugle-horn*, lit. wild-ox-horn, Old Fr. *bugle*, Lat. *buculus*, a diminutive of *bos*, ox, we have perhaps rather an ellipsis, like *waterproof* (coat), than a clipped form—

"Comrades, leave me here a little, while as yet 'tis early morn :
Leave me here, and when you want me, sound upon the *bugle-*
   horn."   *(Locksley Hall.)*

Patter is no doubt for *paternoster*—

   "Fitz-Eustace, you, with Lady Clare,
      May bid your beads and *patter* prayer."

            (Marmion, vi. 27.)

and the use of the word *marble* for a toy sometimes made of that stone makes it very probable that the *alley*, most precious of marbles, is short for *alabaster*.

Less frequently the final syllable is selected, e.g., *bus* for *omnibus*, *loo* for *lanterloo*, variously spelt in the 17th and 18th centuries—

   "Ev'n mighty Pam,[1] that Kings and Queens o'erthrew,
      And mow'd down armies in the fights of *lu*."

            (Rape of the Lock, iii. 62.)

Fr. *lanturelu* was originally the meaningless refrain or "tol de rol" of a popular song in Richelieu's time. *Van* is for *caravan*, a Persian word, properly a company of merchants or ships travelling together, "also of late corruptly used with us for a kind of waggon to carry passengers to and from London" (Blount, *Glosso-graphia*, 1674). *Wig* is for *periwig*, a corruption of Fr. *perruque*, of obscure origin. With the 17th century *'varsity*, for *university*, we may compare Sam Weller's *'Tizer*, for *Morning Advertiser*.

[1] The knave of clubs. The name was also given to Lord Palmerston.

Christian names are treated in the same way. *Alexander* gives *Alec* and *Sandy*, *Herbert*, *'Erb* or *Bert*. *Ib* (see p. 172) was once common for *Isabella*, while the modern language prefers *Bella*; *Maud* for *Matilda* is a telescoped form of Old Fr. *Maheut*, while *'Tilda* is perhaps due to unconscious aphesis, like *Denry*—

"She saved a certain amount of time every day by addressing her son as *Denry*, instead of *Edward Henry*" (ARNOLD BENNETT, *The Card*, Ch. 1.)

Among conscious word-formations may be classed many reduplicated forms, whether riming, as *hurly-burly*, or alliterative, as *tittle-tattle*, though reduplication belongs to the natural speech of children, and, in at least one case, Fr. *tante*, from *ante-ante*, Lat. *amita*, the baby word has prevailed. In a reduplicated form only one half as a rule needs to be explained. Thus *seesaw* is from *saw*, the motion suggesting two sawyers at work on a log. *Zigzag*, from French, and Ger. *zickzack* are of unknown origin. *Shilly-shally* is for *shill I, shall I? Namby-pamby* commemorates the poet Ambrose Philips, who was thus nicknamed by Pope and his friends. The weapon called a *snickersnee*—

"' First let me say my catechism,
    Which my poor mammy taught to me.'
 'Make haste, make haste,' says guzzling Jimmy,
    While Jack pulled out his *snickersnee*."
                              (THACKERAY, *Little Billee*, l. 21.)

is of Dutch origin and means something like "cut and thrust." It is usually mentioned in connection with the Hollanders—

"Among other customs they have in that town, one is, that none must carry a pointed knife about him; which makes the Hollander, who is us'd to *snik* and *snee*, to leave his horn-sheath and knife a ship-board when he comes ashore." (HOWELL, letter from Florence, 1621.)

Here the reduplication is only apparent, for the older form was to *stick* or *snee*, representing the Dutch verbs *steken*, to thrust, *snijden* or *snijen*, to cut. The initial of the first verb has been assimilated to that of the second—

"It is our countrie custome onely to *stick* or *snee*. (GLAPTHORNE, *The Hollander*.)

Reduplication is responsible for *pickaback*, earlier *pick-pack*, from *pack*, bundle. The modern form is due to popular association with *back*.

Occasionally we have what is apparently the arbitrary prefixing of a consonant, e.g., *spruce* for *pruce* (p. 48). *Dapple gray* corresponds so exactly to Fr. *gris pommelé*, Mid. Eng. *pomeli gris*, Ger. *apfelgrau*, and Ital. *pomellato*, "spotted, bespeckled, pide, *dapple-graie*, or fleabitten, the colour of a horse" (Florio), that it is hard not to believe in an unrecorded **apple-gray*, especially as we have *daffodil* for earlier *affodil*, i.e., *asphodel*. Cotgrave has *asphodile* (*asphodèle*), "the *daffadill*, *affodill*, or *asphodill*, flower." The playful elaboration *daffadowndilly* is as old as Spenser.

CHAPTER VI

WORDS AND MEANINGS

WE have all noticed the fantastic way in which ideas are linked together in our thoughts. One thing suggests another with which it is accidentally associated in memory, the second suggests a third, and, in the course even of a few seconds, we find that we have travelled from one subject to another so remote that it requires an effort to reconstruct the series of links which connects them. The same thing happens with words. A large number of words, despite great changes of sense, retain the fundamental meaning of the original, but in many cases this is quite lost. A truer image than that of the linked chain would be that of a sphere giving off in various directions a number of rays each of which may form the nucleus of a fresh sphere. Or we may say that at each link of the chain there is a possibility of another chain branching off in a direction of its own. In Cotgrave's time to *garble* (see p. 21) and to *canvass, i.e.* sift through *canvas,* meant the same thing. Yet how different is their later sense development.

There is a word *ban,* found in Old High German and Anglo-Saxon, and meaning, as far back as it can be traced, a proclamation containing a threat, hence a command or prohibition. We have it in *banish,* to put under the *ban.* The proclamation idea survives in the *banns* of marriage and in Fr. *arrière-ban,* "a proclama-

tion, whereby those that hold authority of the king in
mesne tenure, are summoned to assemble, and serve
him in his warres" (Cotgrave). This is folk-etymology
for Old Fr. *arban*, Old High Ger. *hari-ban*, army
summons. Slanting off from the primitive idea of
proclamation is that of rule or authority. The French
for outskirts is *banlieue*, properly the "circuit of a
league, or thereabouts" (Cotgrave) over which the local
authority extended. All public institutions within such
a radius were associated with *ban*, e.g., *un four, un moulin
à ban*, "a comon oven or mill whereat all men may, and
every tenant and vassall must, bake, and grind"
(Cotgrave). The French adjective *banal*, used in this
connection, gradually developed from the meaning of
"common" that of "common-place," in which sense it
is now familiar in English.[1]

Bureau, a desk, was borrowed from French in the
17th century. In modern French it means not only
the desk, but also the office itself and the authority
exercised by the office. Hence our familiar *bureaucracy*,
likely to become increasingly familiar. The desk was
so called because covered with *bureau*, Old Fr. *burel*,
"a thicke course cloath, of a brown russet, or darke
mingled, colour" (Cotgrave), whence Mid. Eng. *borel*,
rustic, clownish, lit. roughly clad, which occurs as late
as Spenser—

> "How be I am but rude and *borrel*,
>   Yet nearer ways I know."
> > (*Shepherd's Calendar*, July, l. 95.)

With this we may compare the metaphorical use of
home-spun—

> "What hempen *home-spuns* have we swaggering here,
>   So near the cradle of the fairy queen?"
> > (*Midsummer Night's Dream*, iii. 1.)

[1] Archaic Eng. *bannal* already existed in the technical sense.

The source of Old Fr. *burel* is perhaps Lat. *burrus*, fiery, from Gk. πῦρ, fire.

Romance was originally an adverb. To write in the vulgar tongue, instead of in classical Latin, was called *romanice scribere*, Old Fr. *romanz escrire*. When *romanz* became felt as a noun, it developed a "singular" *roman* or *romant*, the latter of which gave the archaic Eng. *romaunt*. The most famous of Old French romances are the epic poems called *Chansons de geste*, songs of exploits, *geste* coming from the Lat. *gesta*, deeds. Eng. *gest* or *jest* is common in the 16th and 17th centuries in the sense of act, deed, and *jest*-book meant a story-book. As the favourite story-books were merry tales, the word gradually acquired its present meaning.

A part of our Anglo-Saxon church vocabulary was supplanted by Latin or French words. Thus Anglo-Sax. *ge-bed*, prayer, was gradually expelled by Old Fr. *preiere* (*prière*), Lat. *precaria*. It has survived in *beadsman*—

> " The *beadsman*, after thousand aves told,
> For aye unsought-for slept among his ashes cold."
>
> (KEATS, *Eve of St Agnes*.)

beadroll, and *bead*, now applied only to the humble device employed in counting prayers.

Not only the Romance languages, but also German and Dutch, adopted, with the Roman character, Lat. *scribere*, to write. English, on the contrary, preserved the native to *write*, *i.e.* to scratch (runes), giving to *scribere* only a limited sense, to *shrive*. The curious change of meaning was perhaps due to the fact that the priestly absolution was felt as having the validity of a "written" law or enactment.

The meaning which we generally give to *pudding* is comparatively modern. The older sense appears in *black pudding*, a sausage made of pig's blood. This is also the meaning of Fr. *boudin*, whence *pudding* comes. A still older meaning of both words is intestine, a sense still common in dialect. The derivation of the word is obscure, but it is probably related to Fr. *bouder*, to pout, whence *boudoir*, lit. a sulking-room.

A *hearse*, now the vehicle in which a coffin is carried, is used by Shakespeare for a coffin or tomb. Its earlier meaning is a framework to support candles, usually put round the coffin at a funeral. This framework was so named from some resemblance to a harrow,[1] Fr. *herse*, Lat. *hirpex*, *hirpic-*, a rake.

Treacle is a stock example of great change of meaning. It is used in Coverdale's Bible (1535) for the "*balm* in Gilead" of the *Authorised Version*—

"There is no more *triacle* at Galaad."[2]   (Jeremiah, vii. 22.)

Old Fr. *triacle* is from Greco-Lat. *theriaca*, a remedy against poison or snake-bite (θήρ, a wild beast). In Mid. English and later it was used of a sovereign remedy. It has, like *sirup* (p. 146), acquired its present meaning *via* the apothecary's shop.

A *stickler* is now a man who is fussy about small points of etiquette or procedure. In Shakespeare he is one who parts combatants—

"The dragon wing of night o'erspreads the earth,
    And, *stickler*-like, the armies separates."
                    (*Troilus and Cressida*, v. 8.)

An earlier sense is that of seeing fair-play. The word has been popularly associated with the *stick*, or staff, used by the umpires in duels, and Torriano gives

---

[1] This is the usual explanation. But Fr. *herse* also acquired the meaning "portcullis," the pointed bars of which were naturally likened to the blades of a harrow; and it seems possible that it is to this later sense that we owe the older English meaning of *hearse* (see p. 154).

[2] "Numquid *resina* non est in Galaad?"   (*Vulgate.*)

stickler as one of the meanings of *bastoniere*, a verger or mace-bearer. But it probably comes from Mid. Eng. *stightlen*, to arrange, keep order (see p. 172, n. 2).

Infantry comes, through French, from Italian. It means a collection of "infants" or juniors, so called by contrast with the proved veterans who composed the cavalry.

The *pastern* of a horse, defined by Dr Johnson as the knee, from "ignorance, madam, pure ignorance," still means in Cotgrave and Florio "shackle." Florio even recognises a verb to *pastern*, e.g., *pastoiare*, "to fetter, to clog, to shackle, to *pastern*, to give (gyve)." It comes from Old Fr. *pasturon* (*paturon*), a derivative of *pasture*, such shackles being used to prevent grazing horses from straying. *Pester* (p. 167) is connected with it. The modern Fr. *paturon* has changed its meaning in the same way.

To *rummage* means in the Elizabethan navigators to stow goods in a hold. A rummager was what we call a *stevedore*.[1] *Rummage* is Old Fr. *arrumage* (*arrimage*), from *arrumer*, to stow, the middle syllable of which is probably cognate with English *room*; cf. *arranger*, to put in "rank."

The Christmas *waits* were originally watchmen, Anglo-Fr. *waite*, Old Fr. *gaite*, from the Old High German form of modern Ger. *Wacht*, watch. Modern French still has the verb *guetter*, to lie in wait for, and *guet*, the watch. *Minstrel* comes from an Old French derivative of Lat. *minister*, servant. Modern Fr. *ménétrier* is only used of a country fiddler who attends village weddings.

The *lumber*-room is supposed to be for *Lombard* room, *i.e.*, the room in which pawnbrokers used to store

---

[1] A Spanish word, Lat. *stipator*, "one that stoppeth chinkes" (Cooper). It came to England in connection with the wool trade.

pledged property. The Lombards introduced into this
country the three balls, said to be taken from the arms
of the Medici family.

Livery is correctly explained by the poet Spenser—

"What *livery* is, we by common use in England know well
enough, namely, that it is allowance of horse - meat, as they
commonly use the word in stabling; as, to keep horses at
livery; the which word, I guess, is derived of *livering* or
delivering forth their nightly food. So in great houses, the
livery is said to be served up for all night, that is, their evening
allowance for drink; and *livery* is also called the upper weed
(see p. 2) which a serving-man wears; so called, as I suppose,
for that it was *delivered* and taken from him at pleasure."
(*View of the State of Ireland.*)

This passage explains also *livery* stable.[1] Our word
comes from Fr. *livrée*, the feminine past participle of
livrer, from Lat. *liberare*, to deliver.

Pedigree was in Mid. English *pedegrew, petigrew*, etc.
It represents Old Fr. *pie* (*pied*) *de grue*, crane's foot,
from the shape of a sign used in showing lines of
descent in genealogical charts. The older form survives
in the family name *Pettigrew*. Here it is a nickname,
like *Pettifer* (pied de fer), iron-foot; cf. *Sheepshanks*.

Fairy is a collective, Fr. *féerie*, its modern use being
perhaps due to its occurrence in such phrases as *Faerie
Queen, i.e.,* Queen of Fairyland. Cf. *paynim*, used by
some poets for *pagan*, but really a doublet of *paganism*,
occurring in *paynim host, paynim knight*, etc. The
correct name for the individual *fairy* is *fay*, Fr. *fée*,
Vulgar Lat. **fata*, connected with *fatum*, fate. This
appears in Ital. *fata*, "a fairie, a witch, an enchantres,
an elfe" (Florio). The *fata morgana*, the mirage some-

---

[1] In "livery and bait" there is pleonasm. *Bait*, connected with *bite*, is
the same word as in bear-*baiting* and fishermen's *bait*. We have it also,
via Old French, in *abet*, whence the aphetic *bet*, originally to egg on.

times seen in the Strait of Messina, is attributed to the fairy Morgana of Tasso, the Morgan le Fay of our own Arthurian legends.

Many people must have wondered at some time why the *clubs* and *spades* on cards are so called. The latter figure, it is true, bears some resemblance to a spade, but no giant of fiction is depicted with a club with a triple head. The explanation is that we have adopted the French pattern, *carreau* (see p. 161), diamond, *cœur*, heart, *pique*, pike, spear-head, *trèfle*, trefoil, clover-leaf, but have given to the two latter the names used in the Italian and Spanish pattern, which, instead of the pike and trefoil, has the sword (Ital. *spada*) and mace (Ital. *bastone*). Etymologically both *spades* are identical, the origin being Greco-Lat. *spatha*, the name of a number of blade-shaped objects; *cf.* the diminutive *spatula*.

Wafer, in both its senses, is related to Ger. *Wabe*, honeycomb. We find Anglo-Fr. *wafre* in the sense of a thin cake, perhaps stamped with a honeycomb pattern. The cognate Fr. *gaufre* is the name of a similar cake, which not only has the honeycomb pattern, but is also largely composed of honey. Hence our verb to *goffer*, to give a cellular appearance to a frill.

The meanings of adjectives are especially subject to change. *Quaint* now conveys the idea of what is unusual, and, as early as the 17th century, we find it explained as "strange, unknown." This is the exact opposite of its original meaning, Old Fr. *cointe*, Lat. *cognitus ;* cf. *acquaint*, Old Fr. *acointier*, to make known. It is possible to trace roughly the process by which this remarkable *volte - face* has been brought about. The intermediate sense of trim or pretty is common in Shakespeare—

"For a fine, *quaint*, graceful, and excellent fashion, yours is worth ten on't." (*Much Ado*, iii. 4.)

We apply *restive* to a horse that will not stand still.
It means properly a horse that will not do anything
else. Fr. *rétif*, Old Fr. *restif*, from *rester*, to remain,
Lat. *re-stare*, has kept more of the original sense of
stubbornness. Scot. *reest*, *reist*, means to stand stock-
still—

"Certain it was that Shagram *reisted*, and I ken Martin thinks
he saw something." (*Monastery*, Ch. 4.)

Dryden even uses *restive* in the sense of sluggish—

"So James the drowsy genius wakes
Of Britain, long entranced in charms,
Restive, and slumbering on its arms."
(*Threnodia Augustalis.*)

Reasty, used of meat that has "stood" too long, is
the same word (cf. *testy*, Old Fr. *testif*, heady), and
rusty bacon is probably folk-etymology for *reasty*
bacon—

"And then came haltyng Jone,
And brought a gambone
Of bakon that was *reasty*."
(SKELTON, *Elynour Rummyng*.)

Sterling has an obscure history. It is from Old Fr.
esterlin, a coin which etymologists of an earlier age
connected with the *Easterlings*, or Hanse merchants, who
formed one of the great mercantile communities of
the Middle Ages; and perhaps some such association
is responsible for the meaning that *sterling* has acquired ;
but chronology shows this traditional etymology to be
impossible. We find *unus sterlingus* in a medieval Latin
document of 1184, and the Old Fr. *esterlin* occurs in
Wace's *Roman de Rou* (Romaunt of Rollo the Sea King),
which was written before 1175. Hence it is conjectured
that the original coin was named from the *star* which
appears on some Norman pennies.

When Horatio says—

"It is a nipping and an *eager* air." (*Hamlet*, i. 4.)

we are reminded that *eager* is identical with the second part of vin-*egar*, Fr. *aigre*, sour, Lat. *acer*, keen. It seems hardly possible to explain the modern sense of *nice*, which in the course of its history has traversed nearly the whole diatonic scale between "rotten" and "ripping." In Mid. English and Old French it means foolish. Cotgrave explains it by "lither, lazie, sloathful, idle; faint, slack; dull, simple," and Shakespeare uses it in a great variety of meanings. It is supposed to come from Lat. *nescius*, ignorant. The transition from *fond*, foolish, which survives in "*fond* hopes," to *fond*, loving, is easy. French *fou* is used in exactly the same way. *Cf.* also to *dote* on, *i.e.*, to be foolish about. *Puny* is Fr. *puîné*, from *puis né*, later born, junior, whence the *puisne* justices. Milton uses it of a minor—

"He must appear in print like a *puny* with his guardian."
(*Areopagitica.*)

Petty, Fr. *petit*, was similarly used for a small boy.

In some cases a complimentary adjective loses its true meaning and takes on a contemptuous or ironic sense. None of us care to be called *bland*, and to describe a man as *worthy* is to apologise for his existence. We may compare Fr. *bonhomme*, which now means generally an old fool, and *bonne femme*, good-wife, goody. *Dapper*, the Dutch for brave (*cf.* Ger. *tapfer*), and *pert*, Mid. Eng. *apert*, representing in meaning Lat. *expertus*, have changed much since Milton wrote of—

"The *pert* fairies and the *dapper* elves." (*Comus*, l. 118.)

Pert seems in fact to have acquired the meaning of its opposite *malapert*, though the older sense of brisk, sprightly, survives in dialect—

"He looks spry and *peart* for once."
(Phillpotts, *American Prisoner*, Ch. 3.)

Smug, cognate with Ger. *schmuck*, trim, elegant, beautiful, has its original sense in Shakespeare—

"And here the *smug* and silver Trent shall run
In a new channel, fair and evenly."

(1 *Henry IV.*, iii. 1.)

The degeneration of an adjective is sometimes due
to its employment for euphemistic purposes. The
favourite substitute for *fat* is *stout*, properly strong,[1]
dauntless, etc., cognate with Ger. *stolz*, proud. Pre-
cisely the same euphemism appears in French, e.g.,
"une dame un peu *forte*." *Ugly* is replaced in English
by *plain*, and in American by *homely*—

"She is not so handsome as these, maybe, but her *homeliness*
is not actually alarming." (MAX ADELER, *Mr Skinner's Night in
the Underworld*.)

In the case of this word, as in many others, the
American use preserves a meaning which was once
common in English. Kersey's *Dictionary* (1720) explains
homely as "ugly, disagreeable, course (coarse), mean."

Change of meaning may be brought about by
association. A *miniature* is a small portrait, and we
even use the word as an adjective meaning small, on a
reduced scale. But the true sense of *miniature* is
something painted in *minium*, red lead. Florio explains
miniatura as "a limning (see p. 63), a painting with
vermilion." Such paintings were usually small, hence
the later meaning. The word was first applied to the
ornamental red initial capitals in manuscripts. *Vignette*
still means technically in French an interlaced vine-

---

[1] Hence the use of *stout* for a "strong" beer. *Porter* was once the
favourite tap of *porters*, and a mixture of stout and ale, now known as *cooper*,
was especially relished by the brewery *cooper*.

pattern on a frontispiece.[1] Cotgrave has *vignettes*, "vignets; branches, or branch-like borders, or flourishes in painting, or ingravery."

The degeneration in the meaning of a noun may be partly due to frequent association with disparaging adjectives. Thus *hussy*, *i.e.* housewife, *quean*,[2] woman, *wench*, child, have absorbed such adjectives as impudent, idle, light, saucy, etc. Shakespeare uses *quean* only three times, and these three include "cozening *quean*" (*Merry Wives*, iv. 2) and "scolding *quean*" (*All's Well*, ii. 2). With *wench*, still used without any disparaging sense by country folk, we may compare Fr. *garce*, lass, and Ger. *Dirne*, maid-servant, both of which are now insulting epithets, but, in the older language, could be applied to Joan of Arc and the Virgin Mary respectively. *Garce* was replaced by *fille*, which has acquired in its turn a meaning so offensive that it has now given way to *jeune fille*. *Minx*, earlier *minkes*, is probably the Low Ger. *minsk*, Ger. *Mensch*, lit. human, but used also in the sense of "wench." For the consonantal change cf. *hunks*, Dan. *hundsk*, stingy, lit. doggish. These examples show that the indignant "Who are you calling a *woman?*" is, philologically, in all likelihood a case of intelligent anticipation.

Adjectives are affected in their turn by being regularly coupled with certain nouns. A *buxom* helpmate was once obedient, the word being cognate with Ger. *biegsam*, flexible, yielding—

> "The place where thou and Death
> Shall dwell at ease, and up and down unseen
> Wing silently the *buxom* air."
>
> (*Paradise Lost*, ii. 840.)

[1] Folk-etymology for *frontispice*, Lat. *frontispicium*, front view.
[2] Related to, but not identical with, *queen*.

An obedient nature is "*buxom*, blithe and debonair," qualities which affect the physique and result in heartiness of aspect and a comely plumpness. An *arch* damsel is etymologically akin to an *arch*bishop, both descending from the Greek prefix ἀρχι, from ἀρχή, a beginning, first cause. Shakespeare uses *arch* as a noun—

> "The noble duke my master,
> My worthy *arch* and patron comes to-night."
>
> (*Lear*, ii. 1.)

Occurring chiefly in such phrases as *arch* enemy, *arch* heretic, *arch* hypocrite, *arch* rogue, it acquired a depreciatory sense, which has now become so weakened that *archness* is not altogether an unpleasing attribute. We may compare the cognate German prefix *Erz*. Ludwig has, as successive entries, *Ertz-dieb*, "an archthief, an arrant thief," and *Ertz-engel*, "an arch-angel." The meaning of *arrant* is almost entirely due to association with "thief." It means lit. wandering, vagabond, so that the *arrant* thief is nearly related to the knight *errant*, and to the Justices in *eyre*, Old Fr. *eire*, Lat. *iter*, a way, journey. Fr. *errer*, to wander, stray, is compounded of Vulgar Lat. *iterare*, to journey, and Lat. *errare*, to stray, and it would be difficult to calculate how much of each enters into the composition of *le Juif errant*.

As I have suggested above, association accounts to some extent for changes of meaning, but the process is in reality more complex, and usually a number of factors are working together or in opposition to each other. A low word may gradually acquire right of citizenship. "That article blackguardly called *pluck*" (Scott) is now much respected. It is the same word as *pluck*, the heart, liver, and lungs of an animal—

"During the Crimean war, *plucky*, signifying courageous, seemed likely to become a favourite term in Mayfair, even among the ladies." (HOTTEN'S *Slang Dictionary*, 1864.)

Having become respectable, it is now replaced in sporting circles by the more emphatic *guts*, which reproduces the original metaphor. A word may die out in its general sense, surviving only in some special meaning. Thus the poetic *sward*, scarcely used except with "green," meant originally the skin or crust of anything. It is cognate with Ger. *Schwarte*, "the *sward*, or rind, of a thing" (Ludwig), which now means especially bacon-rind. Related words may meet with very different fates in kindred languages. Eng. *knight* is cognate with Ger. *Knecht*, servant, which had, in Mid. High German, a wide range of meanings, including "warrior, hero." There is no more complimentary epithet than *knightly*, while Ger. *knechtisch* means servile. The degeneration of words like *boor*,[1] *churl*, farmer, is a familiar phenomenon (cf. *villain*, p. 150). The same thing has happened to *blackguard*, the modern meaning of which bears hardly on a humble but useful class. The name *black guard* was given collectively to the kitchen detachment of a great man's retinue. The *scavenger* has also come down in the world, rather an unusual phenomenon in the case of official titles. The medieval *scavager*[2] was an important official who seems to have been originally a kind of inspector of customs. He was called in Anglo-French *scawageour*, from the noun *scawage*, showing. The Old French dialect verb *escauwer* is of Germanic origin and cognate with Eng. *show* and Ger. *schauen*, to look. The *cheater*, now usually *cheat*, probably deserved his fate. The *escheators* looked after *escheats*, *i.e.*, estates or property that lapsed and were forfeited. The origin of

---

[1] The older meaning of *boor* survives in the compound *neighbour*, i.e., *nigh boor*, the farmer near at hand. Du. *boer* is of course the same word.

[2] English regularly inserts *n* in words thus formed; cf. *harbinger*, *messenger*, *passenger*, *pottinger*, etc.

the word is Old Fr. *escheoir* (*échoir*), to fall due, Vulgar
Lat. *ex *cadēre* for *cadĕre*. Their reputation was
unsavoury, and *cheat* has already its present meaning in
Shakespeare. He also plays on the double meaning—

> "I will be *cheater* to them both, and they shall be exchequers
> to me." (*Merry Wives*, i. 3.)

Beldam implies "hag" as early as Shakespeare, but
he also uses it in its proper sense of "grandmother,"
e.g., Hotspur refers to "old *beldam* earth" and "our
grandam earth" in the same speech (I *Henry IV.*, iii. I),
and Milton speaks of "*beldam* nature"—

> "Then sing of secret things that came to pass
> When *Beldam* Nature in her cradle was."
> (*Vacation Exercise*, l. 46.)

It is of course from *belle-dame*, used in Mid. English for
grandmother, as *belsire* was for grandfather. Hence
it is a doublet of *belladonna*. The masculine *belsire*
survives as a family name, *Belcher*[1]; and to Jim Belcher,
most gentlemanly of prize-fighters, we owe the *belcher*
handkerchief, which had large white spots with a
dark blue dot in the centre of each on a medium
blue ground. It was also known to the "fancy" as a
"bird's-eye wipe."

---

[1] Other forms of the same name are *Bowser* and *Bewsher*. The form
Belcher is Picard—

> "On assomma la pauvre bête.
> Un manant lui coupa le pied droit et la tête.
> Le seigneur du village à sa porte les mit ;
> Et ce dicton picard à l'entour fut écrit :
> ' *Biaux chires* leups, n'écoutez mie
> Mère tenchent (grondant) chen fieux (son fils) qui crie.' "
> (LA FONTAINE, *Fables*, iv. 16.)

CHAPTER VII

SEMANTICS

THE convenient name semantics has been applied of late to the science of meanings, as distinguished from phonetics, the science of sound. The comparative study of languages enables us to observe and codify the general laws which govern sense development, and to understand why meanings become extended or restricted. One phenomenon which seems to occur normally in language results from what we may call the simplicity of the olden times. Thus the whole vocabulary which is etymologically related to *writing* and *books* has developed from an old Germanic verb that means to *scratch* and the Germanic name for the *beech*. Our earliest books were wooden tablets on which inscriptions were scratched. The word *book* itself comes from Anglo-Sax. *bōc*, beech; *cf*. Ger. *Buchstabe*, letter, lit. beech-stave. Lat. *liber*, book, whence a large family of words in the Romance languages, means the inner bark of a tree, and *bible* is ultimately from Greek βύβλος, the inner rind of the *papyrus*, the Egyptian rush from which *paper* was made.[1]

The earliest measurements were calculated from the human body. All European languages use the *foot*, and

---

[1] Parchment (see p. 49) was invented as a substitute when the supply of papyrus failed.

we still measure horses by *hands*, while *span* survives in
table-books. *Cubit* is Latin for *elbow*, the first part of
which is the same as *ell*, cognate with Lat. *ulna*, also
used in both senses. Fr. *brasse*, fathom, is Lat. *brachia*,
the two arms, and *pouce*, thumb, means inch. A further
set of measures are represented by simple devices:
a *yard*[1] is a small "stick," and the *rod, pole,* or *perch* (cf.
perch for birds, Fr. *perche*, pole) which gives charm to
our arithmetic is a larger one. A *furlong* is a *furrow-
long*. For weights common objects were used, *e.g.*, a
grain, or a *scruple*, Lat. *scrupulus*, "a little sharpe stone
falling sometime into a man's shooe" (Cooper), for very
small things, a *stone* for heavier goods. Gk. δραχμά,
whence our *dram*, means a handful. Our decimal
system is due to our possession of ten *digits*, or
fingers, and *calculation* comes from Lat. *calculus*, a
pebble.

A modern Chancellor of the Exchequer, considering
his budget, is not so near the reality of things as his
medieval predecessor, who literally sat in his counting-
house, counting up his money. For the *exchequer*,
named from the Old Fr. *eschequier* (*échiquier*), chess-board,
was once the board marked out in squares on which the
treasurer reckoned up with counters the king's taxes.
This Old Fr. *eschequier*, which has also given *chequer*, is
a derivative of Old Fr. *eschec* (*échec*), check. Thus "*check*
trousers" and a "*chequered* career" are both directly
related to an eastern potentate (see *chess*, p. 120.). The

---

[1] The "stick" meaning survives in the *yards* of a ship. *Yard* was once
the general word for rod, wand. Thus the "cheating *yardwand*" of
Tennyson's "smooth-faced snubnosed rogue" (*Maud*, I. i. 16) is a
pleonasm of the same type as *greyhound* (p. 135). *Yard*, an enclosure, is
a separate word, related to *garden*. The doublet *garth*, used in the Eastern
counties, is of Scandinavian origin—

"I climb'd to the top of the *garth*, and stood by the road at the gate."
(TENNYSON, *The Grandmother*, l. 38.)

chancellor himself was originally a kind of door-keeper in charge of a *chancel*, a latticed barrier which we now know in church architecture only. *Chancel* is derived, through Fr. *chancel* or *cancel*, from Lat. *cancellus*, a cross-bar, occurring more usually in the plural in the sense of lattice, grating. We still *cancel* a document by drawing such a pattern on it. In German *cancellus* has given *Kanzel*, pulpit. The *budget*, now a document in which millions are mere items, was the chancellor's little bag or purse—

> " If tinkers may have leave to live,
>   And bear the sow-skin *budget*,
> Then my account I well may give,
>   And in the stocks avouch it."
>
> > (*Winter's Tale*, iv. 2.)

Fr. *bougette*, from which it is borrowed, is a diminutive of *bouge*, a leathern bag, which comes from Lat. *bulga*, "a male or *bouget* of leather; a purse; a bagge" (Cooper). Modern French has borrowed back our *budget*, together with several other words dealing with business and finance.

Among the most important servants of the exchequer were the *controllers*. We now call them officially *comptroller*, through a mistaken association with Fr. *compte*, account. The controller had charge of the *counter-rolls* (cf. *counterfoil*), from Old Fr. *contre-rolle*, " the copy of a role (of accounts, etc.), a paralell of the same quality and content, with the originall " (Cotgrave). In French *contrôle* has preserved the sense of supervision or verification which it has lost in ordinary English.

A very ancient functionary of the exchequer, the tally-cutter, was abolished in the reign of George III. *Tallies* (Fr. *tailler*, to cut) were sticks "scored" across in such a way that the notches could be compared for

purposes of verification.   Jack Cade preferred those
good old ways—

> "Our fore-fathers had no other books but the *score* and the
> *tally;* thou hast caused books to be used."
>
> (2 *Henry VI.*, iv. 7.)

This rudimentary method of calculation was still in use
in the Kentish hop-gardens within fairly recent times;
and some of us can remember very old gentlemen ask-
ing us, after a cricket match, how many "notches" we
had "scored"—

> "The *scorers* were prepared to *notch* the runs."
>
> (*Pickwick*, Ch. 7.)

This use of *score*, for a reckoning in general, or for twenty,
occurs in Anglo-Saxon, but the word is Scandinavian.
The words *score* and *tally*, originally of identical
meaning, were soon differentiated, a common phenomenon in such cases.   For the exchequer *tally* was
substituted an "indented cheque receipt."   An *indenture*,
chiefly familiar to us in connection with apprentice-
ship, was a duplicate document of which the "indented"
or toothed edges had to correspond like the notches
of the score or tally.   *Cheque*, earlier *check*, is
identical with *check*, rebuff.   The metaphor is from the
game of chess (see p. 120), to *check* a man's accounts
involving a sort of control, or pulling up short, if
necessary.   A *cheque* is a method of payment which
makes "checking" easy.   The modern spelling is due
to popular association with *exchequer*, which is etymologically right, though the words have reached their
modern functions by very different paths.

The development of the meaning of *chancellor* can
be paralleled in the case of many other functionaries,
once humble but now important.   The titles of two great
medieval officers, the *constable* and the *marshal*, mean

the same thing. *Constable*, Old Fr. *conestable* (*connétable*), is Lat. *comes stabuli*, stable fellow. *Marshal*, the first element of which is cognate with *mare*, while the second corresponds to modern Ger. *Schalk*, rascal, expresses the same idea in German. Both *constable* and *marshal* are now used of very high positions, but Policeman X. and the *farrier-marshal*, or shoeing-smith, of a troop of cavalry, remind them of the base degrees by which they did ascend. The *Marshalsea* where Little Dorrit lived is for *marshalsy*, marshals' office, etc. The *steward*, or *sty-ward*, looked after his master's pigs. He rose in importance until, by the marriage of Marjorie Bruce to Walter the *Stewart* of Scotland, he founded the most picturesque of royal houses. The *chamberlain*, as his name suggests, attended to the royal comforts long before he became a judge of wholesome literature.

All these names now stand for a great number of functions of varying importance. Other titles which are equally vague are *sergeant* (see p. 148) and *usher*, Old Fr. *uissier*[1] (*huissier*), lit. door-keeper, Lat. *ostiarius*, a porter. Another official was the *harbinger*, who survives only in poetry. He was a forerunner, or vauntcourier, who preceded the great man to secure him "harbourage" for the night, and his name comes from Old Fr. *herberger* (*héberger*), to shelter (see p. 164). As late as the reign of Charles II. we read that—

"On the removal of the court to pass the summer at Winchester, Bishop Ken's house, which he held in the right of his prebend, was marked by the *harbinger* for the use of Mrs Eleanor Gwyn ; but he refused to grant her admittance, and she was forced to seek for lodgings in another place."

(HAWKINS, *Life of Bishop Ken.*)

[1] As Old Fr. *uissier* has given *usher*, I would suggest that the family names *Lush* and *Lusher*, which Bardsley (*Dict. of English Surnames*) gives up, are for Old Fr. *l'uis* (cf. *Laporte*) and *l'uissier*. In modern French *Lhuissier* is not an uncommon name.

PARALLEL METAPHORS 91

One of the most interesting branches of semantics, and the most useful to the etymologist, deals with the study of parallel metaphors in different languages. We have seen (p. 29) how, for instance, the names of flowers show that the same likeness has been observed by various races. The spice called *clove* and the *clove*-pink both belong to Lat. *clavus*, a nail. The German for pink is *Nelke*, a Low German diminutive, *nail-kin*, of *Nagel*, nail. The spice, or *Gewürznelke*, is called in South Germany *Nägele*, little nail. A *clove* of garlic is quite a separate word; but, as it has some interesting cognates, it may be mentioned here. It is so called because the bulb *cleaves* naturally into segments.[1] The German name is *Knoblauch*, for Mid. High Ger. *klobe-louch*, clove-leek, by dissimilation of one *l*. The Dutch doublet is *kloof*, a chasm, gully, familiar in South Africa.

Fr. *poison*, Lat. *potio, potion-*, a drink, and Ger. *Gift*, poison, lit. gift, seem to date from treacherous times. On the other hand, Ger. *Geschenk*, a present, means something poured out (see *nuncheon*, p. 124), while a tip is in French *pourboire* and in German *Trinkgeld*, even when accepted by a lifelong abstainer. In English we "ride a *hobby*," i.e., a hobby-horse, or wooden horse. German has the same metaphor, "ein *Steckenpferd* reiten," and French says "enfourcher un *dada*," i.e., to bestride a gee-gee. *Hobby*, for Mid. Eng. *hobin*, a nag, was a proper name for a horse. Like *Dobbin* and *Robin*, it belongs to the numerous progeny of Robert.

In some cases the reason for a metaphor is not quite clear to the modern mind. The bloodthirsty weasel is called in French *belette*,[2] little beauty, in Italian

---

[1] The *onion*, Fr. *oignon*, Lat. *unio, union-*, is so named because successive skins form an harmonious one-ness. It is a doublet of *union*.

[2] Perhaps a diminutive of Cymric *bele*, marten, but felt as from Fr. *belle*.

donnola, in Portuguese *doninha*, little lady, in Spanish *comadreja*, gossip (Fr. *commère*, Scot. *cummer*, p. 94), in Bavarian *Schöntierlein*, beautiful little animal, in Danish *kjönne*, beautiful, and in older English *fairy*.[1] From Lat. *medius* we get *mediastinus*, " a drugge (drudge) or lubber to doe all vile service in the house ; a kitching slave" (Cooper). Why this drudge should have a name implying a middle position I cannot say ; but to-day in the North of England a maid-of-all-work is called a *tweeny* (between maid).

A stock semantic parallel occurs in the relation between age and respectability. All of us, as soon as we get to reasonable maturity, lay great stress on the importance of deference to "elders." It follows naturally that many titles of more or less dignity should be evolved from this idea of seniority. The Eng. *alderman* is obvious. *Priest*, Old Fr. *prestre*[2] (*prêtre*), from Gk. πρεσβύτερος, comparative of πρέσβυς, old, is not so obvious. In the Romance languages we have a whole group of words, *e.g.*, Fr. *sire, sieur, seigneur*, Ital. *signor*, Span. *señor*, with their compounds *monsieur, messer*, etc., all representing either *senior* or *seniorem*. Ger. *Eltern*, parents, is the plural comparative of *alt*, old, and the first element of *seneschal* (see *marshal*, p. 90) is cognate with Lat. *senex*. From Fr. *sire* comes Eng. *sir*, and from this was formed the adjective *sirly*,[3] now spelt *surly*, which in Shakespeare still means haughty, arrogant—

" See how the *surly* Warwick mans the wall."
(3 *Henry VI.*, v. 1.)

---

[1] Dozens of similar names for the weasel could be collected from the European languages and dialects. It is probable that these complimentary names were propitiatory, the weasel being an animal regarded with superstitious dread.

[2] Cf. *Prester* John, the fabulous priest monarch of Ethiopia.

[3] Cf. *lordly, princely*, etc., and Ger. *herrisch*, imperious, from *Herr*, sir.

A *list*, in the sense of enumeration, is a "strip." The cognate German word is *Leiste*, border. We have the original meaning in "*list* slippers." Fr. *bordereau*, a list, which became very familiar in connection with the Dreyfus case, is a diminutive of *bord*, edge. *Label* is the same word as Old Fr. *lambel* (*lambeau*), rag. *Scroll* is an alteration, perhaps due to *roll*, of Mid. Eng. *scrow* or *escrow*, from Old Fr. *escroue*,[1] rag, shred. *Docket*, earlier *dogget*, is from an old Italian diminutive of *doga*, cask-stave, which meant a bendlet in heraldry. *Schedule* is a diminutive of Lat. *scheda*, "a scrowe" (Cooper), properly a strip of papyrus. Ger. *Zettel*, bill, ticket, is the same word. Thus all these words, more or less kindred in meaning, can be reduced to the primitive notion of strip or scrap.

Farce, from French, means stuffing. The verb to *farce*, which represents Lat. *farcire*, survives in the perverted *force*-meat. A parallel is *satire*, from Lat. *satura* (*lanx*), a full dish, hence a medley. Somewhat similar is the modern meaning of *magazine*, a "storehouse" of amusement or information.

The closest form of intimacy is represented by community of board and lodging, or, in older phraseology, "bed and board." *Companion*, with its related words, belongs to Vulgar Lat. **companio, companion-*, bread-sharer. The same idea is represented by the pleonastic Eng. *messmate*, the second part of which, *mate*, is related to *meat*. *Mess*, food, Old Fr. *mes* (*mets*), Lat. *missum*, is in modern English only military or naval, but was once the usual name for a dish of food—

> "Herbs and other country *messes*
> Which the neat-handed Phillis dresses."
> (*Allegro*, 1. 85.)

With *mate* we may compare Fr. *matelot*, earlier *matenot*,

---

[1] Modern Fr. *écrou* is used only in the sense of prison register.

representing Du. *maat*, meat, and *genoot*, a companion. The latter word is cognate with Ger. *Genosse*, a companion, from *geniessen*, to enjoy or use together. In early Dutch we find also *mattegenoet*, through popular association with *matte*, hammock, one hammock serving, by a Box and Cox arrangement, for two sailors.

Comrade is from Fr. *camarade*, and this from Span. *camarada*, originally a "room-full," called in the French army *une chambrée*. This corresponds to Ger. *Geselle*, comrade, from *Saal*, room. The reduction of the collective to the individual is paralleled by Ger. *Bursche*, fellow, from Mid. High Ger. *burse*, college hostel ; cf. *Frauenzimmer*, wench, lit. women's room. It can hardly be doubted that *chum* is a corrupted clip from *chamber-fellow*.[1] It is thus explained in a *Dictionary of the Canting Crew* (1690), within a few years of its earliest recorded occurrence, and the reader will remember Mr Pickwick's introduction to the *chummage* system in the Fleet (Ch. 42).

English *gossip*, earlier *god-sib*, related in God, a sponsor, soon developed the subsidiary meanings of boon companion, crony, tippler, babbler, etc., all of which are represented in Shakespeare. The case of Fr. *compère* and *commère*, godfather and godmother, is

[1] The vowel is not so great a difficulty as it might appear, and we actually have the same change in *comrade* itself, formerly pronounced *cumrade*. In the London pronunciation the *u* of such words as *but, cup, hurry*, etc., represents roughly a continental short *a*. This fact, familiar to phoneticians but disbelieved by others, is one of the first peculiarities noted by foreigners beginning to learn English. It is quite possible that *chum* is an accidental spelling for *cham, just as we write *bungalow* for *bangla* (Bengal), *pundit* for *pandit*, and *Punjaub* for *Panjab*, five rivers, whence also probably the liquid called *punch*, from its five ingredients. *Cf.* also American to *slug*, *i.e.* to *slog*, which appears to represent Du. *slag*, blow—"That was for *slugging* the guard" (Kipling, *An Error in the Fourth Dimension*)—and the adjective *bluff*, from obsolete Du. *blaf*, broad-faced.

similar. Cotgrave explains *commérage* as "gossiping;
the acquaintance, affinity, or league that growes
betweene women by christning a child together, or
one for another." Ger. *Gevatter*, godfather, has also
acquired the sense of Fr. *bonhomme* (p. 80), Eng. *daddy*.
From *commère* comes Scot. *cummer* or *kimmer*—

> "A canty quean was Kate, and a special *cummer* of my ain."
> (*Monastery*, Ch. 8.)

While christenings led to cheerful garrulity, the wilder
fun of weddings has given the Fr. *faire la noce*, to go on
the spree. In Ger. *Hochzeit*, wedding, lit. high time,
we have a converse development of meaning.

Parallel sense development in different languages
sometimes gives us a glimpse of the life of our
ancestors. Our verb to *curry* (leather) comes from
Old Fr. *corréer*[1] (*courroyer*), to make ready, put in
order, which represents a theoretical **con-red-are*, the
root syllable of which is Germanic and cognate with
our *ready*. Ger. *gerben*, to tan, Old High Ger. *garawen*,
to make ready, is a derivative of *gar*, ready, complete,
now used only as an adverb meaning "quite," but
cognate with our *yare*—

> "Our ship—
> Which, but three glasses since, we gave out split—
> Is tight, and *yare*, and bravely rigg'd."
> (*Tempest*, v. i.)

Both *curry* and *gerben* must have acquired their restricted
meaning at a time when there was literally nothing like
leather.

Even in slang we find the same parallelism exempli-
fied. We call an old-fashioned watch a *turnip*. In
German it is called *Zwiebel*, onion, and in French *oignon*.
Eng. *greenhorn* likens an inexperienced person to an

---

[1] *Array*, Old Fr. *arréer*, is related.

animal whose horns have just begun to sprout. In Ger.
Gelbschnabel, yellow-bill, and Fr. *bec-jaune*, we have
the metaphor of the fledgling. Ludwig explains
Gelbschnabel by "chitty-face," *chit*, cognate with *kit*-ten,
being a general term in Mid. English for a young
animal. From *bec-jaune* we have archaic Scot. *beejam*,
university freshman. Cotgrave spells the French word
bejaune, and gives, as he usually does for such words,[1]
a very full gloss, which happens, by exception, to be
quotable—

> "A novice ; a late prentice to, or young beginner in, a trade,
> or art ; also, a simple, ignorant, unexperienced, asse ; a rude,
> unfashioned, home-bred hoydon ; a sot, ninny, doult, noddy ; one
> that's blankt, and hath nought to say, when he hath most need
> to speake."

The Englishman intimates that a thing has ceased
to please by saying that he is "fed up" with it. The
Frenchman says, "J'en ai soupé." Both these metaphors are quite modern, but they express in flippant
form the same figure of physical satiety which is as old as
language. *Padding* is a comparatively new word in connection with literary composition, but it reproduces,
with a slightly different meaning, the figure expressed by
bombast, lit. wadding, a derivative of Greco-Lat. *bombyx*,
originally "silk-worm," whence also *bombasine*. We
may compare also "*fustian* eloquence"—

> "And he, whose *fustian*'s so sublimely bad,
>   It is not poetry, but prose run mad."
>   (POPE, *Prologue to the Satires*, l. 187.)

[1] This is a characteristic of the old dictionary makers. The gem of my
collection is Ludwig's gloss for *Lümmel*, "a long lubber, a lazy lubber, a
slouch, a lordant, a lordane, a looby, a booby, a tony, a fop, a dunce, a
simpleton, a wise-acre, a sot, a logger-head, a block-head, a nickampoop, a
lingerer, a drowsy or dreaming lusk, a pill-garlick, a slowback, a lathback, a
pitiful sneaking fellow, a lungis, a tall slim fellow, a slim longback, a great
he-fellow, a lubberly fellow, a lozel, an awkward fellow."

And a very similar image is found in the Latin poet
Ausonius—

> "At nos illepidum, rudem libellum,
> *Burras*, quisquilias ineptiasque
> Credemus gremio cui fovendum?"
>
> (*Drepanio Filio.*)

Even to "take the cake" is paralleled by the Gk. λαβεῖν
τὸν πυραμοῦντα, to be awarded the cake of roasted
wheat and honey which was originally the prize of him
who best kept awake during a night-watch.

In the proverbial expressions which contain the con-
centrated wisdom of the ages we sometimes find exact
correspondences.   Thus "to look a gift-horse in the
mouth" is literally reproduced in French and German.
Sometimes the symbols vary, *e.g.*, the risk one is exposed
to in acquiring goods without examination is called by
us "buying a pig in a poke."[1]   French and German
substitute the cat.   We say that "a cat may look at
a king."   The French *dramatis personæ* are a dog and
a bishop.   The "bird in hand" which we regard as the
equivalent of two in the bush is in German compared
advantageously with ten on the roof.

Every language has an immense number of metaphors
to describe the various stages of intoxication.   We, as a
seafaring nation, have naturally a set of such metaphors
taken from nautical English.   In French and German
the state of being "half-seas over" or "three sheets in
the wind," and the practice of "splicing the main-brace"
are expressed by various land metaphors.   But the
more obvious nautical figures are common property.
We speak of being *stranded;* French says "*échouer* (to
run ashore) dans une entreprise," and German uses
scheitern, to strand, split on a rock, in the same way.

---

[1] *Poke*, sack, is still common in dialect, *e.g.* in the Kentish hop-gardens.
It is a doublet of *pouch*, and its diminutive is *pocket*.

Finally, we observe the same principle in euphemism, or that form of speech which avoids calling things by their names. Euphemism is the result of various human instincts which range from religious reverence down to common decency. There is, however, a special type of euphemism which may be described as the delicacy of the partially educated. It is a matter of common observation that for educated people a spade is a spade, while the more outspoken class prefers to call it a decorated shovel. Between these two classes come those delicate beings whose work in life is—

> "le retranchement de ces syllabes sales
> Qui dans les plus beaux mots produisent des scandales ;
> Ces jouets éternels des sots de tous les temps ;
> Ces fades lieux-communs de nos méchants plaisants ;
> Ces sources d'un amas d'équivoques infâmes,
> Dont on vient faire insulte à la pudeur des femmes."
>
> (MOLIÈRE, *Les Femmes savantes*, iii. 2.)

In the United States refined society has succeeded in banning as improper the word *leg*, which must now be replaced by *limb*, even when the possessor is a boiled fowl, and this refinement is not unknown in England. The coloured ladies of Barbados appear to have been equally sensitive—

> "Fate had placed me opposite to a fine turkey. I asked my partner if I should have the pleasure of helping her to a piece of the breast. She looked at me indignantly, and said, 'Curse your impudence, sar ; I wonder where you larn manners. Sar, I take a lilly turkey *bosom*, if you please.'" (*Peter Simple*, Ch. 31.)

This tendency shows itself especially in connection with the more intimate garments and articles intended for personal use. We have the absurd name *pocket handkerchief*, *i.e.*, pocket hand-cover-head, for a comparatively modern convenience, the earlier names of which have more of the directness of the Artful Dodger's "wipe." Ben Jonson calls it a *muckinder*. In 1829 the use of the word *mouchoir* in a French adaptation of *Othello* caused a riot at the Comédie Française. History repeats itself, for, in 1907, a play by J. M. Synge was produced in Dublin, but—

> "The audience broke up in disorder at the word *shift*."
> (*Academy*, 14th Oct. 1911.)

This is all the more ludicrous when we reflect that *shift*, *i.e.* change of raiment, is itself an early euphemism for *smock*; *cf.* Ital. *mutande*, "thinne under-breeches" (Florio), from a country and century not usually regarded as prudish. The fact is that, just as the low word, when once accepted, loses its primitive vigour (see *pluck*, p. 83), the euphemism is, by inevitable association, doomed from its very birth.

I will now give a few examples of the way in which the study of semantics helps the etymologist. The *antlers* of a deer are properly the lowest branches of the horns, what we now call brow-antlers. The word comes from Old Fr. *antoilliers*, which answers phonetically to a conjectured Lat. **ante-oculares*, from *oculus*, eye. This conjecture is confirmed by the Ger. *Augensprosse*, brow-antler, lit. eye-sprout.

Eng. *plover*, from Fr. *pluvier*, could come from a Vulgar Lat. **pluviarius*, belonging to rain. The German name *Regenpfeifer*, lit. rain-piper, shows this to be correct. It does not matter, etymologically, whether the bird really has any connection with rain, for rustic observation, interesting as it is, is essentially unscientific. The *honey*suckle is useless to the bee. The *slow-worm*, which appears to be for *slay-worm*, strike-serpent,[1] is

---

[1] The meaning of *worm* has degenerated since the days of the *Lindwurm*, the dragon slain by Siegfried. The Norse form survives in *Great Orme's Head*, the dragon's head.

perfectly harmless, and the toad, though ugly, is not venomous, nor does he bear a jewel in his head.

Kestrel, a kind of hawk, represents Old Fr. *quercerelle* (*crécerelle*), "a kastrell" (Cotgrave). *Crécerelle* is a diminutive of *crécelle*, a rattle, used in Old French especially of the leper's rattle or clapper, with which he warned people away from his neighbourhood. It is connected with Lat. *crepare*, to resound. The Latin name for the kestrel is *tinnunculus*, lit. a little ringer, derived from the verb *tinnire*, to clink, jingle, "tintinnabulate." Cooper tells us that "they use to set them (kestrels) in pigeon houses, to make doves to love the place, bicause they feare away other haukes with their ringing voyce." This information is obtained from the Latin agriculturist Columella. This parallel makes it clear that Fr. *crécerelle*, kestrel, is a metaphorical application of the same word, meaning a leper's "clicket."

The curious word *akimbo* occurs first in Mid. English in the form *in kenebowe*. In half a dozen languages we find this attitude expressed by the figure of a jug-handle, or, as it used to be called, a pot-ear. The oldest equivalent is Lat. *ansatus*, used by Plautus, from *ansa*, a jug-handle. *Ansatus homo* is explained by Cooper as "a man with his arms *on kenbow*." Archaic French for to stand with arms akimbo is "faire le pot a deux *anses*," and the same striking image occurs in German, Dutch, and Spanish. Hence it seems a plausible conjecture that *kenebowe* means "jug-handle." This is confirmed by the fact that Dryden translates *ansa*, "the eare or handle of a cuppe or pot" (Cooper), by "*kimbo* handle" (Vergil, *Ecl.* iii. 44). Eng. *bow*, meaning anything bent, is used in many connections for handle. The first element may be *can*, applied to every description of vessel in earlier English, as it still is in Scottish, or it may be some Scandinavian word. In fact the whole compound may be Scandinavian. Thomas' *Latin Dictionary* (1644) explains *ansatus homo* as " one that in bragging manner strowteth up and down with his armes *a-canne-bow*."

Demure has been explained as from Mid. Eng. *mure*, ripe, mature, with prefixed *de*. But *demure* is the older word of the two, and while the loss of the atonic first syllable is normal in English (p. 61), it would be hard to find a case in which a meaningless prefix has been added. Nor does the meaning of *demure* approximate very closely to that of ripe. It now has a suggestion of slyness, but in Milton's time meant sedate—

> " Come, pensive nun, devout and pure,
> Sober, stedfast, and *demure*." (*Penseroso*, l. 31.)

and its oldest meaning is calm, settled, used of the sea. When we consider that it is nearly equivalent to *staid*, earlier *stayed*, and compare the equivalent terms in other languages, *e.g.*, Lat. *sedatus*, Fr. *rassis*, Ger. *gesetzt*, etc., it seems likely that it is formed from the Old Norman *demurer* (*demeurer*), to " stay," just as *stale* is formed from Old Fr. *estaler* (*étaler*), to display on a *stall*, or *trove*, in " treasure *trove*," from Old Fr. *trover* (*trouver*).

The origin of *lugger* is unknown, but the word is recorded a century later than *lugsail*, whence it is probably derived. The explanation of *lugsail* as a *sail* that is *lugged* seems to be a piece of folk-etymology. The French for *lugsail* is *voile de fortune*, and a still earlier name, which occurs also in Tudor English, is *bonaventure*, *i.e.*, good luck. Hence it is not unreasonable to conjecture that *lugsail* stands for **luck-sail*, just as the name *Higson* stands for *Hickson* (see p. 172).

G 2

The *pips* on cards or dice have nothing to do with apple pips. The oldest spelling is *peeps*. In the Germanic languages they are called "eyes," and in the Romance languages "points"; and the Romance derivatives of Lat. *punctus*, point, also mean "*peep* of day." Hence the *peeps* are connected with the verb to *peep*.

The game called *dominoes* is French, and the name is taken from the phrase *faire domino*, to win the game. *Domino*, a hooded cloak worn by priests in winter, is an Italian word, apparently connected with Lat. *dominus*. French also has, in various games, the phrase *faire capot*, with a meaning like that of *faire domino*. *Capot*, related to Eng. *cap* and Fr. *chapeau*, means properly a hooded cloak. The two metaphors are quite parallel, but it is impossible to say what was the original idea. Perhaps it was that of extinguishing the opponent by putting, as it were, his head in a bag.

The card game called *gleek* is often mentioned in Tudor literature. It is derived from Old Fr. *glic*, used by Rabelais, and the word is very common in the works of the more disreputable French poets of the 15th century. According to French archæologists the game was also called *bonheur*, *chance*, *fortune*, and *hasard*. Hence *glic* represents in all probability Ger. *Glück*, luck.[1] The Old French form *ghelicque* would correspond to Mid. High Ger. *gelücke*. The history of *tennis* (p. 10) and *trump* (p. 9) shows that it is not necessary to find the German word recorded in the same sense.

The word *sentry*, which occurs in English only, has no connection at all with *sentinel*, the earliest form of which is Ital. *sentinella*, of unknown origin. The older lexicographers obscured the etymology of *sentry*, which is really quite simple, by always attempting to treat it

---

[1] Some derive it from Ger. *gleich*, like, used of a "flush."

along with *sentinel.* It is a common phenomenon in military language that the abstract name of an action is applied to the building or station in which the action is performed, then to the group of men thus employed, and finally to the individual soldier. Thus Lat. *custodia* means (1) guardianship, (2) a ward-room, watch-tower, (3) the watch collectively, (4) a watchman. Fr. *vigie*, the look-out man on board ship, can be traced back in a similar series of meanings to Lat. *vigilia*, watching.[1] A *sentry*, now a single soldier, was formerly a band of soldiers—

> "What strength, what art can then
> Suffice, or what evasion bear him safe
> Through the strict *senteries* and stations thick
> Of angels watching round?"
>
> (*Paradise Lost*, ii. 410.)

and earlier still a watch-tower, *e.g.*, Cotgrave explains Old Fr. *eschauguette* (*échauguette*) as "a *sentrie*, watch-tower, beacon." The purely abstract sense survives in the phrase "to keep *sentry*," *i.e.* guard—

> "Here toils, and Death, and Death's half-brother, Sleep,
> Forms terrible to view their *centry* [2] keep."
>
> (DRYDEN, *Æneid*, vi. 277.)

It is a contracted form of *sanctuary.* In the 17th century it is a pretty familiar word in this sense.[2] The earliest example I have come across is in Nashe—

> "He hath no way now to slyppe out of my hands, but to take *sentrie* in the Hospital of Warwick."
>
> (First Part of PASQUIL'S *Apologie*, 1590.)

Fr. *guérite*, a sentry box, can be traced back in the

---

[1] This is why so many French military terms are feminine, e.g., *recrue*, *sentinelle*, *vedette*, etc.

[2] Skinner's *Etymologicon* (1671) has the two entries, *centry pro sanctuary* and *centry v. sentinel.* The spellings *centry* and *centinel*, which were common when the words still had a collective sense, are perhaps due to some fancied connection with *century*, a hundred soldiers.

same way to Old Fr. *garir* (*guérir*), to save. Cotgrave
explains it as "a place of refuge, and of safe retyrall,"
also "a *sentrie*, or little lodge for a sentinell, built on
high." It is to this latter sense that we owe Eng
garret.   In medieval French *guérite* means refuge,
sanctuary—

"Ceste roche est Ihesucrist meismes qui est li refuges et la
garite aus humbles."[1]

If French had not borrowed *sentinelle* from Italian,
guérite would probably now mean "sentry"; *cf.* the
history of *vigie* (p. 103), or of *vedette*, a cavalry sentry,
but originally "a prying or peeping hole" (Florio),
from Ital. *vedere*, to see.

[1] "This rock is Jesus Christ himself, who is the refuge and sanctuary
of the humble."

CHAPTER VIII

METAPHOR

EVERY expression that we employ, apart from those that are connected with the most rudimentary objects and actions, is a metaphor, though the original meaning is dulled by constant use. Thus, in the above sentence, *expression* means what is " squeezed out," to *employ* is to "twine in" like a basket maker, to *connect* is to "weave together," *rudimentary* means "in the rough state," and an *object* is something "thrown in our way." A classification of the metaphors in use in the European languages would show that a large number of the most *obvious* kind, *i.e.* of those which "come to meet" one, are common property, while others would reflect the most striking habits and pursuits of the various races. It would probably be found that in the common stock of simple metaphor the most important contribution would come from agriculture, while in English the nautical element would occur to an extent quite unparalleled in other European languages.[1] A curious agricultural

---

[1] It would be interesting to trace the rise and spread of nautical metaphor in English. We have a good example of the transition from the bucolic to the nautical in the expression "To lose the *ship* for a ha'porth of tar." Few people who use this metaphor know that *ship* is here the dialect pronunciation of *sheep*; cf. *Ship Street*, at Oxford (and elsewhere), for *Sheep Street*. Tar was, and is, used as a medicine for sheep, but in this particular case the allusion seems to be rather to the marking of sheep with tar ; *cf.* "tarred with the same brush," *i.e.*, members of the same flock.

metaphor which, though of Old French origin, now appears to be peculiar to English, is to *rehearse*, lit. to harrow over again (see *hearse*, p. 75).

Some metaphors are easy to track. It does not require much philological knowledge to see that *astonish*, *astound*, and *stun* all contain the idea of "thunder - striking," Vulgar Lat. **ex - tonare*. To *embarrass* is obviously connected with *bar*, and to *interfere* is to "strike between," Old Fr. *entreferir*. This word was especially used in the 16th century of a horse knocking its legs together in trotting, "to *interfeere*, as a horse" (Cotgrave). When we speak of a *prentice-hand*, sound *journeyman* work, and a *masterpiece*, we revive the medieval classification of artisans into learners, qualified workmen, and those who, by the presentation to their guild of a finished piece of work, were recognised as past (passed) masters.

But many of our metaphors are drawn from pursuits with which we are no longer familiar, or from arts and sciences no longer practised. *Disaster*, *ill-starred*, and such adjectives as *jovial*, *mercurial*, are reminiscent of astrology. To bring a thing to the *test* is to put it in the alchemist's or metallurgist's *test* or trying - pot (cf. *test*-tube), Old Fr. *test* (*têt*). This is related to Old Fr. *teste* (*tête*), head, from Lat. *testa*, tile, pot, etc., used in Roman slang for *caput*. Shakespeare has the complete metaphor—

> "Let there be some more *test* made of my metal,[1]
> Before so noble and so great a figure
> Be stamp'd upon it."
>
> (*Measure for Measure*, i. 1.)

The old butchers' shops which adjoin Nottingham Market Place are still called the *Shambles*. The word

---

[1] See *mettle*, p. 144.

is similarly used at Carlisle, and probably elsewhere; but to most people it is familiar only in the metaphorical sense of place of slaughter, generally regarded as a singular. Thus Denys of Burgundy says—

> "The beasts are in the *shambles*."
> (*Cloister and Hearth*, Ch. 33.)

etymologically misusing the word, which does not mean slaughter-house, but the bench on which meat is exposed for sale. It is a very early loan from Lat. *scamnum*, a bench or form, also explained by Cooper as "a step or grice (see p. 118) to get up to bedde." The same diminutive form occurs in Fr. *escabeau*, an office stool, and Ger. *Schemel*, a stool.

Fusty, earlier *foisty*, is no longer used in its proper sense. It comes from Old Fr. *fusté*, "*fusty*; tasting of the caske, smelling of the vessell wherein it hath been kept" (Cotgrave), a derivative of Old Fr. *fust* (*fût*), a cask.[1]

The smith's art has given us *brand-new*, often corrupted into *bran-new*. Shakespeare uses *fire-new*—

> "You should then have accosted her; and with some excellent jests, *fire-new* from the mint, you should have banged the youth into dumbness." (*Twelfth Night*, iii. 2.)

Modern German has *funkelnagelneu*, spark nail new; but in older German we find also *spanneu*, *splinterneu*, chip new, splinter new; which shows the origin of our *spick and span* (new), *i.e.*, spike and chip new. French has *tout battant neuf*, beating new, *i.e.*, fresh from the anvil.

Many old hunting terms survive as metaphors. To

---

[1] Lat. *fustis*, a staff, cudgel, gave also Old Fr. *fust*, a kind of boat, whence obsolete Eng. *foist* in the same sense. Both meanings seem to go back to a time when casks and boats were "dug out" instead of being built up.

be *at bay*, Fr. *aux abois*, is to be facing the baying
hounds. The fundamental meaning of Old Fr. *abaier*
(*aboyer*), of obscure origin, is perhaps to gape at.[1] Thus
a right or estate which is in *abeyance* is one regarded
with open-mouthed expectancy. The *toils* are Fr.
toiles, lit. cloths, Lat. *tela*, the nets put round a thicket
to prevent the game from escaping. To "beat about
the bush" seems to be a mixture of two metaphors
which are quite unlike in meaning. To "beat the
bush" was the office of the beaters, who started the
game for others, hence an old proverb, "I will not beat
the bush that another may have the birds." To "go
about the bush" would seem to have been used
originally of a hesitating hound. The two expressions
have coalesced to express the idea for which French
says "y aller par quatre chemins." *Crestfallen* and
white feather belong to the old sport of cock-fighting.
Jeopardy is Old Fr. *jeu parti*, a divided game, hence an
equal encounter. To run full *tilt* is a jousting phrase.
To *pounce* upon is to seize in the *pounces*, the old word
for a hawk's claws. The ultimate source is Lat.
pungere, to prick, pierce. A goldsmith's *punch* was
also called a *pounce*, hence the verb to *pounce*, to make
patterns on metal. The northern past participle
pouncet[2] occurs in *pouncet-box*, a metal perforated globe
for scents—

> "And 'twixt his finger and his thumb he held
> A *pouncet-box*, which ever and anon
> He gave his nose, and took't away again."
>
> (1 *Henry IV.*, i. 3.)

To the language of hawking belongs also *haggard*.
Cotgrave defines *faulcon* (*faucon*) *hagard*, as "a faulcon

---

[1] Related are *bouche béante*, or *bée*, mouth agape ; *bâiller*, to yawn ; and
badaud, "a gaping hoydon" (Cotgrave, *badauld*).

[2] *Cf.* the *Stickit* Minister.

that preyed for her selfe long before she was taken."
Hence the sense of wild, untameable. The original
meaning is hedge-hawk, the first syllable representing
Old High Ger. *hag*, hedge.   *Hag*, a witch, is of cognate
origin.

The antiquity of dicing appears in the history of
Ger. *gefallen*, to please, originally used of the "fall" of
the dice.   In Mid. High German it is always used
with *wohl*, well, or *übel*, ill; e.g., *es gefällt mir wohl*, it
"falls out" well for me.   There can be no reasonable
doubt that the *deuce !* is a dicer's exclamation at making
the lowest throw, two, Fr. *deux*.   We still use *deuce* for
the two in cards, and German has *Daus* in both senses.
Tennis has given us *bandy*, Fr. *bander*, "to *bandie*, at
tennis" (Cotgrave).   We now only bandy words or
reproaches, but Juliet understood the word in its literal
sense—

> "Had she affections and warm youthful blood,
>   She'd be as swift in motion as a ball ;
>   My words would *bandy* her to my sweet love,
>   And his to me."   (*Romeo and Juliet*, ii. 5.)

Fowling has given us *cajole*, *decoy*, and *trepan*.   Fr.
cajoler, which formerly meant to chatter like a jay in a
cage, has in modern French assumed the meaning of
enjôler, earlier *engeoler*, "to incage, or ingaole"
(Cotgrave), hence to entice.   Fr. *geôle*, gaol, represents
Vulgar Lat. *caveola*.   *Decoy*, earlier also *coy*, is Du.
kooi, cage.   The later form is perhaps due to *duck-coy*.
Du. *kooi* is also of Latin origin.   It comes, like Fr.
cage, from Vulgar Lat. *cavea*, and has a doublet *kevie*,
whence Scot. *cavie*, a hen-coop.   *Trepan* was formerly
trapan, and belongs to *trap*—

> "Some by the nose with fumes *trapan* 'em,
>   As Dunstan did the devil's grannam."
>   (*Hudibras*, ii. 3.)

It is now equivalent to *kidnap*, *i.e.* to *nab kids* (children),
once a lucrative pursuit. The surgical *trepan* is a
different word altogether, and belongs to Greco-Lat.
trypanon, an auger, piercer. To *allure* is to bring to the
lure, or bait. To the same group of metaphors belongs
inveigle, which corresponds, with altered prefix, to Fr.
aveugler, to blind, Vulgar Lat. **ab-oculare*.[1] A distant
relative of this word is *ogle*, which is of Low German
origin; *cf.* Ger. *liebäugeln* " to *ogle*, to smicker, to
look amorously, to cast sheeps-eyes, to cast amorous
looks " (Ludwig).

The archaic verb to *cozen* is a metaphor of quite
another kind. Every young noble who did the grand
tour in the 16th and 17th centuries spent some time
at Naples, " where he may improve his knowledge
in horsemanship " (Howell, *Instructions for Forreine
Travell*, 1642). Now the Italian horse-dealers were so
notorious that Dekker, writing about 1600, describes a
swindling " horse-courser " as a " meere jadish Non-
politane," a play on Neapolitan. The Italian name is
cozzone, " a horse-courser, a horse-breaker, a craftie
knave " (Florio), whence the verb *cozzonare*, " to have
perfect skill in all *cosenages* " (Torriano). The essential
idea of to *cozen* in the Elizabethans is that of selling
faulty goods in a bad light, a device said to be
practised by some horse-dealers. At any rate the
words for horse-dealer in all languages, from the Lat.
mango to the Amer. *horse-swapper*, mean swindler and
worse things. *Cozen* is a favourite word with the
Elizabethan dramatists, because it enables them to bring
off one of those stock puns that make one feel " The
less Shakespeare he "—

---

[1] Or perhaps **alboculare*, as *albus oculus*, lit. white eye, is used of
blindness in an early Vulgar Latin glossary.

> "*Cousins*, indeed ; and by their uncle *cozen'd*
> Of comfort, kingdom, kindred, freedom, life."
>
> (*Richard III.*, iv. 4.)

In the *Merry Wives of Windsor* (iv. 5) there is a
lot of word-play on "cousins-german" and "German
cozeners." An exact parallel to the history of *cozen* is
furnished by the verb to *jockey*, from *jockey*, in its older
sense of horse-dealer.

Scion is a metaphor from the garden. It is Fr.
scion, "a scion ; a young and tender plant; a shoot,
sprig, or twig" (Cotgrave). Ger. *Sprössling*, sprout-
ling, is also used of an "offshoot" from a "stock." We
have a similar metaphor in the word *imp*. We now
graft trees, a misspelling of older *graffe*, Fr. *greffe*,
Greco-Lat. *graphium*, a pencil, from the shape of the
slip. But the older word was *imp*, which we find also
used of inserting a new feather into the wing or tail of
a hawk, or fitting a small bell-rope to a larger one.
The art of grafting was learnt from the Romans, who
had a post-classical verb *imputare*,[1] to graft, which
has given Eng. *imp*, Ger. *impfen*, Fr. *enter*, and is represented in most other European languages. *Imp* was
used like *scion*, but degenerated in meaning. In
Shakespeare it has already the somewhat contemptuous
shade of meaning which we find in Ger. *Sprössling*,
and is only used by comic characters. Thus Pistol
addresses Prince Hal—

> "The heavens thee guard and keep, most royal *imp* of fame."
>
> (2 *Henry IV.*, v. 5.)

But Thomas Cromwell, in his last letter to Henry
VIII., speaks of—

> "That most noble *imp*, the prince's grace, your most dear son."

The special sense of "young devil" appears to be due

---

[1] Of uncertain origin. Lat. *putare*, to cut (cf. *amputate*), or Gk.
ἔμφυτος, implanted ?

to the frequent occurrence of such phrases as "*imps* (children) of Satan," "the devil and his *imps*," etc. Ger. *impfen* also means to vaccinate. Our earlier term *inoculate*[1] originally meant to graft, and, in fact, *engraft* was also used in this sense.

Zest is quite obsolete in its original meaning of a piece of orange peel used to give piquancy to wine. It is a French word of unknown origin, properly applied to the inner skin of fruit and nuts. Cotgrave explains it as "the thick skinne, or filme whereby the kernell of a wallnut is divided."

[1] From *oculus*, eye, in the sense of bud.

CHAPTER IX

FOLK-ETYMOLOGY

THE sound, spelling, and even the meaning of a word are often perverted by influences to which the collective name of folk-etymology has been given. I here use the term to include all phenomena which are due to any kind of misunderstanding of a word. A word beginning with *n* sometimes loses this sound through its being confused with the *n* of the indefinite article *an*. Thus *an adder* and *an auger* are for *a nadder* (*cf*. Ger. *Natter*) and *a nauger*, Mid. Eng. *navegor*, properly an instrument for piercing the *nave* of a wheel. *Apron* was in Mid. English *naprun*, from Old Fr. *naperon*, a derivative of *nappe*, cloth. The *aitch-bone* was formerly the *nache-bone*, from Old Fr. *nache*, buttock, Vulgar Lat. **natica* for *nates*. *Nache* is still used by French butchers. *Humble-pie* is a popular perversion of *umble-pie*, *i.e.*, a pie made from the *umbles*, or inferior parts of the stag. But *umble* is for earlier *numble*, Old Fr. *nomble*, formed, with dissimilation, from Lat. *lumbulus*, diminutive of *lumbus*, loin; cf. *niveau* (p. 58). Thus *humble-pie* has etymologically no connection with humility. *Umpire* represents Old Fr. *non per* (*pair*), not equal, the *umpire* being a third person called in when arbitrators could not agree. This appears clearly in the following extract from a medieval letter—

"And if so be that the said arbitrators may not accord before the said feast of Allhalowes, then the said parties be

H

the advise abovesaid are agreed to abide the award and ordin-
ance of an *noumper* to be chosen be the said arbitrators."

(*Plumpton Correspondence*, 1431.)

For the sense we may compare Span. *tercero*, "the
third, a broaker, a mediator" (Percyvall). *An eyas*
falcon is for *a neyas* falcon, Fr. *niais*, foolish, lit. nestling,
related to *nid*, nest. Rosenkrantz uses it in the literal
sense—

"But there is, sir, an aiery of children, little *eyases*, that cry
out on the top of question, and are most tyranically clapped for't."
(*Hamlet*, ii. 2.)

Somewhat similar is the loss in French of initial *a* in
la boutique for *l'aboutique*, Greco-Lat. *apotheca*, and *la
Pouille* for *l'Apouille*, Apulia, or of the initial *l* in *ounce*,
a kind of tiger-cat, from Fr. *once*, earlier *lonce*, "the
ounce, a ravenous beast" (Cotgrave), taken as *l'once*.
It is almost a doublet of *lynx*.

The opposite has happened in the case of *a newt*
for *an ewt* and *a nick-name* for *an eke-name*. *Eke*, also,
occurs in the first stanza of John Gilpin. It is cognate
with Ger. *auch*, also, and Lat. *augere*, to increase. *Nuncle*,
the customary address of a court fool to his superiors—

"How now, *nuncle!* Would I had two coxcombs and two
daughters."   (*Lear*, i. 4.)

is for *mine uncle*. We also find *naunt*. *Nonce* occurs
properly only in the phrase *for the nonce*, which is for
earlier *for then ones*, where *then* is the dative of the
definite article. Family names like *Nash*, *Nokes* are
aphetic for *atten ash*, at the ash, *atten oakes*, at the oaks.
The creation of such forms was perhaps helped by our
tendency to use initial *n* in Christian names, e.g., *Ned*
for *Edward*, *Noll* for *Oliver*, *Nell* for *Ellen*.

Agglutination of the definite article is common in French, e.g., *lingot*, ingot, *lierre*, ivy, for *l'ierre*, Lat. *hedera*, and the dialect *lévier*, sink, for *évier*, Lat. *aquarium*, whence Eng. *ewer*. The derivation of Fr. *landier*, andiron, is unknown, but the *iron* of the English word is due to folk-etymology. Such agglutination occurs often in family names such as *Langlois*, lit. the Englishman, *Lhuissier*, the usher (see p. 90), and some of these have passed into English, e.g., *Levick* for *l'évêque*, the bishop.

The two words *alarm* and *alert* include the Italian definite article. The first is Ital. *all'arme*, to arms, for *a le arme*, and the second is *all'erta* for *alla (a la) erta*, the last word representing Lat. *erecta*. With rolled *r*, *alarm* becomes *alarum*, whence the aphetic *larum*—

> "Then we shall hear their *larum*, and they ours."
> (*Coriolanus*, i. 4.)

Ger. *Lärm*, noise, is the same word. In Luther's time we also find *Allerm*.

We have the Arabic definite article in a great many words borrowed from Spanish. *Alcalde*, or *alcade*, and *alguazil*, common in Elizabethan literature, are two old friends from the *Arabian Nights*, the *cadi* and the *wazir*, or *vizier*. The Arabic article also occurs in *acton*, Old Fr. *auqueton*, now *hoqueton*, for *al qutn* (cotton), because originally used of a wadded coat—

> "But Cranstoun's lance, of more avail,
> Pierced through, like silk, the Borderer's mail ;
> Through shield, and jack, and *acton* past,
> Deep in his bosom broke at last."
> (SCOTT, *Lay*, iii. 6.)

In *alligator*, Span. *el lagarto*, the lizard, from Lat. *lacertus*, we have the Spanish definite article. See also *lariat*, p. 24.

A foreign word ending in a sibilant is sometimes mistaken for a plural. Thus Old Fr. *assets* (*assez*), enough, Lat. *ad satis*, has given Eng. *assets*, plural, with a barbarous, but useful, singular *asset*. *Cherry* is for *cheris*, from a dialect form of Fr. *cerise*, and *sherry* for *sherris*, from *Xeres* in Spain (see p. 51). Falstaff opines that—

> "A good *sherris*-sack[1] hath a twofold operation in it."
> (2 *Henry IV*., iv. 3.)

Pea is a false singular from older *pease*, Lat. *pisum*. Perhaps the frequent occurrence of *pease-soup*, not to be distinguished from *pea-soup*, is partly responsible for this mistake. *Marquee*, a large tent, is from Fr. *marquise*. With this we may class the heathen *Chinee* and the *Portugee*. Milton wrote correctly of—

> "The barren plains
> Of Sericana, where *Chineses* drive
> With sails and wind their cany waggons light."
> (*Paradise Lost*, iii. 438.)

It has been ingeniously suggested that *Yankee* has been derived in the same way from Du. *Jan Kees*, John Cornelius, supposed to have been a nickname for early Dutch colonists. It is more probably the Dutch dim. *Janke*, i.e. Johnny. The vulgarism *shay* for *chaise*[2] is of similar formation. *Corp*, for *corpse*, is also used provincially. *Kickshaws* is really a singular from Fr. *quelque chose*—

> "Art thou good at these *kickshawses*, knight?"
> (*Twelfth Night*, i. 3.)

Cotgrave spells it *quelkchoses* (s.v. *fricandeau*).

---

[1] *Sack*, earlier also *seck*, is Fr. *sec*, dry, which, with spurious *t*, has also given Ger. *Sekt*, now used for champagne.

[2] Fr. *chaise*, chair, for older *chaire*, now used only of a pulpit or professorial chair, Lat. *cathedra*, is due to an affected pronunciation that prevailed in Paris in the 16th century.

Skate has a curious history.   It is a false singular
from Du. *schaats*.   This is from *escache*, an Old French
dialect form of *échasse*, stilt, which was used in the
Middle Ages for a wooden leg.   It is of German origin,
and is related to *shank*.   *Cf.*, for the sense development, Eng. *patten*, from Fr. *patin*, a derivative of *patte*,
foot, cognate with *paw*.   *Skates* are still called *pattens*
by the fenmen of Cambridgeshire.   We also had
formerly a doublet from Old Fr. *escache* directly, but
in the older sense, for Cotgrave has *eschasses* (*échasses*),
"stilts, or *scatches* to go on."   *Row*, a disturbance,
belongs to *rouse*, a jollification—

> "The king doth wake to-night and takes his *rouse*."
> (*Hamlet*, i. 4.)

of uncertain origin, but probably aphetic for *carouse*,
drink carouse being wrongly separated as *drink a rouse*.
The bird called a *wheatear* was formerly called
wheatears, a corruption of a name best explained
by its French equivalent *cul blanc*, "the bird called
a whittaile" (Cotgrave).   We may compare the bird-
name *redstart*, where *start* means rump.

Conversely a word used in the plural is sometimes
regarded as a singular, the result being a double
plural.   Many Latin neuter plurals were adopted into
French as feminine singulars, e.g., *cornua*, *corne*, horn;
labra, *lèvre*, lip; *vela*, *voile*, sail.   It is obvious that this
is most likely to occur in the case of plurals which are
used for a pair, or set, of things, and thus have a kind
of collective sense.   *Breeches* or *breeks* is a double plural,
Anglo-Sax. *brēc* being already the plural of *brōc*.   In
Mid. English we still find *breche* or *breke* used of this
garment.   *Trousers* was earlier *trouses*, plural of *trouse*,
now *trews*, and was used especially of Irish native
costume.   The latest researches throw doubt on the

identity of these words with Fr. *trousse*, a page's short breeches. The etymology which now finds most favour is Irish and Gaelic *triubhas*, from Late Lat. *tubracci* or *tribracci*, which is supposed to be a corrupted compound from *tibia*, leg, shank, and *braccæ*, breeches. *Bodice* is for *bodies*, as *pence* is for *pennies*. Cotgrave explains *corset* by "a paire of *bodies* for a woman," and the plural sense occurs as late as Harrison Ainsworth—

"A *pair of bodice* of the cumbrous form in vogue at the beginning of the last century." (*Jack Sheppard*, Ch. 1.)

Trace, of a horse, is the Old Fr. plural *trais*[1] (*traits*) of *trait*, "a teame-trace" (Cotgrave). *Apprentice* is the plural of Fr. *apprenti*, formerly *apprentif*, a derivative of *apprendre*, to learn, hence a disciple. *Invoice* is the plural of the obsolete *invoy*, from Fr. *envoi*, sending.

In the *Grecian steps*, at Lincoln, we have a popular corruption of the common Mid. Eng. and Tudor *grece*, *grese*, plural of Old Fr. *gré*, step, from Lat. *gradus*. Shakespeare spells it *grize*—

"Let me speak like yourself; and lay a sentence,
Which, as a *grize*, or step, may help these lovers
Into your favour."

(*Othello*, i. 3.)

Scot. *brose*, or *brewis*, was in Mid. Eng. *browes*, from Old Fr. *brouez*, plural of *brouet*, a word cognate with our *broth*. From this association comes perhaps the use of *broth* as a plural in some of our dialects. *Porridge*, not originally limited to oatmeal, seems to be combined from *pottage* and Mid. Eng. *porrets*, plural of *porret*, leek,

---

[1] The fact that in Old French the final consonant of the singular disappeared in the plural form helped to bring about such misunderstandings.

a diminutive from Lat. *porrum*. *Porridge* is sometimes used as a plural in Scottish—

"They're fine, halesome food, they're grand food, *parritch*."
(*Kidnapped*, Ch. 3.)

and in the northern counties of England people speak of taking "a few" porridge, or broth. *Baize*, now generally green, is for earlier *bayes*, the plural of the adjective *bay*, now used only of horses; *cf.* Du. *baai*, baize. The origin of the adjective *bay*, Fr. *bai*, forms of which occur in all the Romance languages, is Lat. *badius*, "of bay colour, bayarde" (Cooper). Hence the name *Bayard*, applied to FitzJames' horse in *The Lady of the Lake* (v. 18), and earlier to the steed that carried the four sons of Aymon. *Quince* is the plural of *quin*, from the Norman form of Old Fr. *coin* (*coing*), which is derived from Gk. κυδώνιον. *Truce* is the plural of Mid. Eng. *trewe* (lit. truth, faith) with the same meaning. Already in Anglo-Saxon it is found in the plural, probably as rendering Lat. *induciæ*. *Lettuce*, Mid. Eng. *letows*, seems also to be a plural, from Fr. *laitue*, Lat. *lactuca*.

Earnest in the sense of pledge—

"And, for an *earnest* of a greater honour,
He bade me, from him, call thee Thane of Cawdor."
(*Macbeth*, i. 3.)

has nothing to do with the adjective *earnest*. It is the Mid. Eng. *ernes*, earlier *erles*, which survives as *arles* in some of our dialects. The verb to *earl* is still used in Cumberland of "enlisting" a servant with a shilling in the open market. The Old French word was *arres* or *erres*, now written learnedly *arrhes*, a plural from Lat. *arrha*, "an *earnest* penny, *earnest* money" (Cooper). The existence of Mid. Eng. *erles* shows that there must have been also an Old French diminutive form. For the apparently arbitrary change of *l* to *n* we may compare *banister* for *baluster* (see p. 60).

The *jesses* of a hawk—

> "If I do prove her haggard,[1]
> Though that her *jesses* were my dear heart-strings,
> I'd whistle her off, and let her down the wind,
> To prey at fortune."
>
> (*Othello*, iii. 3.)

were the thongs by which it was held or "thrown" into the air. *Jess* is the Old Fr. *jes*, the plural of *jet*, from *jeter*, to throw. In Colman's *Elder Brother* we read of a gentleman who lounged and chatted, "not minding time a *souse*," where *souse* is the plural of Fr. *sou*, halfpenny. From Fr. *muer*, to moult, Lat. *mutare*, we get Fr. *mue*, moulting, later applied to the coop or pen in which moulting falcons were confined, whence the phrase "to *mew* (up)"—

> "More pity, that the eagles should be *mew'd*,
> While kites and buzzards prey at liberty."
>
> (*Richard III.*, i. 1.)

When, in 1534, the royal *mews*, or hawk-houses, near Charing Cross were rebuilt as stables, the word acquired its present meaning.

Chess, Old Fr. *esches* (*échecs*), is the plural of *check*, Fr. *échec*, from Persian *shāh*, king. By analogy with the "game of kings," the name *jeu des dames* was given in French to draughts, still called *dams* in Scotland. *Draught*, from *draw*, meant in Mid. English a "move" at chess. The etymology of *tweezers* can best be made clear by starting from French *étui*, a case, of doubtful origin. This became in English *etwee*, or *twee*, *e.g.*, Cotgrave explains *estui* (*étui*) as "a sheath, case, or box to put things in; and (more particularly) a case of little instruments, as sizzars, bodkin, penknife,

---

[1] For *haggard* see p. 108.

etc., now commonly termed an *ettwee.*" Such a case
generally opens book-fashion, each half being fitted
with instruments. Accordingly we find it called a
surgeon's "pair of *twees*," or simply *tweese*, and later a
"pair of *tweeses.*" The implement was named from
the case (*cf.* Fr. *boussole*, p. 127), and became *tweezers*
by association with *pincers* (Fr. *pinces*), *scissors*, etc.

The form of a word is often affected by association
with some other word with which it is instinctively
coupled. Thus *larboard*, for Mid. Eng. *ladeboard*, *i.e.*
loading side, is due to *starboard*, steering side. *Bridal*,
for *bride-ale*, from the liquid consumed at marriage
festivities, is due to analogy with *betrothal*, *espousal*,
etc. A 16th-century Puritan records with satisfaction
the disappearance of—

"Church-ales, helpe-ales, and soule-ales, called also dirge-ales,
and heathenish rioting at *bride-ales.*"

(HARRISON, *Description of England*, 1577.)

Rampart is from Old Fr. *rempar*, a verbal noun
from *remparer*, to repair; *cf.* Ital. *riparo*, "a *rampire*,
a fort, a banke" (Florio). By analogy with Old Fr.
boulevart (*boulevard*), of German origin and identical
with our *bulwark*,[1] *rempar* became *rempart*. The older
English form occurs in the obsolete *rampier* or *rampire*,
which survive in the dialect *ramper*, embankment,
causeway. For the spelling *rampire* we may compare
umpire (p. 113). The apple called a *jenneting*, sometimes
"explained" as for *June-eating*, was once spelt *geniton*,
no doubt for Fr. *jeanneton*, a diminutive of *Jean*. It
is called in French *pomme de Saint-Jean*, and in German
Johannisapfel, because ripe about St John's Day (June 24).

---

[1] In Old French confusion sometimes arose with regard to final consonants, because of their disappearance in the plural (see p. 118, *n.*). In
gerfaut, gerfalcon, for Old Fr. *gerfauc*, the less familiar final *-c* was, as in
boulevart, replaced by the more usual *-t*.

The modern form is due to such apple names as *golding*, *sweeting*, *codlin*, *pippin*.

In the records of medieval London we frequently come across the distinction made between people who lived "in the city," Anglo-Fr. *deinz* (*dans*) *la cité*, and "outside the city," Anglo-Fr. *fors* (*hors*) *la cité*. The former were called *deinzein*, whence our *denizen*, and the latter *forein*.[1] The Anglo-French form of modern Fr. *citoyen* was *citein*, which became *citizen* by analogy with *denizen*. The following passage from a medieval London by-law shows how rigid was the division between "denizen" and "foreign" traders—

"Item, qe nulle pulletere *deinzeyn* n'estoise a Carfeux del Ledenhalle deins mesoun ne dehors, ove conilles, volatilie, n'autre pulletrie pur vendre . . . issint qe les *forreins* pulleters, ove lour pulletrie, estoisent par eux mesmes, et vendent lour pulletrie sur le cornere de Ledenhalle, sanz ceo qe ascuns pulletere *deinzein* viegne ou medle en vent ou en achate ove eux, ne entre eux."[2] (*Liber Albus*.)

Even words which have opposite meanings may affect each other by association. Thus Lat. *reddere*, to give back, became Vulgar Lat. **rendere* by analogy with *prendere* (*prehendere*), to take away; hence Fr. *rendre*. Our word *grief*, from Fr. *grief*, is derived

---

[1] An unoriginal *g* occurs in many English words derived from French, e.g., *foreign*, *sovereign*, older *sovran*, *sprightly* for *spritely*, i.e., *sprite-like*, *delight*, from Old Fr. *delit*, which belongs to Lat. *delectare*.

[2] "Also, that no 'denizen' poulterer shall stand at the 'Carfax' of Leadenhall in a house or without, with rabbits, fowls, or other poultry to sell . . . and that the 'foreign' poulterers, with their poultry, shall stand by themselves, and sell their poultry at the corner of Leadenhall, without any 'denizen' poulterer coming or meddling in sale or purchase with them, or among them."

The word *carfax*, once the usual name for a "cross-way," survives at Oxford and Exeter. It is a plural, from Fr. *carrefour*, Vulgar Lat. **quadrifurcum* (for *furca*), four-fork.

from a Vulgar Lat. *grĕvis*, heavy (for *grăvis*), which is due to *lĕvis*, light.

The plural of *titmouse* is now usually *titmice*, by analogy with *mouse*, *mice*, with which it has no connection. The second part of the word is Anglo-Sax. *māse*, used of several small birds. It is cognate with Ger. *Meise*, titmouse, and Fr. *mésange*, "a titmouse, or tittling" (Cotgrave). *Tit*, of Norse origin, is applied to various small animals, and occurs also as a prefix in *titbit* or *tidbit*. Cf. *tomtit* (p. 37).

The Spanish word *salva*, "a taste, a salutation" (Percyvall), was used of the pregustation of a great man's food or drink. We have given the name to the tray or dish from which the "assay" was made, but, by analogy with *platter*, *trencher*, we spell it *salver*. In another sense, that of a "salutation" in the form of a volley of shot, we have corrupted it into *salvo*. With the use of Span. *salva* we may compare that of Ital. *credenza*, lit. faith, "the taste or assaie of a princes meate and drinke" (Florio), whence Fr. *crédence*, sideboard, used in English only in the ecclesiastical compound *credence table*, and Ger. *credenzen*, to pour out.

In spoken English the ending -*ew*, -*ue*, of French origin, has been often changed to -*ee*, -*ey*. Thus *pedigree* was formerly *pedigrew* (see p. 77). The fencing term *veney*—

"I bruised my shin the other day with playing at sword and dagger with a master of fence—three *veneys* for a dish of stewed prunes." (*Merry Wives*, i. 1.)

also spelt *venew*, is from Fr. *venue*, "a *venny* in fencing" (Cotgrave). *Carew* has become *Carey*, and *Beaulieu*, in Hampshire, is called *Bewley*. Under the influence of these double forms we sometimes get the opposite change, e.g., *purlieu*, now generally used of the outskirts of a town, is for *purley*, a strip of disforested woodland. This is a contraction of Anglo-Fr. *pour-allée*, used to translate the legal Lat. *perambulatio*, a going through. A change of *venue*[1] is sometimes made when it seems likely that an accused person, or a football team, will not get justice from a local jury. This *venue* is in law Latin *vicinetum*, neighbourhood, which gave Anglo-Fr. *visné*, and this, perhaps by confusion with the *venire facias*, or jury summons, became *venew*, *venue*.

In the preceding examples the form has been chiefly affected. In the word *luncheon* both form and meaning have been influenced by the obsolete *nuncheon*, a meal at noon, Mid. Eng. *none-chenche*, for *none-schenche, noon draught, from Anglo-Sax. *scencan*,[2] to pour. Drinking seems to have been regarded as more important than eating, for in some counties we find this *nuncheon* replaced by *bever*, the Anglo-French infinitive from Lat. *bibere*, to drink. *Lunch*, a piece or hunk, especially of bread, also used in the sense of a "snack" (*cf.* Scot. "piece"), was extended to *luncheon* by analogy with *nuncheon*, which it has now replaced—

> "So munch on, crunch on, take your *nuncheon*,
> Breakfast, supper, dinner, *luncheon*."
> (BROWNING, *Pied Piper of Hamelin.*)

The term folk-etymology is often applied in a narrower sense to the corruption of words through a mistaken idea of their etymology or origin. The tendency of the uneducated is to distort an unfamiliar or unintelligible word into some form which suggests a meaning. Some cases may have originated in a kind

[1] This word is getting overworked, *e.g.,* "The Derbyshire Golf Club links were yesterday the *venue* of a 72-hole match" (*Nottingham Guardian,* 21st Nov. 1911).

[2] *Cf.* Ger. *schenken*, to pour, and the Tudor word *skinker*, a drawer, waiter (1 *Henry IV.*, ii. 4).

of heavy jocularity, as in *sparrow-grass* for *asparagus* or *sparagus* (see p. 66), or Rogue Riderhood's *Alfred David* for *affidavit*—

"'Is that your name?' asked Lightwood. 'My name?' returned the man. 'No; I want to take a *Alfred David*.'"
(Our Mutual Friend, Ch. 12.)

In others there has been a wrong association of ideas, *e.g.*, the *primrose*, *rosemary*, and *tuberose* have none of them originally any connection with the *rose*. *Primrose* was earlier *primerole*, an Old French derivative of Latin *primula*; *rosemary*, French *romarin*, is from Lat. *ros marinus*, sea-dew; *tuberose* is the Latin adjective *tuberosus*, bulbous, tuberous. Or attempts are made at translation, such as Sam Weller's *Have his carcase* for *Habeas Corpus*, or the curious names which country folk give to such complaints as *bronchitis*, *erysipelas*, etc. To this class belongs Private Mulvaney's perversion of *locomotor ataxy*—

"'They call ut *Locomotus attacks us*,' he sez, 'bekaze,' sez he, 'it attacks us like a locomotive.'" (*Love o' Women*.)

Our language is, owing to our borrowing habits, particularly rich in these gems. Examples familiar to everybody are *crayfish* from Fr. *écrevisse*, *gilly-flower* from Fr. *giroflée*, *shame-faced* for *shamefast*. Other words in which the second element has been altered are *causeway*, earlier *causey*, from the Picard form of Fr. *chaussée*, Lat. (*via*) *calciata*, *i.e.*, made with lime, *calx*; *penthouse*, for *pentice*, Fr. *appentis*, "the *penthouse* of a house" (Cotgrave), a derivative of Old Fr. *appendre*, to hang to. Fr. *hangar*, a shed, now introduced into English by aviators as unnecessarily as *garage* by motorists, may also contain the same idea of "hanging."

In *hiccough*, for earlier *hickup*, an onomatopœic word, the spelling, suggested by *cough*, has not affected the pronunciation. *Surcease* is Fr. *sursis*, past participle of *surseoir*, "to *surcease*, pawse, intermit, leave off, give over, delay or stay for a time" (Cotgrave), Lat. *supersedere*. *Taffrail* has been confused with *rail*, its older form being *tafferel*, from Du. *tafereel*, diminutive of *tafel*, picture, from Lat. *tabula*. It meant originally the flat part of the stern of a ship ornamented with carvings or pictures. This is called *tableau* in nautical French. Fr. *coutelas*, an augmentative of Old Fr. *coutel* (*couteau*), knife, gave Eng. *cutlass*, which has no more etymological connection with "cutting" than a *cutler*, Fr. *coutelier*, or a *cutlet*, Fr. *côtelette*, little rib, Lat. *costa*. *Cutlas* was popularly corrupted into *curtal-axe*, the form used by Rosalind—

> "A gallant *curtal-axe* upon my thigh,
>   A boar-spear in my hand."
>
> (*As You Like It*, i. 3.)

We have a similar corruption in *pick-axe*, Mid. Eng. *pikeys*, Old Fr. *piquois*, *picquois*, "a pickax" (Cotgrave), from the verb *piquer*. The word *posthumous* has changed its meaning through folk-etymology. It represents the Latin superlative *postumus*, latest born. By association with *humus*, ground, earth, it came to be used of a child born, or a work published, after its author's death, a meaning which the derivatives of *postumus* have in all the Romance languages.

The first part of the word has been distorted in *pursy*, short-winded—

> "And *pursy* insolence shall break his wind
>   With fear and horrid flight."
>
> (*Timon of Athens*, v. 5.)

Fr. *poussif*, from Lat. *pulsus*, throbbing. It was formerly used also in connection with horses—

> "You must warrant this horse clear of the glanders, and *pursyness*." (*The Gentleman's Dictionary*, 1705.)

Arquebus, Fr. *arquebuse*, is a doublet of *hackbut*, Old Fr. *haquebute*, " an *haquebut*, or *arquebuse ;* a caliver" (Cotgrave). The corruption is due to *arcus*, bow. Both *arquebus* and *hackbut* are common in Scott—

> " His arms were halbert, axe, or spear,
> A cross-bow there, a *hackbut* here,
> A dagger-knife, and brand."
>
> (*Marmion*, v. 3.)

The origin is Du. *haakbus*, hook-gun, the second element of which appears in *blunderbuss*. The first part of this word has undergone so many popular transformations that it is difficult to say which was the original form. Ludwig has *Donner-büchs, Blunder-büchs, oder Muszketon*, " a thunder-box ; a *blunder-buss ;* a musketoon ; a wide-mouthed brass-gun, carrying about twenty pistol bullets at once." It was also called in German *Plantier-büchs*, from *plantieren*, to plant, set up, because fired from a rest. Du. *bus*, like Ger. *Büchse*, means both " box " and " gun." In the *bushes*, or axle-boxes, of a cart-wheel, we have the same word. The ultimate origin is Greek πύξος, the box-tree, whence also the learned word *pyx*. Fr. *boîte*, box, is cognate, and Fr. *boussole*, mariners' compass, is from the Italian diminutive *bossola*, " a boxe that mariners keepe their compasse in. Also taken for the compasse" (Florio).

Scissors were formerly *cizars* (*cf.* Fr. *ciseaux*), connected with Lat. *cædere*, to cut. The modern spelling is due to association with Lat. *scissor*, a cutter, tailor, from *scindere*, to cut. *Runagate* is well known to be a corrupt doublet of *renegade*, one who has " denied " his faith. *Recreant*, the present participle of Old Fr. *recreire*, Vulgar Lat. **recredere*, to change one's faith, contains very much the same idea ; cf. *miscreant*, lit. unbeliever. *Jaunty*, spelt *janty* by

Wycherley and *genty* by Burns, is Fr. *gentil*, wrongly
brought into connection with *jaunt*.

In some cases of folk-etymology it is difficult to see
to what idea the corruption is due.[1] The mollusc called
a *periwinkle* was in Anglo-Saxon *pinewincla*, which still
survives in dialect as *pennywinkle*. It appears to have
been influenced by the plant-name *periwinkle*, which is
itself a corruption of Mid. Eng. *pervenke*, from Lat.
pervinca; *cf.* Fr. *pervenche*. The material called
lutestring was formerly *lustring*, Fr. *lustrine*, from its
glossiness. A *wiseacre* is "one that knows or tells
truth; we commonly use it *in malam partem* for a
fool" (Blount, *Glossographia*, 1674). This comes,
through Dutch, from Ger. *Weissager*, commonly understood as *wise-sayer*, but really unconnected with *sagen*,
to say. The Old High Ger. *wīzago*, prophet, is cognate
with Eng. *witty*. The military and naval word *ensign*
is in Shakespeare corrupted, in both its meanings, into
ancient. Thus Falstaff describes his tatterdemalion
recruits as—

"Ten times more dishonourable ragged than an old-faced *ancient*."
(1 *Henry IV.*, iv. 2.)

while *Ancient* Pistol is familiar to every reader. A
cordwainer, from Old Fr. *cordouanier*, "a shoomaker,
a *cordwainer*" (Cotgrave), worked with *cordouan*, "Cor-
dovan leather; which is properly a goat's skin tanned."
The modern French form *cordonnier* is due to association with *cordon*, a thong, bootlace, etc. *Witch-elm*
has nothing to do with witches. It is for older
weech-elm, *wiche-elm*, and belongs to Anglo-Sax. *wīcan*,

---

[1] Perhaps it is the mere instinct to make an unfamiliar word "look like
something." Thus Fr. *beaupré*, from Eng. *bowsprit*, cannot conceivably
have been associated with a fair meadow ; and *accomplice*, for *complice*, La*,
complex, *complic-*, can hardly have been confused with *accomplish*.

to bend. *Service-tree* is a meaningless corruption of Mid. Eng. *serves*, an early loan word from Lat. *sorbus*.

In the case of a double-barrelled word, folk-etymology usually affects one half only, e.g., *verdigris* is for Fr. *vert-de-gris*, for Old Fr. *vert de Grece*, Greek green. The reason for the name is unknown. Cotgrave calls it "Spanish green." Mid. English had the more correct *vertegresse* and *verte Grece* (*Promptorium Parvulorum*, 1440). The cavalry trumpet-call *boot and saddle* is for Fr. *boute-selle*, lit. "put saddle." *Court card* is for *coat card*, a name given to these cards from the dresses depicted on them. Florio has *carta di figura*, "a *cote* carde." The card game called *Pope Joan* would appear to be in some way corrupted from *nain jaune*, lit. "yellow dwarf," its French name.

But occasionally the results of folk-etymology are literally *preposterous*.[1] The Fr. *choucroute* is from *sūrkrūt*, a dialect pronunciation of Ger. *Sauer-kraut*, sour cabbage, so that the first syllable, meaning "sour," has actually been corrupted so as to mean "cabbage." Another example, which I have never seen quoted, is the name of a beech-wood near the little town of Remilly in Lorraine. The trees of this wood are very old and curiously twisted, and they are called in French *les jolis fous*, where *fou* (Lat. *fagus*) is the Old French for "beech" (*fouet*, whip, is its diminutive). This is rendered in German as *tolle Buchen*, mad beeches, the *fou* having been misunderstood as referring to the fantastic appearance of the trees.

Forlorn hope is sometimes used metaphorically as though the *hope* were of the kind that springs eternal in

---

[1] Lat. *præposterus*, from *præ*, before, and *posterus*, behind.

I

the human breast.   In military language it now means
the leaders of a storming party—

"The *forlorn hope* of each attack consisted of a sergeant and
twelve Europeans." (*Wellington's Despatches*, 1799.)

but was earlier used of soldiers in any way exposed
to special danger.   Cotgrave has *enfans perdus*, "perdus ;
or the *forlorne hope* of a campe (are commonly gentlemen of companies)."   It is from obsolete Du. *verloren
hoop*, where *hoop*, cognate with Eng. *heap*, is used for a
band or company.   In 16th-century German we find
ein verlorener Haufe.   Both the Dutch and German
expressions are obsolete in this sense.

The military phrase *to run the gauntlet* has no connection with *gauntlet*, glove.   The older form is *gantlope*—

"Some said he ought to be tied neck and heels ; others that
he deserved to *run the gantlope*." (*Tom Jones*, vii. 1.)

It is a punishment of Swedish origin from the period
of the Thirty Years' War.   The Swedish form is *gat-
lopp*, in which *gat* is cognate with Eng. *gate*, in its
northern sense of "street," and *lopp* with Eng. *leap* and
Ger. *laufen*, to run.

The *press-gang* had originally nothing to do with
"pressing."   When soldiers or seamen were engaged,
they received earnest money called *prest*-money, *i.e.*, an
advance on "loan," Old Fr. *prest* (*prêt*), and the engage-
ment was called *presting* or *impresting*.   Florio explains
soldato (see p. 154), lit. "paid," by "*prest* with paie as
soldiers are."   The popular corruption to *press* took
place naturally as the method of enlistment became
more "pressing."

The *black art* is a translation of Old Fr. *nigromance*,
"nigromancie, conjuring, the *black art*" (Cotgrave); but
this is folk-etymology for *nécromantie*, Greco-Lat. *necro-
mantia*, divination by means of the dead.   The popular

form *négromancie* still survives in French. To *curry favour* is a corruption of Mid. Eng. "to curry *favel*." The expression is translated from French. Palsgrave has *curryfavell*, a flatterer, "estrille faveau," *estriller* (*étriller*) meaning "to curry (a horse)." *Faveau*, earlier *fauvel*, is the name of a horse in the famous *Roman de Fauvel*, a satirical Old French poem of the early 14th century. He symbolises worldly vanity carefully tended by all classes of society. The name is a diminutive of Fr. *fauve*, tawny, cognate with Eng. *fallow* (deer). (See also p. 192, *n.*)

A very curious case of folk-etymology is seen in the old superstition of the *hand of glory*. This is understood to be a skeleton hand from the gallows which will point out hidden treasure—

> "Now mount who list,
> And close by the wrist
> Sever me quickly the Dead Man's fist."
> (INGOLDSBY, *The Hand of Glory*.)

It is simply a translation of Fr. *main de gloire*. But the French expression is a popular corruption of *mandragore*, from Lat. *mandragora*, the mandragore, or mandrake, to the forked roots of which a similar virtue was attributed, especially if the plant were obtained from the foot of the gallows.

Akin to folk-etymology is contamination, *i.e.*, the welding of two words into one. This can often be noticed in children, whose linguistic instincts are those of primitive races. I have heard a child, on her first visit to the Zoo, express great eagerness to see the *canimals* (*camels* × *animals*), which, by the way, turned out to be the giraffes. A small boy who learnt English and German simultaneously evolved, at the age of two, the word *spam* (*sponge* × Ger. *Schwamm*). In a college in the English midlands, a student named *Constantine*, who sat next to a student named *Turpin*, once heard himself startlingly addressed by a lecturer as *Turpentine*. People who inhabit the frontier of two languages, and in fact all who are in any degree bilingual, must inevitably form such composites occasionally. The *h* aspirate of Fr. *haut*, Lat. *altus*, high, can only be explained by the influence of Old High Ger. *hŏh* (*hoch*). The poetic word *glaive* cannot be derived from Lat. *gladius*, sword, which has given Fr. *glai*, an archaic name for the gladiolus. We must invoke the help of a Gaulish word *cladebo*, sword, which is related to Gaelic *clay-more*, big sword. It has been said that in this word the swords of Cæsar and Vercingetorix still cross each other. In Old French we find *oreste*, a storm, combined from *orage* and *tempeste* (*tempête*). Fr. *orteil*, toe, represents the mixture of Lat. *articulus*, a little joint, with Gaulish *ordag*. A *battledore* was in Mid. English a washing beetle, which is in Provençal *batedor*, lit. beater. Hence it seems that this is one of the very few Provençal words which passed directly into English during the period of our occupation of Guienne. It has been contaminated by the cognate *beetle*.

Cannibal is from Span. *canibal*, earlier *caribal*, i.e. *Carib*, the *n* being perhaps due to contamination with Span. *canino*, canine, voracious. It can hardly be doubted that this word suggested Shakespeare's *Caliban*. *Seraglio* is due to confusion between the Turkish word *serai*, a palace, and Ital. *serraglio*, "an inclosure, a close, a padocke, a parke, a cloister or secluse" (Florio), which belongs to Lat. *sera*, a bolt or bar.

Anecdotage is a deliberate coinage ascribed to John Wilkes—

"When a man fell into his *anecdotage*, it was a sign for him to retire from the world." (DISRAELI, *Lothair*, Ch. 28.)

In some cases it is impossible to estimate the

different elements in a word. *Arbour* certainly owes its modern spelling to Lat. *arbor*, a tree, but it represents also Mid. Eng. *herbere*, *erbere*, which comes, through French, from Lat. * *herbarium*. But this can only mean herb-garden, so that the sense development of the word must have been affected by *harbour*, properly "army-shelter," ultimately identical with Fr. *auberge* (p. 164). When Dryden wrote—

> "Tardy of aid, *unseal* thy heavy eyes,
>   Awake, and with the dawning day arise."
>   (*The Cock and the Fox*, 247.)

he was expressing a composite idea made up from the verb *seal*, Old Fr. *seeler* (*sceller*), Lat. *sigillare*, and *seel*, Old Fr. *ciller*, Vulgar Lat. * *ciliare*, from *cilium*, eyebrow. The latter verb, meaning to sew together the eyelids of a young falcon, was once a common word—

> "Come, *seeling* night,
> Scarf up the tender eye of pitiful day."
>   (*Macbeth*, iii. 2.)

The verb *fret* is Anglo-Sax. *fretan*, to eat away (*cf.* Ger. *fressen*). *Fret* is also used of interlaced bars in heraldry, in which sense it corresponds to Fr. *frette* with the same meaning; for this word, which also means ferrule, a Vulgar Lat. * *ferritta* (*ferrum*, iron) has been suggested. When Hamlet speaks of—

> "This majestical roof *fretted* with golden fire,"
>   (*Hamlet*, ii. 3)

is he thinking of *frets* in heraldry, or of *fretwork*, or are these two of one origin? Why should *fret*, in this sense, not come from *fret*, to eat away, since *fretwork* may be described as the "eating away" of part of the material? Cf. *etch*, which comes, through Dutch, from Ger. *ätzen*, the factitive of *essen*, to eat. But the German for *fretwork* is *durchbrochene Arbeit*, "broken-through" work, and Old Fr. *fret* or *frait*, Lat. *fractus*, means "broken." Who shall decide how much our *fretwork* owes to each of these possible etymons?

That form of taxation called excise, which dates from the time of Charles I., has always been unpopular. Andrew Marvell says that *Excise*—

> "With hundred rows of teeth the shark exceeds,
> And on all trades like cassowar she feeds."

Dr Johnson defines it as "a hateful tax levied upon commodities, and adjudged not by the common judges of property, but wretches hired by those to whom excise is paid," an outburst which Lord Mansfield considered "actionable." The name, like the tax, came from the Netherlands, where it was called *accijs*—

> "'Twere cheap living here, were it not for the monstrous *excises* which are impos'd upon all sorts of commodities, both for belly and back." (HOWELL, *Letter from Amsterdam*, 1619.)

In modern Dutch it has become *accijns*, through confusion with *cijns,* tax (Lat. *census*; *cf.* Ger. *Zins*, interest). But the Dutch word is from Fr. *accise*, which appears in medieval Latin as *accisia*, as though connected with "cutting" (cf. *tallage*, from Fr. *tailler*, to cut), or with the "incidence" of the tax. It is perhaps a perversion of Ital. *assisa*, "an imposition, or taxe, or assesment" (Torriano); but there is also an Old Fr. *aceis* which must be related to Latin *census*.

When folk-etymology and contamination work together, the result is sometimes bewildering. Thus *equerry* represents an older *querry* or *quirry*, still usual in the 18th century. Among my books is—

> "The Compleat Horseman, or Perfect Farrier, written in French by the Sieur de Solleysell, *Querry* to the Present King of France" (1702).

The modern spelling is due to popular association with

Lat. *equus.* But this *querry* is identical with French *écurie,* stable, just as in Scottish the *post* often means the *postman.* And *écurie,* older *escurie,* is from Old High Ger. *scura*[1] (*Scheuer,* barn). The word used in modern French in the sense of our *equerry* is *écuyer,* older *escuier,* Lat. *scutarius,* shield-bearer, whence our word *esquire.* This *écuyer* is in French naturally confused with *écurie,* so that Cotgrave defines *escuyrie* as " the stable of a prince, or nobleman; also, a *querry*-ship; or the duties, or offices belonging thereto; also (in old authors) a *squire's* place; or, the dignity, title, estate of an esquire."

Ignorance of the true meaning of a word often leads to pleonasm. Thus *greyhound* means *hound-hound,* the first syllable representing Icel. *grey,* a dog. *Peajacket* is explanatory of Du. *pij,* earlier *pye,* " py-gown, or rough gown, as souldiers and seamen wear " (Hexham). *On Greenhow Hill* means " on green hill hill," and *Buckhurst Holt Wood* means " beech wood wood wood," an explanatory word being added as its predecessor became obsolete. The second part of *salt-cellar* is not the same word as in *wine-cellar.* It comes from Fr. *salière,* "a salt-*seller*" (Cotgrave), so that the *salt* is unnecessary. We speak pleonastically of " *dishevelled* hair," while Old Fr. *deschevelé,* lit. dis-haired, now replaced by *échevelé,* can only be applied to a person, e.g., *une femme toute deschevelée,* " discheveled, with all her haire disorderly falling about her eares " (Cotgrave). The word *cheer* meant in Mid. English " face." Its French original *chère* scarcely survives except in the phrase *faire bonne chère,* lit. " make a good face," a meaning preserved in " to be of good *cheer.*" In both languages the meaning has been

---

[1] This etymology is, however, now regarded as doubtful, and it seems likely that Old Fr. *escurie* is really derived from *escuyer.* If so, there is no question of contamination.

transferred to the more substantial blessings which the pleasant countenance seems to promise, and also to the felicity resulting from good treatment. The true meaning of the word is so lost that we can speak of a "*cheerful* face," *i.e.*, a face full of face.

But there are many words whose changes of form cannot be altogether explained by any of the influences that have been discussed in this and the preceding chapters. Why should *cervelas*, "a large kind of sausage, well season'd, and eaten cold in slices" (Kersey's *Eng. Dict.*, 1720), now be *saveloy?* We might invoke the initial letters of *sausage* to account for part of the change, but the *oy* remains a mystery. *Cervelas*, earlier *cervelat*, comes through French from Ital. *cervellato*, "a kinde of dry sausage" (Florio), said to have been originally made from pig's brains.　For *hatchment* we find in the 16th century *achement*, and even *achievement*.　It is archaic Fr. *hachement*, the ornamental crest of a helmet, etc., probably derived from Old Fr. *achemer*, variant of *acesmer*, to adorn.　Hence both the French and English forms have an unexplained *h-*, the earlier *achement* being nearer the original.　French *omelette* has a bewildering history, but we can trace it almost to its present form.　To begin with, an *omelet*, in spite of proverbs, is not necessarily associated with eggs.　The origin is to be found in Lat. *lamella*, a thin plate,[1] which gave Old Fr. *lamelle*.　Then *la lamelle* was taken as *l'alamelle*, and the new *alamelle* or *alemelle* became, with change of suffix, *alemette*.　By metathesis (see p. 59) this gave

[1] We have a parallel in Fr. *flan*, Eng. *flawn*, Ger. *Fladen*, etc., a kind of omelet, ultimately related to Eng. *flat*—

"The feast was over, the board was clear'd,
　　The *flawns* and the custards had all disappear'd.
　　　　　　　　　(INGOLDSBY, *Jackdaw of Rheims*.)

Cotgrave has *flans*, "flawnes, custards, eggepies ; also, round planchets, or plates of metall."

amelette, still in dialect use, for which modern French has substituted *omelette*.   The *o* then remains unexplained, unless we admit the influence of the old form *œuf-mollet*, a product of folk-etymology.

Counterpane represents Old Fr. *coute-pointe*, now corruptly *courte-pointe*, from Lat. *culcita puncta*, lit. "stitched quilt"; *cf.* Ger. *Steppdecke*, counterpane, from *steppen*, to stitch.   In Old French we also find the corrupt form *contrepointe* which gave Eng. *counterpoint*—

> "In ivory coffers I have stuff'd my crowns;
>   In cypress chests my arras, *counterpoints*,
>   Costly apparel, tents and canopies."
>   (*Taming of the Shrew*, ii. 1).

in modern English replaced by *counterpane*.   Mid. English has also the more correct form *quilt-point*, from the Old Norman *cuilte (pur)pointe*, which occurs in a 12th-century poem on St Thomas of Canterbury.   The hooped petticoat called a *farthingale* was spelt by Shakespeare *fardingale* and by Cotgrave *vardingall.* This is Old Fr. *verdugalle*, of Spanish origin and derived from Span. *verdugo*, a (green) wand, because the circumference was stiffened with flexible switches before the application of whalebone or steel to this purpose. The *crinoline*, as its name implies, was originally strengthened with horse-hair, Lat. *crinis*, hair.   To return to the *farthingale*, the insertion of an *n* before *g* is common in English (see p. 84, *n.* 2), but the change of the initial consonant is baffling.   The modern Fr. *vertugadin* is also a corrupt form.   *Isinglass* seems to be an arbitrary perversion of obsolete Du. *huyzenblas* (*huisblad*), sturgeon bladder; *cf.* the cognate Ger. *Hausenblase*.

Few words have suffered so many distortions as *liquorice*.   The original is Greco-Lat. *glycyrrhiza*, lit. "sweet root," corrupted into late Lat. *liquiritia*, whence Fr. *réglisse*, Ital. *legorizia, regolizia*, and Ger. *Lakritze*. The Mid. English form *licoris* would appear to have been influenced by *orris*, a plant which also has a sweet root, while the modern spelling is perhaps due to *liquor*.

CHAPTER X

DOUBLETS

THE largest class of doublets is formed by those words of Latin origin which have been introduced into the language in two forms, the popular form through Anglo-Saxon or Old French, and the learned through modern French or directly from Latin. Obvious examples are *caitiff*, *captive*; *chieftain*, *captain*; *frail*, *fragile*. Lat. *discus*, a plate, quoit, gave Anglo-Sax. *disc*, whence Eng. *dish*. In Old French it became *deis* (*dais*), Eng. *dais*, and in Ital. *desco*, "a deske, a table, a boord, a counting boord" (Florio), whence our *desk*. We have also the learned *disc* or *disk*, so that the one Latin word has supplied us with four vocables, differentiated in meaning, but each having the fundamental sense of a flat surface.

Dainty, from Old Fr. *deintié*, is a doublet of *dignity*. *Ague* is properly an adjective equivalent to *acute*, as in Fr. *fièvre aigue*. The *paladins* were the twelve peers of Charlemagne's *palace*, and a Count *Palatine* is a later name for something of the same kind. One of the most famous bearers of the title, Prince Rupert, is usually called in contemporary records the *Palsgrave*, from Ger. *Pfalzgraf*, lit. palace count, Ger. *Pfalz* being a very early loan from Lat. *palatium*. *Trivet*, Lat. *tripes*, *triped-*, dates back to Anglo-Saxon, its "rightness" being due to the fact that a three-legged stool stands firm on any surface. In the learned doublets *tripod* and *tripos* we have the Greek form. *Spice*, Old Fr. *espice* (*épice*), is a doublet of *species*. The medieval merchants recognised four "kinds" of spice, viz., saffron, cloves, cinnamon, nutmegs.

Coffin is the learned doublet of *coffer*, Fr. *coffre*, from Lat. *cophinus*. It was originally used of a basket or case of any kind, and even of a pie-crust—

> " Why, thou say'st true ; it is a paltry cap ;
> A custard-*coffin*, a bauble, a silken pie."
>
> (*Taming of the Shrew*, iv. 3.)

Its present meaning is an attempt at avoiding the mention of the inevitable, a natural human weakness which has popularised in America the horrible word *casket* in this sense. The Greeks, fearing death less than do the moderns, called a coffin plainly σαρκοφάγος, flesh-eater, whence indirectly Fr. *cercueil* and Ger. *Sarg*.

The homely *mangle*, which comes to us from Dutch, is a doublet of the warlike engine called a *mangonel*—

> " You may win the wall in spite both of bow and *mangonel*."
>
> (*Ivanhoe*, Ch. 27.)

which is Old French. The source is Greco-Lat. *manganum*, apparatus, whence Ital. *mangano*, with both meanings. The verb *mangle*, to mutilate, is unrelated.

Sullen, earlier *soleyn*, is a popular doublet of *solemn*, in its secondary meaning of glum or morose. In the early Latin-English dictionaries *solemn*, *soleyn*, and *sullen* are used indifferently to explain such words as *acerbus*, *agelastus*, *vultuosus*. Shakespeare speaks of "customary suits of *solemn* black" (*Hamlet*, i. 2), but makes Bolingbroke say—

> " Come, mourn with me for that I do lament,
> And put on *sullen* black incontinent."
>
> (*Richard II.*, v. 6.)

while the "*solemn* curfew" (*Tempest*, v. 1) is described by Milton as "swinging slow with *sullen* roar" (*Penseroso*, l. 76). The meaning of *antic*, a doublet of *antique*, has changed considerably, but the process is easy to follow. From meaning simply ancient it acquired the sense of quaint or odd, and was applied to grotesque[1] work in art or to a fantastic disguise. Then it came to mean buffoon, in which sense Shakespeare applies it to grim death—

> "For within the hollow crown
> That rounds the mortal temples of a king,
> Keeps death his court ; and there the *antic* sits,
> Scoffing his state, and grinning at his pomp."
>
> (*Richard II.*, iii. **2.**)

and lastly the meaning was transferred to the capers of the buffoon. From Old High Ger. *faltan* (*falten*), to fold, and *stuol* (*Stuhl*), chair, we get Fr. *fauteuil*. Medieval Latin constructed the compound *faldestolium*, whence our ecclesiastical *faldstool*, a litany desk. *Revel* is from Old Fr. *reveler*, Lat. *rebellare*, so that it is a doublet of *rebel*. Holyoak's *Latin Dictionary* (1612) has *revells or routs*, "concursus populi illegitimus." Its sense development, from a riotous concourse to a festive gathering, has perhaps been affected by Fr. *réveiller*, to wake, whence *réveillon*, a Christmas Eve supper, or "wake." Cf. Ital. *vegghia*, "a watch, a wake, a *revelling a nights*" (Florio).

The very important word *money* has acquired its meaning by one of those accidents which are so common in word-history. The Roman *mint* was attached to the temple of Juno *Moneta*, *i.e.*, the admonisher, from *monēre*, and this name was transferred to the building. The Romans introduced *moneta*, in the course of their

---

[1] *I.e.*, grotto painting, Ital. *grottesca*, "a kinde of rugged unpolished painters worke, anticke worke" (Florio).

conquests, into French (*monnaie*), German (*Münze*), and
English (*mint*). The French and German words still
have three meanings, viz., mint, coin, change. We have
borrowed the French word and given it the general
sense represented in French by *argent*, lit. silver. The
Ger. *Geld*, money, has no connection with *gold*, but is
cognate with Eng. *yield*, as in "the *yield* of an invest-
ment," of which we preserve the old form in *wergild*,
payment for having killed a man (Anglo-Sax. *wer*). To
return to *moneta*, we have a third form of the word
in *moidore*—

> "And fair rose-nobles and broad *moidores*
>   The waiter pulls out of their pockets by scores."
>   (INGOLDSBY, *The Hand of Glory*.)

from Port. *moeda de ouro*, money of gold.

Sometimes the same word reaches us through
different languages. Thus *charge* is French and *cargo*
is Spanish, both belonging to a Vulgar Lat. **carricare*
from *carrus*, vehicle. In old commercial records we often
find the Anglo-Norman form *cark*, a load, burden, which
survives now only in a metaphorical sense, e.g. *carking*,
i.e. burdensome, care. Lat. *domina* has given us through
French both *dame* and *dam*,[1] and through Spanish
duenna; while Ital. *donna* occurs in the compound
madonna and the *donah* of the East End costermonger.
Lat. *datum*, given, becomes Fr. *dé* and Eng. *die* (plural
dice). Its Italian doublet is *dado*, originally cubical
pedestal, hence part of wall representing continuous
pedestal. *Scrimmage* and *skirmish* are variant spellings
of Fr. *escarmouche*, from Ital. *scaramuccia*, of German
origin (see p. 64, *n.*). But we have also, more immediately
from Italian, the form *scaramouch*. Blount's *Glossographia*

---

[1] See p. 120. The aristocracy of the horse is still testified to by the use
of *sire* and *dam* for his parents.

(1674) mentions *Scaramoche*, "a famous Italian Zani (see p. 45), or mimick, who acted here in England, 1673." *Scaramouch* was one of the stock characters of the old Italian comedy, which still exists as the harlequinade of the Christmas pantomime, and of which some traces survive in the Punch and Judy show. He was represented as a cowardly braggart dressed in black. The golfer's *stance* is a doublet of the poet's *stanza*, both of them belonging to Lat. *stare*, to stand. *Stance* is Old French and *stanza* is Italian, "a *stance* or staffe of verses or songs" (Florio). A *stanza* is then properly a pause or resting place, just as a *verse*, Lat. *versus*, is a "turning" to the beginning of the next line.

Different French dialects have supplied us with many doublets. Old Fr. *chacier* (*chasser*), Vulgar Lat. **captiare*, for *captare*, a frequentative of *capere*, to take, was in Picard *cachier*. This has given Eng. *catch*, which is thus a doublet of *chase*. In *cater* (see p. 63) we have the Picard form of Fr. *acheter*, but the true French form survives in the family name *Chater*.[1] In late Latin the neuter adjective *capitale*, capital, was used of property. This has given, through Old Fr. *chatel*, our *chattel*, while the doublet *catel* has given *cattle*, now limited to what was once the most important form of property. Fr. *cheptel* is still used of cattle farmed out on a kind of profit-sharing system. This restriction of the meaning of *cattle* is paralleled by Scot. *avers*, farm beasts, from Old Fr. *aver*[2] (*avoir*), property, goods. The history of the word *fee*, Anglo-Sax. *feoh*, cattle, cognate with Lat. *pecus*, whence *pecunia*, money, also takes us back to the times when a man's wealth was estimated by his flocks and herds; but, in this case, the sense development is exactly reversed.

[1] Sometimes this name is for *cheater*, *escheatour* (p. 84).
[2] Cf. *avoirdupois*, earlier *avers de pois* (*poids*), goods sold by weight.

Fr. *jumeau*, twin, was earlier *gemeau*, still used by Corneille, and earlier still *gemel*, Lat. *gemellus*, diminutive of *geminus*, twin. From one form we have the *gimbals*, or twin pivots, which keep the compass horizontal. Shakespeare uses it of clockwork—

> " I think, by some odd *gimmals*, or device,
>   Their arms are set like clocks, still to strike on."
>   (1 *Henry VI.*, i. 2.)

and also speaks of a *gimmal* bit (*Henry V.*, iv. 2). In the 17th century we find numerous allusions to *gimmal* rings (variously spelt). The toothsome *jumble*, known to the Midlands as " brandy-snap," is the same word, this delicacy having apparently at one time been made in links. We may compare the obsolete Ital. *stortelli*, lit. " little twists," explained by Torriano as " winding simnels, wreathed *jumbals*."

An accident of spelling may disguise the origin and meaning of a word. *Tret* is Fr. *trait*, in Old French also *tret*, Lat. *tractus*, pull (of the scale). It was usually an allowance of four pounds in a hundred and four, which was supposed to be equal to the sum of the " turns of the scale" which would be in the purchaser's favour if the goods were weighed in small quantities. *Trait* is still so used in modern French.

A difference in spelling, originally accidental, but perpetuated by an apparent difference of meaning, is seen in *flour, flower; metal, mettle.* *Flour* is the *flower*, *i.e.* the finest part, of meal, Fr. *fleur de farine*, "*flower*, or the finest meale*" (Cotgrave). In the *Nottingham Guardian* (29th Aug. 1911) I read that—

> " Mrs Kernahan is among the increasing number of persons who do not discriminate between *metal* and *mettle*, and writes 'Margaret was on her *metal*.'"

It might be added that this author is in the excellent company of Shakespeare—

> "See whe'r their basest *metal* be not mov'd."
> (*Julius Cæsar*, i. 1.)

There is no more etymological difference between *metal* and *mettle* than between the "temper" of a cook and that of a sword-blade.

Parson is a doublet of *person*, the priest perhaps being taken as "representing" the Church, for Lat. *persona*, an actor's mask, from *per*, through, and *sonare*, to sound,[1] was also used of a costumed character or *dramatis persona*. *Mask*, which ultimately belongs to an Arabic word meaning buffoon, has had a sense development exactly opposite to that of *person*, its modern meaning corresponding to the Lat. *persona* from which the latter started. *Parson* shows the popular pronunciation of *er*, now modified by the influence of traditional spelling. We still have it in *Berkeley*, *clerk*, *Derby*, *sergeant*, as we formerly did in *merchant*. Proper names, in which the orthography depends on the "taste and fancy of the speller," or the phonetic theories of the old parish clerk, are often more in accordance with the pronunciation, *e.g.*, *Barclay*, *Clark*, *Darby*, *Sargent*, *Marchant*. *Posy*, in both its senses, is a contraction of *poesy*, the flowers of a nosegay expressing by their arrangement a sentiment like that engraved on a ring. The latter use is perhaps obsolete—

> "A hoop of gold, a paltry ring
> That she did give me ; whose *posy* was
> For all the world like cutler's *poetry*
> Upon a knife : 'Love me and leave me not.'"
> (*Merchant of Venice*, v. 1.)

The poetic word *glamour* is the same as *grammar*,

---

[1] It is possible that this is a case of early folk-etymology and that *persona* is an Etruscan word.

K

which had in the Middle Ages the sense of mysterious learning. From the same source we have the French corruption *grimoire*, "a booke of conjuring" (Cotgrave). *Glamour* and *gramarye* were both revived by Scott—

> "A moment then the volume spread,
>   And one short spell therein he read ;
>   It had much of *glamour* might."
>   (*Lay of the Last Minstrel*, iii. 9.)

> "And how he sought her castle high,
>   That morn, by help of *gramarye*."
>   (*Ibid.*, v. 27.)

For the change of *r* to *l* we have the parallel of *flounce* for older *frounce* (p. 60). *Quire* is the same word as *quair*, in the "King's *Quair*," *i.e.* book. Its Mid. English form is *quayer*, Old Fr. *quaer*, *caer* (*cahier*), Vulgar Lat. **quaternum*, for *quaternio*, "a *quier* with foure sheetes" (Cooper).

Oriental words have sometimes come into the language by very diverse routes. *Sirup*, or *syrup*, *sherbet*, and (*rum*)-*shrub* are of identical origin, ultimately Arabic. *Sirup*, which comes through Spanish and French, was once used, like *treacle* (p. 75), of medicinal compounds—

> "Not poppy, nor mandragora,
>   Nor all the drowsy *syrups* of the world,
>   Shall ever medicine thee to that sweet sleep
>   Which thou ow'dst yesterday."

>   (*Othello*, iii. 3.)

Sherbet and *shrub* are directly borrowed through the medium of travellers—

> "'I smoke on *srub* and water, myself,' said Mr Omer."
>   (*David Copperfield*, Ch. 30.)

Sepoy, used of Indian soldiers in the English service, is the same as *spahi*, the French name for the Algerian cavalry. Both come ultimately from a Persian adjective meaning "military," and the French form was at one time used also in English in speaking of Oriental soldiery—

"The Janizaries and *Spahies* came in a tumultuary manner to the Seraglio." (HOWELL, *Familiar Letters*, 1623.)

Tulip is from Fr. *tulipe*, formerly *tulipan*, " the delicate flower called a *tulipa*, *tulipie*, or Dalmatian cap" (Cotgrave). It is a doublet of *turban*. The German *Tulpe* was also earlier *Tulipan*.

The humblest of medieval coins was the *maravedi*, which came from Spain at an early date, though not early enough for Robin Hood to have said to Isaac of York—

"I will strip thee of every *maravedi* thou hast in the world."
                                              (*Ivanhoe*, Ch. 33.)

The name is due to the Moorish dynasty of the *Al-maravides* or *Marabouts*. This Arabic name, which means hermit, was given also to a kind of stork, the *marabout*, on account of the solitary and sober habits which have earned in India for a somewhat similar bird the name *adjutant* (p. 34).

Cipher and *zero* do not look like doublets, but both of them come from the same Arabic word. The medieval Lat. *zephyrum* connects the two forms. *Crimson* and *carmine*, both of them ultimately from Old Spanish, are not quite doublets, but both belong to *kermes*, the cochineal insect, of Arabic origin.

The relationship between *cipher* and *zero* is perhaps better disguised than that between *furnish* and *veneer*, though this is by no means obvious. *Veneer*, spelt *fineer* by Smollett, is Ger. *fournieren*, borrowed from Fr.

fournir[1] and specialised in meaning. Ebers' *German Dict.* (1796) has *furnieren*, "to inlay with several sorts of wood, to *veneer*."

The doublets selected for discussion among the hundreds which exist in the language reveal many etymological relationships which would hardly be suspected at first sight. Many other words might be quoted which are almost doublets. Thus *sergeant*, Fr. *sergent*, Lat. *serviens, servient-*, is almost a doublet of *servant*, the present participle of Fr. *servir*. The fabric called *drill* or *drilling* is from Ger. *Drillich*, "tick, linnen-cloth woven of *three* threads" (Ludwig). This is an adaptation of Lat. *trilix, trilic-*, which, through Fr. *treillis*, has given Eng. *trellis*. We may compare the older *twill*, of Anglo - Saxon origin, cognate with Ger. *Zwilch* or *Zwillich*, "linnen woven with a *double* thread" (Ludwig). *Robe*, from French, is cognate with *rob*, and with Ger. *Raub*, booty, the conqueror decking himself in the spoils of the conquered. *Musk* is a doublet of *meg* in *nutmeg*, Fr. *noix muscade*. In Mid. English we find *note-mugge*, and Cotgrave has the diminutive *muguette*, "a nutmeg"; *cf.* modern Fr. *muguet*, the lily of the valley. Fr. *dîner* and *déjeuner* both represent Vulgar Lat. **dis-junare*, to break fast, from *jejunus*, fasting. The difference of form is due to the shifting of the accent in the Latin conjugation, e.g., *dis-junáre* gives Old Fr. *disner* (*dîner*), while *dis-júnat* gives Old Fr. *desjune* (*déjeune*).

Admiral, earlier *amiral*, comes through French from the Arab. *amir*, an emir. Its Old French forms are numerous, and the one which has survived in English may be taken as an abbreviation of Arab. *amir al bahr*, emir on the sea. Greco-Lat. *pandura*, a stringed instru-

---

[1] This is the accepted etymology; but it is more probable that *furnieren* comes from Fr. *vernir*, to varnish.

ment, has produced an extraordinary number of corruptions, among which some philologists rank *mandoline*.
Eng. *bandore*, now obsolete, was once a fairly common
word, and from it, or from some cognate Romance form,
comes the negro corruption *banjo*—

"'What is this, mamma? it is not a guitar, is it?' 'No, my
dear, it is called a *banjore*; it is an African instrument, of which
the negroes are particularly fond.'" (MISS EDGEWORTH, *Belinda*,
Ch. 18.)

Florio has *pandora*, *pandura*, "a musical instrument
with three strings, a kit, a croude,[1] a rebecke." *Kit*,
used by Dickens—

"He had a little fiddle, which at school we used to call a *kit*,
under his left arm." (*Bleak House*, Ch. 14.)

seems to be a clipped form from Old French dialect
quiterne, for *guiterne*, Greco-Lat. *cithara*. Cotgrave
explains *mandore* as a "*kitt*, small gitterne." The
doublet *guitar* is from Spanish.

The two pretty words *dimity* and *samite*—

> "An arm
> Rose up from out the bosom of the lake,
> Clothed in white *samite*, mystic, wonderful,
> Holding the sword."
>
> (TENNYSON, *Morte d'Arthur*, l. 29.)

are both connected with Gk. μίτος, thread. *Dimity* is
the plural, *dimiti*, of Ital. *dimito*, "a kind of course cotton
or flanell" (Florio), from Greco-Lat. *dimitus*, double
thread (cf. *twill*, p. 148). *Samite*, Old Fr. *samit*, whence
Ger. *Samt*, velvet, is in medieval Latin *hexamitus*,
six-thread; this is Byzantine Gk. ἑξάμιτον, whence also
Old Slavonic *aksamitu*. The Italian form is *sciamito*,
"a kind of sleave, feret, or filosello silke" (Florio). The
word *feret* used here by Florio is from Ital. *fioretto*, little

---

[1] See *Crowther*, p. 176.

K 2

flower. It was also called *floret* silk. Florio explains the plural *fioretti* as "a kind of course silke called *f[l]oret* or *ferret* silke," and Cotgrave has *fleuret*, "course silke, *floret* silke." This doublet of *floweret* is not obsolete in the sense of tape—

> "'Twas so fram'd and express'd no tribunal could shake it,
> And firm as red wax and black *ferret* could make it."
> (INGOLDSBY, *The Housewarming*.)

Parish and *diocese* are closely related, *parish*, Fr. *paroisse*, representing Greco-Lat. *par-oikia* (οἶκος, a house), and *diocese* coming through Old French from Greco-Lat. *di-oikesis*. *Skirt* is the Scandinavian doublet of *shirt*, from Vulgar Lat. *ex-curtus*, which has also given us *short*. The form without the prefix appears in Fr. *court*, Ger. *kurz*, and the English diminutive *kirtle*—

> "What stuff wilt have a *kirtle* of?"
> (2 *Henry IV.*, ii. 4.)

These are all very early loan words.

A new drawing-room game for amateur philologists would be to trace relationships between words which have no apparent connection. In discussing, a few years ago, a lurid book on the "Mysteries of Modern London," *Punch* remarked that the existence of a *villa* seemed to be proof presumptive of that of a *villain*. This is etymologically true. An Old French *vilain*, "a villaine, slave, bondman, servile tenant" (Cotgrave), was a peasant attached to his lord's *ville* or domain, Lat. *villa*. For the degeneration in meaning we may compare Eng. *boor* and *churl* (p. 84), and Fr. *manant*, a clodhopper, lit. a dweller (see *manor*, p. 9). A *butcher*, Fr. *boucher*, must originally have dealt in goat's flesh, Fr. *bouc*, goat; *cf.* Ital. *beccaio*, butcher, and *becco*, goat. Hence *butcher* and *buck* are related. The extension of meaning of *broker*, an Anglo-Norman form of *brocheur*,

shows the importance of the wine trade in the Middle
Ages.   A *broker* was at first[1] one who " broached " casks
with a *broche*, which means in modern French both brooch
and spit.   The essential part of a *brooch* is the pin or spike.

When   Kent   says   that   Cornwall   and   Regan—

> " Summon'd up their *meiny*, straight took horse."
>   (*Lear*, ii. 4.)

he is using a common Mid. English and Tudor
word which comes, through Old Fr. *maisniee*, from
Vulgar Lat. **mansionata*, a houseful. A *menial* is a
member of such a body.   An Italian cognate is
masnadiere, " a ruffler, a swashbuckler, a swaggerer,
a high way theefe, a hackster " (Florio).   Those inclined
to moralise may see in these words a proof that the
arrogance of the great man's flunkey was curbed in
England earlier than in Italy.   Old Fr. *maisniee* is now
replaced by *ménage*, Vulgar Lat. **mansionaticum*.   A
derivative of this word is *ménagerie*, first applied to the
collection of household animals, but now to a " wild
beast show."

A *bonfire* was formerly a *bone-fire*.   We find *bane-
fire*, " ignis ossium," in a Latin dictionary of 1483, and
Cooper explains *pyra* by " *bone-fire*, wherein men's
bodyes were burned."   Apparently the word is due to
the practice of burning the dead after a victory.
Hexham has *bone-fire*, " een *been-vier*, dat is, als men
victorie brandt."   *Walnut* is related to *Wal*es, Corn*wall*,
the *Wall*oons, *Wall*achia and Sir William *Wall*ace.   It
means " foreign " nut.   This very wide spread *wal* is
supposed to represent the Celtic tribal name *Volcæ*.   It
was applied by the English to the Celts, and by the
Germans to the French and Italians, especially the

---

[1] But the early use of the word in the sense of middle-man points to
contamination with some other word of different meaning.

latter, whence the earlier Ger. *welsche Nuss*, for *Walnuss*. The German Swiss use it of the French Swiss, hence the canton *Wallis* or *Valais*. The Old French name for the *walnut* is *noix gauge*, Lat. *Gallica*. The relation of *umbrella* to *umber* is pretty obvious. The former is Italian—

> "A little shadow, a little round thing that women bare in their hands to shadow them. Also a broad brimd hat to keepe off heate and rayne. Also a kinde of round thing like a round skreene that gentlemen use in Italie in time of sommer or when it is very hote, to keepe the sunne from them when they are riding by the way." (Florio.)

Umber is Fr. *terre d'ombre*, shadow earth—

> "I'll put myself in poor and mean attire,
>   And with a kind of *umber* smirch my face."
>   (*As You Like It*, i. 3.)

Ballad, originally a dancing song, Prov. *ballada*, is a doublet of *ballet*, and thus related to *ball*. We find a late Lat. *ballare*, to dance, in Saint Augustine, but the history of this group of words is obscure. The sense development of *carol* is very like that of ballad. It is from Old Fr. *carolle*, "a kinde of dance wherein many may dance together; also, a *carroll*, or Christmas song" (Cotgrave). The form *corolla* is found in Provençal, and *carolle* in Old French is commonly used, like Ger. *Kranz*, garland, and Lat. *corona*, of a social or festive ring of people. Hence it seems a reasonable conjecture that the origin of the word is Lat. *corolla*, a little garland.

Many "chapel" people would be shocked to know that *chapel* means properly the sanctuary in which a saint's relics are deposited. The name was first applied to the chapel in which was preserved the *cape* or cloak of St Martin of Tours. The doublet *capel* survives in *Capel Court*, near the Exchange. Ger. *Kapelle* also means orchestra or military band. *Tocsin* is literally "touch sign." Fr. *toquer*, to tap, beat, cognate with *touch*, survives in "*tuck* of drum" and *tucket*—

> "Then let the trumpets sound
> The *tucket* sonance and the note to mount."
> (*Henry V.*, iv. 2.)

while *sinet*, the diminutive of Old Fr. *sin*, sign, has given *sennet*, common in the stage directions of Elizabethan plays in a sense very similar to that of *tucket*.

Junket is from Old Fr. *joncade*, "a certaine spoone-meat, made of creame, rose-water, and sugar" (Cotgrave), Ital. *giuncata*, "a kinde of fresh cheese and creame, so called bicause it is brought to market upon rushes; also a *junket*" (Florio). It is thus related to *jonquil*, which comes, through French, from Span. *junquillo*, a diminutive from Lat. *juncus*, rush. The plant is named from its rush-like leaves. *Ditto*, Italian, lit. "said," and *ditty*, Old Fr. *dité*, are both past participles,[1] from the Latin verbs *dico* and *dicto* respectively. The *nave* of a church is from Fr. *nef*, still occasionally used in poetry in its original sense of ship, Lat. *navis*. It is thus related to *navy*, Old Fr. *navie*, a derivative of *navis*. Similarly Ger. *Schiff* is used in the sense of nave, though the metaphor is variously explained.

The old word *cole*, cabbage, its north country and Scottish equivalent *kail*, Fr. *chou* (Old Fr. *chol*), and Ger. *Kohl*, are all from Lat. *caulis*, cabbage; cf. *cauli-*flower. We have the Dutch form in *colza*, which comes, through French, from Du. *kool-zaad*, cabbage seed. *Cabbage* itself is Fr. *caboche*, a Picard derivative of Lat. *caput*, head. In modern French *caboche* corresponds to our vulgar "chump." A *goshawk* is a *goose hawk*, so called from its preying on poultry. *Merino* is related to *mayor*, which comes, through French, from Lat. *maior*,

[1] But the usual Italian past participle of *dire* is *detto*.

greater. Span. *merino*, Vulgar Lat. * *majorinus*, means both a magistrate and a superintendent of sheep-walks. From the latter meaning comes that of " sheepe driven from the winter pastures to the sommer pastures, or the wooll of those sheepe" (Percyvall). *Portcullis* is from Old Fr. *porte coulisse*, sliding door. Fr. *coulisse* is still used of many sliding contrivances, especially in connection with stage scenery, but in the portcullis sense it is replaced by *herse* (see p. 75), except in the language of heraldry. The masculine form *coulis* means a clear broth, or *cullis*, as it was called in English up to the 18th century. This suggests *colander*, which, like *portcullis*, belongs to Lat. *colare*, "to streine" (Cooper), whence Fr. *couler*, to flow.

Solder, formerly spelt *sowder* or *sodder*, and still so pronounced by the plumber, represents Fr. *soudure*, from the verb *souder ;* cf. *batter* from Old Fr. *batture*, *fritter* from Fr. *friture*, and *tenter* (hooks)[1] from Fr. *tenture*. Fr. *souder* is from Lat. *solidare*, to consolidate. Fr. *sou*, formerly *sol,* a halfpenny, comes, like Ital. *soldo*, from Lat. *solidus*, the meaning of which appears also in the Italian participle *soldato*, a soldier, lit. a paid man. This Italian word has passed into French and German, displacing the older cognates *soudard* and *Söldner*, which now have a depreciatory sense. Eng. *soldier* is of Old French origin. It is represented in medieval Latin by *sol[i]darius*, glossed *sowdeor* in a vocabulary of the 15th century. As in *solder*, the *l* has been re-introduced by learned influence, but the vulgar *sodger* is nearer the original pronunciation.

[1] Hooks used for stretching cloth.

CHAPTER XI

HOMONYMS

MODERN English contains some six or seven hundred pairs or sets of homonyms, *i.e.*, of words identical in sound and spelling but differing in meaning and origin. The *New English Dictionary* recognises provisionally nine separate nouns *rack*. The subject is a difficult one to deal with, because one word sometimes develops such apparently different meanings that the original identity becomes obscured, and even, as we have seen in the case of *flour* and *mettle* (p. 144), a difference of spelling may result. When Denys of Burgundy said to the physician—

"Go to! He was no fool who first called you *leeches*."
(*Cloister and Hearth*, Ch. 26.)

he was unaware that both *leeches* represent Anglo-Sax. *læce*, healer. On the other hand, a resemblance of form may bring about a contamination of meaning. The verb to *gloss*, or *gloze*, means simply to explain or translate, from Greco-Lat. *glossa*, tongue; but, under the influence of the unrelated *gloss*, superficial lustre, it has acquired the sense of specious interpretation. That part of a helmet called the *beaver*—

"I saw young Harry, with his *beaver* on,
His cuisses on his thigh, gallantly arm'd,
Rise from the ground like feather'd Mercury."
(1 *Henry IV.*, iv. 1.)

has, of course, no connection with the animal whose
fur has been used for some centuries for expensive
hats. It comes from Old Fr. *bavière*, a child's bib, now
replaced by *bavette*, from *baver*, to slobber.

It may be noted *en passant* that many of the
revived medieval words which sound so picturesque
in Scott are of very prosaic origin. Thus the *basnet*—

> "My *basnet* to a prentice cap,
> Lord Surrey's o'er the Till."
>
> (*Marmion*, vi. 21.)

or close-fitting steel cap worn under the ornamental
helmet, is Fr. *bassinet*, a little basin. It was also called
a *kettle hat*, or *pot*. Another obsolete name given to
a steel cap was a privy *pallet*, from Fr. *palette*, a barber's
bowl, a "helmet of Mambrino." To a brilliant living
monarch we owe the phrase "mailed fist," a translation
of Ger. *gepanzerte Faust*. *Panzer*, a cuirass, is etymologically a *pauncher*, or defence for the paunch. We
may compare an article of female apparel, which took
its name from a more polite name for this part of
the anatomy, and which Shakespeare uses even in the
sense of *Panzer*. Imogen, taking the papers from her
bosom, says—

> "What is here?
> The scriptures of the loyal Leonatus,
> All turn'd to heresy? Away, away,
> Corrupters of my faith! You shall no more
> Be *stomachers* to my heart."
>
> (*Cymbeline*, iii. 4.)

Sometimes homonyms seem to be due to the lowest
type of folk-etymology, the instinct for making an
unfamiliar word "look like something" (see p. 128, *n.*).
To this instinct we owe the nautical *companion* (p. 165).
Trepan, for *trapan*, to entrap, cannot have been confused with the surgical *trepan* (p. 109), although it has

been assimilated to it. The *compound* in which the victims of " Chinese slavery " languished is the Malay *kampong*, an enclosure.

The scent called *bergamot* takes its name from *Bergamo*, in Italy, whence also Shakespeare's *bergomask* dance—

> " Will it please you to see the epilogue, or hear a *Bergomask* dance between two of our company ? "
>
> (*Midsummer Night's Dream*, v. 1.)

but the *bergamot* pear is derived from Turkish *beg armudi*, prince's pear. With *beg*, prince, cf. *bey* and *begum*. The *burden* of a song is from Fr. *bourdon*, " a drone, or dorre-bee ; also, the humming, or buzzing, of bees ; also, the drone of a bag-pipe " (Cotgrave). It is of doubtful origin, but is not related to *burden*, a load, which is connected with the verb to *bear*.

To *cashier*, *i.e.*, break, a soldier, is from Du. *casseeren*, which is borrowed from Fr. *casser*, to break, Lat. *quassare*, frequentative of *quatere*, to shatter. In the 16th and 17th centuries we also find *cass* and *cash*, which come immediately from French, and are thus doublets of *quash*. Cotgrave has *casser*, " to *casse*, *cassere*, discharge." The past participle of the obsolete verb to *cass* is still in military use—

> " But the colonel said he must go, and he (the drum horse) was *cast* in due form and replaced by a washy, bay beast, as ugly as a mule." (KIPLING, *The Rout of the White Hussars*.)

The other *cashier* is of Italian origin. He takes charge of the *cash*, which formerly meant " counting-house," and earlier still " safe," from Ital. *cassa*, " a merchant's *cashe*, or counter" (Florio). This comes from Lat. *capsa*, a coffer, so that *cash* is a doublet of *case*, Fr. *caisse*. The goldsmith's term *chase* is for *enchase*, Fr. *enchâsser*, " to *enchace*, or set, in gold, etc. " (Cotgrave), from *châsse*, coffer, shrine, also from Lat. *capsa*. From the same word comes (window) *sash*.

Gammon, from Mid. Eng. *gamen*, now reduced to *game*, survives as a slang word and also in the compound *backgammon*. In a *gammon* of bacon we have the Picard form of Fr. *jambon*, a ham, an augmentative of *jambe*, leg. Cotgrave has *jambon*, "a *gammon*." *Gambit* is related, from Ital. *gambetto*, "a tripping up of one's heels" (Torriano). A *game* leg is in dialect a *gammy* leg. This is Old Fr. *gambi*, "bent, crooked, bowed" (Cotgrave), which is still used in some French dialects in the sense of lame. It comes from the same Celtic root as *jambe*.

Host, an army, now used only poetically or metaphorically, is from Old Fr. *ost*, army, Lat. *hostis*, enemy. The *host* who receives us is Old Fr. *oste* (*hôte*), Lat. *hospes, hospit-*, guest. These two *hosts* are, however, ultimately related. It is curious that, while modern Fr. *hôte* (*hospes*) means both "host" and "guest," the other *host* (*hostis*) is, very far back, a doublet of *guest*, the ground meaning of both being "stranger." "It is remarkable in what opposite directions the Germans and Romans have developed the meaning of the old hereditary name for 'stranger.' To the Roman the stranger becomes an enemy; among the Germans he enjoys the greatest privileges, a striking confirmation of what Tacitus tells us in his *Germania*."[1] In a dog *kennel* we have the Norman form of Fr. *chenil*, related to *chien;* but *kennel*, a gutter—

> "Go, hop me over every *kennel* home."
>
> (*Taming of the Shrew*, iv, 3.)

is a doublet of *channel* and *canal*.

> "Oh villain ! thou stolest a cup of sack eighteen years ago, and wert taken with the *manner*." (1 *Henry IV*., ii. 4.)

[1] Kluge, *Etymologisches Wörterbuch.*

says Prince Hal to Bardolph.   In the old editions this
is spelt *manour* or *mainour* and means "in the act."
It is an Anglo-French doublet of *manœuvre*, late
Lat. *manu-opera*, handiwork, and is thus related to
its homonym *manner*, Fr. *manière*, from *manier*, to
handle.   Another doublet of *manœuvre* is *manure*, now
a euphemism for dung, but formerly used of the act of
tillage—

 "The *manuring* hand of the tiller shall root up all that burdens
the soil."   (MILTON, *Reason of Church Government.*)

Inure is similarly formed from Old Fr. *enœuvrer*, literally "to work in," hence to accustom to toil.

John Gilpin's "good friend the *calender*," *i.e.* the
cloth-presser, has nothing to do with the *calendar* which
indicates the *calends* of the month, nor with the *calender*,
or Persian monk, of the *Arabian Nights*, whom Mr
Pecksniff described as a "one-eyed *almanack*"—

 "'A one-eyed *calender*, I think, sir,' faltered Tom.
 "'They are pretty nearly the same thing, I believe,' said Mr
Pecksniff, smiling compassionately ; 'or they used to be in my
time.'"   (*Martin Chuzzlewit*, Ch. 6.)

The verb to *calender*, to press and gloss cloth, etc., is
from Old Fr. *calendrer* (*calandrer*), "to sleeke, smooth,
plane, or polish, linnen cloth, etc." (Cotgrave).   This
word is generally considered to be related to *cylinder*,
a conjecture which is supported by obsolete Fr. *calende*,
used of the "rollers" by means of which heavy stones
are moved.

A craft, or association of *masters*, was once called
a *mistery* (for *mastery* or *maistrie*), usually misspelt
mystery by association with a word of quite different
origin and meaning.   This accidental resemblance is
often played on—

 "Painting, sir, I have heard say, is a *mystery* ; but what

mystery there should be in hanging, if I should be hanged, **I cannot**
imagine." (*Measure for Measure*, iv. 2.)

For the pronunciation, cf. *mister*, for *master*, and
mistress.[1] The French for "mistery" is *métier*, earlier
mestier, "a trade, occupation, *misterie*, handicraft"
(Cotgrave), from Old Fr. *maistier*, Lat. *magisterium*.
In its other senses Fr. *métier* represents Lat. *ministerium*,
service.

Pawn, a pledge, is from Old Fr. *pan*, with the same
meaning. The origin of this word, cognates of which
occur in the Germanic languages, is unknown. The
pawn at chess is Fr. *pion*, a pawn, formerly also a foot-
soldier, used contemptuously in modern French for a
junior assistant master. This represents a Vulgar Lat.
**pedo, pedon-*, from *pes*, foot; *cf.* Span. *peon*, "a footeman,
a *pawne* at chesse, a pioner, or laborer" (Percyvall).
In German the *pawn* is called *Bauer*, peasant, a name
also given to the knave in the game of euchre, whence
American *bower*[2]—

> "At last he put down a *right bower*[3]
> Which the same Nye had dealt unto me."
> <div align="right">(BRET HARTE, <i>The Heathen Chinee.</i>)</div>

When Jack Bunce says—

"If they hurt but one hair of Cleveland's head, there will be
the devil to *pay*, and no pitch hot." (*Pirate*, Ch. 36.)

he is using a nautical term which has no connection with
Fr. *payer*. To *pay*, *i.e.* to pitch (a ship), is from Old Fr.
peier or *poier*, Lat. *picare*, from *pix*, pitch. Fr. *limon*, a
lime, has given Eng. *lemon*,[4] but "*lemon* sole" is from
Fr. *limande*, a flat-fish, dab. A *quarry* from which stone

---

[1] Now abbreviated to *miss* in a special sense.
[2] The *Bowery* of New York was formerly a homestead.
[3] Knave of trumps.
[4] In modern French the lemon is called *citron* and the citron *cédrat*.

is obtained was formerly *quarrer*, Old Fr. *quarrière* (*carrière*), a derivative of Lat. *quadrus ;* cf. *quadratarius*, "a squarer of marble" (Cooper). The *quarry* of the hunter has changed its form and meaning. In Mid. English we find *quarré* and *quirré*, from Old Fr. *cuirée*, now *curée*, "a (dog's) reward; the hounds' fees of, or part in, the game they have killed" (Cotgrave). The Old French form means "skinful" (cf. *poignée*, fistful), the hounds' reward being spread on the skin of the slain animal. It is thus related to *cuirass*, originally used of leathern armour. In Shakespeare *quarry* usually means a heap of dead game—

> "Would the nobility lay aside their ruth,
>   And let me use my sword, I'd make a *quarry*
>   With thousands of these quarter'd slaves, as high
>   As I could pick my lance."
>
> (Coriolanus, i. 1.)

In modern English it is applied rather to the animal pursued. Related to the first *quarry* is *quarrel*, the square-headed bolt shot from a crossbow—

> "It is reported by William Brito that the arcubalista or arbalist was first shewed to the French by our king Richard the First, who was shortly after slain by a *quarrel* thereof."
>
> (CAMDEN, Remains concerning Britain.[1])

It comes from Old Fr. *carrel*, of which the modern form, *carreau*, is used of many four-sided objects, *e.g.*, a square tile, the diamond at cards, a pane of glass. In the last sense both *quarrel* and *quarry* are still used by glaziers.

---

[1] In the chapter on "*Artillery.*" So also, in the *Authorised Version*— "Jonathan gave his *artillery* (his bow and arrows) unto his lad, and said unto him, 'Go, carry them into the city.'" (1 Samuel, xx. 40.) It is curious that the words *artillery* and *gun* both belong to the pre-gunpowder period.

In a "*school* of porpoises" we have a Dutch word for crowd.   The older spelling is *scull*—

> "And there they fly, or die, like scaled *sculls*,
>   Before the belching whale."
> > (*Troilus and Cressida*, v. 5.)

A *sorrel* horse and the plant called *sorrel* are both French words of German origin.   The adjective, used in venery of a buck of the third year, is a diminutive of Old Fr. *sor*, which survives in *hareng saur*, red herring, and is perhaps cognate with Eng. *sear*—

> "The *sere*, the yellow leaf."
> > (*Macbeth*, v. 3.)

The plant name is related to *sour*.   Its modern French form *surelle* occurs now only in dialect, having been superseded by *oseille*, which appears to be due to the mixture of two words meaning sour, sharp, viz., Vulgar Lat. **acetula* and Greco-Lat. *oxalis*.

The verb *tattoo*, to adorn the skin with patterns, is Polynesian.   The military *tattoo* is Dutch.   It was earlier *tap-to*, and was the signal for closing the "taps," or taverns.   The first recorded occurrence of the word is in Colonel Hutchinson's orders to the garrison of Nottingham, the original of which hangs in the Nottingham City Library—

> "If any-one shall bee found tiplinge or drinkinge in any taverne, inne, or alehouse after the houre of nyne of the clock at night, when the *tap-too* beates, he shall pay 2s. 6d."   (1644.)

Cf. Ger. *Zapfenstreich*, lit. tap-stroke, the name of a play which was produced some years ago in London under the title "Lights Out."   Ludwig explains *Zapfenschlag* or *Zapfenstreich* as "die Zeit da die Soldaten aus den Schencken heimgehen müssen, the *taptow*."

Tassel, in " *tassel* gentle "—

> " O, for a falconer's voice,
> To lure this *tassel*-gentle back again."
>
> *(Romeo and Juliet*, ii. 2.)

is for *tercel* or *tiercel*, the male hawk, " so tearmed, because he is, commonly, a third part less than the female" (Cotgrave, s.v. *tiercelet*). The true reason for the name is doubtful. The pendent ornament called a *tassel* is a diminutive of Mid. Eng. *tasse*, a heap, bunch, Fr. *tas*. *Tent* wine is Span. *vino tinto, i.e.*, coloured—

> "Of this last there's little comes over right, therefore the vintners make *Tent* (which is a name for all wines in Spain, except white) to supply the place of it " (Howell, *Familiar Letters*, 1634).

The other *tent* is from the Old French past participle of *tendre*, to stretch.

The Shakesperian *utterance*—

> " Rather than so, come, fate, into the list,
> And champion me to the *utterance*."
>
> *(Macbeth*, iii. 1.)

is the Fr. *outrance*, in *combat à outrance, i.e.*, to the extreme, which belongs to Lat. *ultra*. It is quite unconnected with the verb to *utter*, from *out*.

We have seen how, in the case of some homonyms, confusion arises, and a popular connection is established, between words which are quite unrelated. The same sort of association often springs up between words which, without being homonyms, have some accidental resemblance in form or meaning, or in both. Such association may bring about curious changes in sound and sense. *Touchy*, which now conveys the idea of sensitiveness to *touch*, is corrupted from *tetchy*—

> " *Tetchy* and wayward was thy infancy." (*Richard III.*, iv. 4.)

The original meaning was something like "infected, tainted," from Old Fr. *teche* (*tache*), a spot. The word *surround* has completely changed its meaning through association with *round*. It comes from Old Fr. *suronder*, to overflow, Lat. *super-undare*, and its meaning and origin were quite clear to the 16th-century lexicographers. Thus Cooper has *inundo*, "to overflowe, to *surround*." A French bishop carries a *crosse*, and an archbishop a *croix*. These words are of separate origin. From *crosse*, which does not mean "cross," comes our derivative *crosier*, carried by both bishops and archbishops. It is etymologically identical, as its shape suggests, with the shepherd's *crook*, and the bat used in playing *lacrosse*.

The prophecy of the pessimistic *ostler* that, owing to motor-cars—

> "'*Osses* soon will all be in the circusses,
> And if you want an *ostler*, try the work'uses."
>
> (E. V. Lucas.)

shows by what association the meaning of *ostler*, Old Fr. *hostelier* (*hôtelier*), has changed. A *belfry* has nothing to do with *bells*. Old Fr. *berfroi* (*beffroi*) was a tower used in warfare. It comes from two German words represented by modern *bergen*, to hide, guard, and *Friede*, peace, so that it means "guard-peace." The triumph of the form *belfry* is due to association with *bell*, but the *l* is originally due to dissimilation, since we find *belfroi* also in Old French. The same dissimilation is seen in Fr. *auberge*, inn, Prov. *alberga*, which comes from Old High Ger. *hari*, an army, and *bergen*; *cf.* our *harbour* (p. 2) and *harbinger* (p. 90). *Scabbard* is from Old Fr. *escauberc*, earlier *escalberc*, by dissimilation for *escarberc*, from Old High Ger. *scār*, a blade (*cf.* plough*share*), and *bergen*. Cf. *hauberk*, guard-neck, from Ger. *Hals*,[1] neck.

---

[1] Hence, or rather from Du. *hals*, the *hawse*-holes, the "throat" through which the cable runs.

The *buttery* is not so named from *butter*, but from *bottles*. It is for *butlery*, as *chancery* (see p. 88) is for *chancelry*. It is not, of course, now limited to bottles, any more than the *pantry* to bread or the *larder* to bacon, Fr. *lard*, Lat. *laridum*. The *spence*, aphetic for *dispense*, is now known only in dialect—

> " I am gaun to eat my dinner quietly in the *spence*."
> (*Old Mortality*, Ch. 3.)

but has given us the name *Spencer*. The *still-room* maid is not extinct, but I doubt whether the *distilling* of strong waters is now carried on in the region over which she presides. A *journeyman* has nothing to do with *journeys* in the modern sense of the word, but works *à la journée*, by the day. *Cf.* Fr. *journalier*, " a *journey man ;* one that workes by the day " (Cotgrave), and Ger. *Tagelöhner*, literally " day-wager." On the other hand, a *day-woman* (*Love's Labour's Lost*, i. 2) is an explanatory pleonasm (cf. *greyhound*, p. 135) for the old word *day*, servant, milkmaid, etc., whence the common surname *Day* and the derivative *dairy*.

A *briar* pipe is made, not from *briar*, but from the root of heather, Fr. *bruyère*, of Celtic origin. A *catchpole* did not catch *polls*, *i.e.* heads, nor did he catch people with a *pole*, although a very ingenious implement, exhibited in the Tower of London Armoury, is catalogued as a *catchpole*. The word corresponds to a French compound *chasse-poule*, catch-hen, in Picard *cache-pole*, the official's chief duty being to collect dues, or, in default, poultry. For *pole*, from Fr. *poule*, cf. *polecat*, also an enemy of fowls. The *companion*-ladder on shipboard is a product of folk-etymology. It leads to the *kampanje*, the Dutch for *cabin*. This may belong, like *cabin*, to a late Lat. *capanna*, hut, which has a very numerous progeny. *Kajuit*, another Dutch word for cabin, earlier *kajute*, has given us *cuddy*.

A *carousal* is now regarded as a *carouse*, but the two are quite separate, or, rather, there are two distinct words *carousal*. One of them is from Fr. *carrousel*, a word of Italian origin, meaning a pageant or carnival with chariot races and tilting. This word, obsolete in this sense, is sometimes spelt *el* and accented on the last syllable—

> "Before the crystal palace, where he dwells,
>   The armed angels hold their *carousels*."
>   (ANDREW MARVELL, *Lachrymæ Musarum*.)

Ger. *Karussell* means a roundabout at a fair. Our *carousal*, if it is the same word, has been affected in sound and meaning by *carouse*. This comes, probably through French, from Ger. *garaus*, quite out, in the phrase *garaus trinken*, *i.e.*, to drink bumpers—

> "The queen *carouses* to thy fortune, Hamlet."
>   (*Hamlet*, v. 2.)

Rabelais says that he is not one of those—

> "Qui, par force, par oultraige et violence, contraignent les compaignons trinquer voyre *carous* et *alluz* [1] qui pis est."
>   (*Pantagruel*, iii., Prologue.)

The spelling *garous*, and even *garaus*, is found in 17th-century English.

It is perhaps unnecessary to say that a *maul-stick*, Dutch *maal-stok*, paint-stick, has nothing to do with the verb to *maul*, formerly to *mall*,[2] *i.e.*, to hammer. Nor is the painter's *lay-figure* connected with our verb to *lay*. It is also, like so many art terms, of Dutch origin, the *lay* representing Du. *lid*, limb, cognate with Ger. *Glied*.[3] The German for lay-figure is *Gliederpuppe*,

[1] Ger. *all aus*, all out.
[2] Hence the *Mall* and *Pall-Mall*, where games like croquet were played.
[3] The *g-* represents the Old High German prefix *gi-*, *ge-*. *Cf.* Eng. *luck* and Ger. *Glück*.

joint-doll. Sewel's *Dutch Dict.* (1766) has *leeman*, or *ledeman*, "a statue, with pliant limbs for the use of a painter." A *footpad* is not a rubber-soled highwayman, but a *pad*, or robber, who does his work on foot. He was also called a *padder*—

"'Ye crack-rope *padder*, born beggar, and bred thief!' replied the hag." (*Heart of Midlothian*, Ch. 29.)

i.e., one who takes to the "road," from Du. *pad*, path. *Pad*, an ambling nag, a "roadster," is the same word.

Pen comes, through Old French, from Lat. *penna*, "a penne, quil, or fether" (Cooper), while *pencil* is from Old Fr. *pincel* (*pinceau*), a painter's brush, from Lat. *penicillus*, a little tail. The modern meaning of *pencil*, which still meant painter's brush in the 18th century, is due to association with *pen*. The older sense survives in optics and in the expression "pencilled eyebrows." The *ferrule* of a walking-stick is a distinct word from *ferule*, an aid to education. The latter is Lat. *ferula*, "an herbe like big fenell, and maye be called fenell giant. Also a rodde, sticke, or paulmer, wherewith children are striken and corrected in schooles; a cane, a reede, a walking staffe" (Cooper). *Ferrule* is a perversion of earlier *virrel*, *virrol*, Fr. *virole*, "an iron ring put about the end of a staffe, etc., to strengthen it, and keep it from riving" (Cotgrave).

The modern meaning of *pester* is due to a wrong association with *pest*. Its earlier meaning is to hamper or entangle—

"Confined and *pestered* in this pinfold here."

(*Comus*, l. 7.)

It was formerly *impester*, from Old Fr. *empestrer* (*empêtrer*), "to *pester*, intricate, intangle, trouble, incumber" (Cotgrave), originally to "hobble" a grazing horse with *pasterns*, or shackles (see *pastern*, p. 76).

Mosaic work is not connected with *Moses*, but with the *muses* and *museum*. It comes, through French, from Ital. *mosaico*, "a kinde of curious stone worke, of divers colours, checkie worke" (Florio), which is Vulgar Lat. *musaicum opus*. *Sorrow* and *sorry* are quite unrelated. *Sorrow* is from Anglo-Sax. *sorg, sorh,* cognate with Ger. *Sorge,* anxiety. *Sorry,* Mid. Eng. *sori,* is a derivative of *sore,* cognate with Ger. *sehr,* very, lit. "painfully"; *cf.* English "*sore* afraid," or the modern "*awfully* nice," which is in South Germany *arg nett,* "*vexatiously* nice."

It is probable that *vagabond,* Lat. *vagabundus,* has no etymological connection with *vagrant,* which appears to come from Old Fr. *waucrant,* present participle of *waucrer,* a common verb in the Picard dialect, perhaps related to Eng. *walk.* Cotgrave spells it *vaucrer,* "to range, roame, vagary, wander, idly (idle) it up and down." Cotgrave also attributes to it the special meaning of a ship sailing "whither wind and tide will carry it," the precise sense in which it is used in the 13th-century romance of *Aucassin et Nicolette.*

Other examples of mistaken association are *scullion* and *scullery* (p. 43), and *sentry* and *sentinel* (p. 102). Many years ago *Punch* had a picture by Du Maurier called the "*Vikings* of Whitby," followed by a companion picture, the "*Viqueens.*" The word is not *vi-king* but *vik-ing,* the first syllable probably representing an Old Norse form of Anglo-Sax. *wīc,* encampment.

CHAPTER XII

FAMILY NAMES

IN the study of family names we come across very much the same phenomena as in dealing with other words. They are subject to the same phonetic accidents and to the distortions of folk-etymology, being "altered strangely to significative words by the common sort, who desire to make all to be significative" (Camden, *Remains concerning Britain*). Doublets and homonyms are of frequent occurrence, and the origin of some names is obscured by the well-meaning efforts of early philologists. It might be expected that a family name would by its very nature tend to preserve its original form. This is, however, not the case. In old parish registers one often finds on one page two or three different spellings for the same name, and there are said to be a hundred and thirty variants of *Mainwaring*.[1] The telescoped pronunciation of long names such as Cholmondeley, Daventry, Marjoribanks, Strachan, is a familiar phenomenon, and very often the shorter form persists separately, *e.g.*, *Posnett* and *Poslett* occur often in Westmoreland for *Postlethwaite; Beecham* exists by the side of *Beauchamp; Saint Clair* and *Saint Maur* are usually reduced to *Sinclair* and *Seymour;*

[1] This is probably the record for a proper name, but does not by any means equal that of the word *cushion*, of the plural of which about four hundred variants are found in old wills and inventories.

Boon[1] and *Moon* disguise the aristocratic *Bohun* and *Mohun*. In a story by Mr Wells, *Miss Winchelsea's Heart*, the name *Snooks* is gradually improved to *Sevenoaks*, from which in all probability it originally came, via *Senoaks;* cf. *sennight* for *seven-night*, and such names as *Fiveash*, *Twelvetrees*, etc. Folk-etymology converts *Arblaster*, the cross-bowman, into *Alabaster*, *Thurgod* into *Thoroughgood*, and the Cornish *Hannibal* into *Honeyball*. *Beaufoy* is a grammatical monstrosity. Its older form is *Beaufou*, fine beech (see p. 129), with an ambiguous second syllable. *Malthus* looks like Latin, but is identical with *Malthouse*, just as *Bellows* is for *Bellhouse*, *Loftus* for *Lofthouse*, and *Bacchus*, fined for intoxication, Jan. 5, 1911, for *Bakehouse*. But many odd names which are often explained as corruptions may also have their face-value. The first *Gotobed* was a sluggard, *Godbehere* was fond of this pious form of greeting, and *Goodbeer* purveyed sound liquor. With *Toogood*, perhaps ironical, we may compare Fr. *Troplong*, and with *Goodenough* a lady named *Belle-assez*, often mentioned in the Pipe Rolls. *Physick* occurs as a medieval nickname.

Family names fall into four great classes, which are, in descending order of size, local, baptismal, functional, and nicknames. But we have a great many homonyms, names capable of two or more explanations. Thus *Bell* may be for Fr. *le bel* or from a shop-sign, *Collet* a diminutive of *Nicholas* or an aphetic form of *acolyte*. *Dennis* is usually for *Dionysius*, but sometimes for *le Danois*, the Dane; *Gillott*, and all family names beginning with *Gill-*, may be from *Gillian* (see p. 46), or from Fr. *Guillaume*. A famous member of the latter family was *Guillotin*, the humanitarian doctor who urged the abolition of clumsy methods of decapita-

---

[1] Another origin of this name is Fr. *le bon*.

tion. His name is a double diminutive, like Fr. *diablotin*, goblin. *Leggatt* is a variant of *Lidgate*, swing gate, and of *Legate*. *Lovell* is an affectionate diminutive or is for Old Fr. *louvel*, little wolf. It was also in Mid. English a dog's name, hence the force of the rime—

> "The Rat (Ratcliffe), the Cat (Catesby), and *Lovell*, our dog,
> Rule all England under the Hog." (1484.)

It has a doublet *Lowell*. The name *Turney*, well known in Nottingham, is from the town of *Tournay*, or is aphetic for *attorney*. In the following paragraphs I generally give only one source for each name, but it should be understood that in many cases two or more are possible. The forms also vary.

Baptismal names often give surnames without any suffix. Sometimes these are slightly disguised, e.g., *Cobbett* (Cuthbert), *Garrett* (Gerard), *Hammond*, Fr. *Hamon* (Hamo), *Hibbert* (Hubert), *Jessop* (Joseph), *Neil* (Nigel), *Custance* (Constance); or they preserve a name no longer given baptismally, e.g., *Aldridge* (Alderic), *Bardell* (Bardolph), *Goodeve* (Godiva), *Goodlake* (Guthlac), *Goodrich* (Goderic), *Harvey*[1] (Hervey, Fr. *Hervé*), *Mayhew* (Old Fr. *Mahieu*, Matthew). With the help of diminutive suffixes we get *Atkin* (Adam), *Bodkin* (Baldwin), *Larkin* (Lawrence), *Perkin*, *Parkin* (Peter), *Hackett* (Haco), *Huggin*, *Hutchin*, *Hewett*, *Hewlett*, *Howitt* (Hugh), *Philpot* (Philip), *Tibbet* (Theobald or Isabella), *Tillet* (Matilda), *Wilmot* (William), *Wyatt* (Guy), *Gilbey*,

---

[1] "The last two centuries have seen the practice made popular of using surnames for baptismal names. Thus the late Bishop of Carlisle was Harvey Goodwin, although for several centuries Harvey has been obsolete as a personal name" (Bardsley). Camden already complains that "surnames of honourable and worshipful families are given now to mean men's children for christian names." Forty years ago there was hardly a more popular name than *Percy*, while at the present day the admonition, "Be'ave yerself, '*Oward*," is familiar to the attentive ear.

Gibbon (Gilbert), etc., with numerous variants and further derivatives. The changes that can be rung on one favourite name are bewildering, *e.g.*, from *Robert* we have *Rob*, *Dob*, *Hob*, and *Bob;* the first three with a numerous progeny, while *Bob*, now the favourite abbreviation, came into use too late to found a large dynasty. From *Richard* we have *Richards* and *Richardson*, and from its three abbreviations *Rick*, *Dick*, *Hick*, with their variants *Rich*, *Digg*, *Hig*, *Hitch*, one of the largest families of surnames in the language.[1] As the preceding examples show, family names are frequently derived from the mother. Other examples, which are not quite obvious, are *Betts* (Beatrice), *Sisson* (Cecilia), *Moxon* and *Padgett* (Margaret, Moggy, Madge, Padge), *Parnell* (Petronilla), *Ibbotson* (Ib, Isabella), *Tillotson* (Matilda). One group of surnames is derived from baptismal names given according to the season of the Church. Such are *Pentecost*, *Pascal*, whence Cornish *Pascoe*, *Nowell*, and *Middlemas*, a corruption of *Michaelmas*.[2] With these may be grouped *Loveday*, a day appointed for reconciliations.

Surnames derived from place of residence often contain a preposition, e.g., *Atwood*, *Underhill*, and sometimes the article as well, e.g., *Atterbury*, *Bythesea*. In *Surtees*, on the Tees, we have a French preposition and an English river name. Sometimes they preserve a word otherwise obsolete. *Barton*, a farmyard, originally a barley-field, has given its name to about thirty places in England, and thus, directly or indirectly, to

---

[1] It is even possible that *Hood*, *Hudson*, sometimes belong here, as *Hud* appears to have been used as a North Country alternative for Richard, though it is hard to see why. For proofs see BARDSLEY, *Dict. of English Surnames*, s.v. *Hudd*.

[2] Such a corruption, though difficult to explain phonetically, is not without example in uneducated or childish speech. Cf. *tiddlebat* or *tittlebat*, for *stickleback*. In *stickler* (p. 76) we have the opposite change.

many families. *Bristow* preserves what was once the regular pronunciation of *Bristol*. The famous north country name *Peel* means castle, as still in the Isle of Man. It is Old Fr. *pel* (*pal*), stake, and the name was originally given to a wooden hill-fort or stockade.

Many places which have given family names have themselves disappeared from the map, while others, now of great importance, are of too recent growth to have been used in this way. Many of our family names are taken from those of continental towns, especially French and Flemish. Camden says, " Neither is there any village in Normandy that gave not denomination to some family in England." Such are *Bullen* or *Boleyn* (Boulogne), *Cullen* (Cologne), *Challis* (Calais), *Challen* (Châlon), *Chaworth* (Cahors), *Bridges*[1] (Bruges), *Druce* (Dreux), *Gaunt* (*Gand*, Ghent), *Lubbock* (Lübeck), *Luck* (*Luick*, Liège), *Mann* (le Mans), *Malins* (*Malines*, Mechlin), *Nugent* (Nogent), *Hawtrey* (Hauterive), and *Dampier* (Dampierre). To decide which is the particular *Hauterive* or *Dampierre* in question is the work of the genealogist. *Dampierre* (*Dominus Petrus*) means *Saint Peter*. In some cases these names have been simplified, *e.g.*, Camden notes that *Conyers*, from *Coigniers*, lit. quince-trees, becomes *Quince*.

French provinces have given us *Burgoyne*, *Champain*. *Gascoyne* or *Gaskin*, and *Mayne*, and adjectives formed from names of countries, provinces and towns survive in *Allman* (*Allemand*), *Brabazon* (le *Brabançon*, the Brabanter), *Brett* (*le Bret* or *le Breton*[2]), *Pickard* (*le Picard*), *Poidevin*[3] (*le Poitevin*), *Mansell*, Old Fr. *Mancel* (*le Manceau*, inhabitant of Maine or le Mans), *Hanway*

---

[1] Of course also of English origin.

[2] Hence also the name *Britton*.

[3] Whence the perversion *Portwine*, examples of which occur in the *London Directory*.

and *Hannay* (*le Hannuyer*, the Hainaulter), *Loring*
(*le Lorrain*), assimilated to *Fleming*, *Champneys* (*le
Champenois*), with which we may compare *Cornwallis*,
from the Old French adjective *cornwaleis*, man of
Cornwall. To these may be added *Pollock*, which
occasionally means the Pole, or *Polack*—

> "Why then the *Polack* never will defend it."
>
> (*Hamlet*, iv. 4.)

Janaway, the Genoese, and *Haunce*, from the famous
Hanse confederation. *Morris* means sometimes *Moorish*
(see p. 49), and *Norris*, besides having the meaning
seen in its contracted form *nurse*, Fr. *nourrice*, may
stand for *le Noreis*, the Northener. We still have a
Norroy king-at-arms, lit. north king, who holds office
north of the Trent.

In some cases the territorial *de* remains, e.g.,
Dolman is sometimes the same as *Dalmain*, *d'Allemagne*,
Daubeney is *d'Aubigné*, *Danvers* is *d'Anvers* (Antwerp),
Devereux is *d'Évreux*, a town which takes its name
from the *Eburovices*, and *Disney* is *d'Isigny*. With these
may be mentioned *Dubberley*, Fr. *du Boulay*, of the
birch wood, and *Dawnay*, from Old Fr. *aunai*,[1] a
grove of alders. The last governor of the Bastille
was the Marquis de *Launay* (*l'aunai*). There is a large
group of such words in French, coming from Latin
collectives in *-etum*; *d'Aubray* is from Lat. *arbo-
retum*, and has given also the dissimilated form
Darblay, famous in English literature. Other examples
are *Chesney*, *Chaney*, etc., the oak-grove,[2] *Pomeroy*, the
apple-garden.

Names of French origin are particularly subject to

[1] Old Fr. *vernai*, whence our *Verney*, *Varney*, has the same meaning;
cf. *Duverney*, the name of a famous dancer. Old Fr. *verne*, alder, is of
Celtic origin.

[2] Cf. *Chenevix*, old oak, a name introduced by the Huguenots.

corruption and folk-etymology. We have the classic
example of Tess *Durbeyfield*.[1]   Camden, in his *Remains
concerning Britain*, gives, among other curious instances,
Troublefield for *Turberville*.   *Greenfield* is usually literal
(cf. *Whitfield*, *Whittaker*, *Greenacre*, etc.), but occasionally
for *Grenville*.   *Summerfield* is for *Somerville*.   The
notorious *Dangerfield* was of Norman ancestry, from
Angerville.   *Mullins* looks a very English name, but it
is from Fr. *moulin*, mill, as *Musters* is from Old Fr.
moustier, monastery.   *Phillimore* is a corruption of
Finnemore, Fr. *fin amour*.

When we come to names which indicate office or
trade, we have to distinguish between those that are
practically nicknames, such as *King*, *Duke*, *Bishop*,
Cæsar[2] (Julius Cæsar was a famous cricketer of the old
school), and those that are to be taken literally.   Many
callings now obsolete have left traces in our surnames.
The very common name *Chapman* reminds us that this
was once the general term for a dealer (see p. 67), one
who spends his time in *chaffering* or "*chopping* and
changing."   The *grocer*, or *engrosser*, *i.e.*, the man who
bought wholesale, Fr. *en gros*,[3] came too late to supplant
the family name *Spicer*.   *Bailey*, Old Fr. *bailif* (*bailli*),
represents all sorts of officials from a Scotch magistrate
to a man in possession.   *Bayliss* seems to be formed
from it like Williams from William.   *Chaucer*, Old Fr.

[1] Other examples quoted by Mr Hardy are *Priddle*, from *Paridelle*, and
Debbyhouse—"The *Debbyhouses* who now be carters were once the *de Bayeux*
family" (*Tess of the d'Urbervilles*, v. 35).

[2] These names are supposed to have been generally conferred in consequence of characters represented in public performances and processions. In
some cases they imply that the bearer was in the employment of the dignitary.
We find them in other languages, *e.g.*, Fr. *Leroy*, *Leduc*, *Lévêque*; Ger. *König*,
Herzog, *Bischof*. *Lévêque* has given Eng. *Levick*, *Vick*, and (Trotty) *Veck*.

[3] *Gross*, twelve dozen, seems to be of Germanic origin, the duodecimal
hundred, Ger. *Grosshundert*, being Norse or Gothic. But Ger. *Grosshundert*
means 120 only.

chaucier, now replaced by *chaussetier*, " a hosier, or hose-maker" (Cotgrave), is probably obsolete as an English surname.   Mr *Homer's* ancestors made helmets, Fr. *heaume*.   *Jenner* is for *engenour*, engineer (see *gin*, p. 65). In *Ferrier* traditional spelling seems to have triumphed over popular pronunciation (*farrier*), but the latter appears in *Farrar*.   Chaucer's *somonour* survives as *Sumner*.   *Ark* was once a general name for a bin, hence the name *Arkwright*.   Nottingham still has a Fletcher Gate, Lister Gate, and Pilcher Gate.   It is not surprising that the trade of the *fletcher*, Old Fr. *fleschier* (*Fléchier*), arrow-maker, should be obsolete.   The *Fletchers* have absorbed also the *fleshers*, *i.e.* butchers, which explains why they so greatly outnumber the *Bowyers* (see p. 178), *Boyers*, etc.   *Lister*, earlier *littester*, gave way to *dighester*, whence the name *Dexter*, well known in Nottingham, and this is now replaced by *dyer*.   A *Pilcher* made *pilches*, or mantles; *cf.* the cognate Fr. name *Pelissier*, a maker of *pelisses*.[1]   *Kiddier* was once equivalent to pedlar, from *kid*, a basket.   Sailors still speak of the bread-*kid*.   For the name *Wait*, see p. 76. The ancestor of the *Poyser* family made scales (*poises*), or was in charge of a public balance.   *Faulkner*, falconer, *Foster*, *Forster*, forester, and *Warner*, warrener, go together.   With the contraction of *Warner* we may compare *Marner*, mariner.   *Crowther* means fiddler. The obsolete *crowd*, a fiddle, is of Celtic origin.   It gave Old Fr. *rote*, the name of the instrument played by the medieval minstrels—

"Saxon minstrels and Welsh bards were extracting mistuned dirges from their harps, *crowds*, and *rotes*." (*Ivanhoe*, Ch. 41.)

Kemp is an old English word for warrior, champion.

---

[1] *Surplice*, Old Fr. *surpelis*, is a compound of the same word. It was worn " over fur " in unheated medieval churches.

It represents, like Ger. *kämpfen*, to fight, a very early loan from Lat. *campus*, in the sense of battle-field.

Pinder, the man in charge of the pound or pinfold, was the name of a famous wicket-keeper of the last century. The still more famous cricketing name of *Trumper* means one who blows the trump. Cf. *Horner* and *Corner*, which have, however, alternative origins, a maker of horn cups and a *coroner*[1] respectively. A dealer in *shalloon* (see p. 47) was a *Chaloner* or *Chawner*. *Parminter*, a tailor, is as obsolete as its Old French original *parmentier*, a maker of *parements*, deckings, from *parer*, Lat. *parare*, to prepare. A member of the *Parmentier* family popularised the cultivation of the potato in France just before the Revolution, hence *potage Parmentier*, potato soup. The *white tawer* still plies his trade, but is hardly recognisable in *Whittier*. *Massinger* is a corruption of *messenger*. The *Todhunter*, or fox-hunter, used to get twelve pence per fox-head from the parish warden. *Coltman* is simple, but *Runciman*, the man in charge of the *runcies* or *rouncies*, is less obvious. *Rouncy*, a nag, is a common word in Mid. English. It comes from Old Fr. *roncin* (*roussin*), and is probably a derivative of Ger. *Ross*, horse. The Spanish form is *rocin*, " a horse or jade " (Minsheu, 1623), whence Don Quixote's charger *Rocin-ante*, " a jade formerly."

A park keeper is no longer called a *Parker*, nor a maker of palings and palissades a *Palliser*. An English sea-king has immortalised the trade of the *Frobisher*, or furbisher, and a famous bishop bore the appropriate name of *Latimer*, for *Latiner*. With this we may compare *Lorimer*, for *loriner*, harness-maker, a derivative, through Old French, of Lat. *lorum*, " a thong of leather; a coller or other thing, wherewith beastes are bounden

---

[1] Another, and commoner, source of the name is from residence at a " corner."

or tyed; the reyne of a brydle" (Cooper). The *Loriners* still figure among the London City Livery Companies, as do also the *Bowyers*, *Broderers*, *Fletchers* (see p. 176), *Horners* (see p. 177), *Pattenmakers*, *Poulters* and *Upholders* (see p. 63). *Scriven*, Old Fr. *escrivain* (*écrivain*), is now usually extended to *Scrivener*. For *Cator* see p. 63. In some of the above cases the name may have descended from a female, as we have not usually a separate word for women carrying on trades generally practised by men. In French there is a feminine form for nearly every occupation, hence such names as *Labouchère*, the lady butcher, or the butcher's wife.

The meaning of occupative names is not always on the surface. It would, for instance, be rash to form hasty conclusions as to the pursuits of Richard *Kisser*, whose name occurs in medieval London records. He probably made *cuisses*,[1] thigh armour, Fr. *cuisse*, thigh, Lat. *coxa*. A *Barker* employed bark for tanning purposes. *Booker* is a doublet of *Butcher*. A *Cleaver* was, in most cases, a mace-bearer, Old Fr. *clavier* (*Clavier* is a common family name in France) from Lat. *clava*, a club. He may, however, have sometimes been a porter, as Old Fr. *clavier* also means key-bearer, Lat. *clavis*, a key. A *Croker*, or *Crocker*, sold *crocks*, *i.e.*, pottery. A *Lander*, or *Launder*, was a washer-man, Fr. *lavandier*. A *Sloper* made "slops," *i.e.*, loose upper garments, overalls. A *Reeder* or *Reader* thatched with reeds. A *Walker* walked, but within a circumscribed space. He was also called a *Fuller*, Fr. *fouler*, to trample, or a *Tucker*, from a verb which perhaps meant once to "tug" or "twitch." In the following passage some manuscripts have *toukere* for *walkere*—

"And his clothis ben maad schyninge and white ful moche as snow, and which maner clothis a *fullere*, or *walkere* of cloth, may not make white on erthe." (WYCLIF, *Mark*, ix. 2.)

[1] See quotation from *Henry IV*. (p. 155).

The fuller is still called *Walker* in Germany. *Banister* is a corruption of *balestier*, a cross-bow man; cf. *banister* for *baluster* (p. 60).

Some of the occupative names in *-ward* and *-herd* are rather deceptive. *Hayward* means hedge[1] guard. *Howard* is phonetically the Old French name Huard, but also often represents Hayward, Hereward, and the local Haworth, Howarth. For the social elevation of the *sty-ward*, see p. 90. *Durward* is door-ward. The simple *Ward*, replaced in its general sense by *warden*, *warder*, etc., is one of our commonest surnames. Similarly *Herd*, replaced by *herdsman*, is borne as a surname by one who, if he attains not to the first three, is usually held more honourable than the thirty. The hog-herd survives as *Hoggart*; *Seward* is sometimes for sow-herd; *Calvert* represents calf-herd, and *Stoddart* stot-herd, *i.e.*, bullock-herd :—

"'Shentlemans!' cried Andie, 'Shentlemans, ye hielant *stot!* If God would give ye the grace to see yersel' the way that ithers see ye, ye would throw your denner up.'" (*Catriona*, Ch. 15.)

Lambert is in some cases lamb-herd, and *Nutter* is in all probability a perversion of neat-herd, through the North Country and Scot. *nowt-herd*. It is a common surname in Lancashire, and Alice Nutter was one of the Lancashire Witches.

In a sense all personal names are nicknames (see p. 114), since they all give that additional information which enables us to distinguish one person from another. The practice of giving nicknames suggested by appearance, physique, or habits is common to the European languages; but, on the whole, our nicknames compare very unfavourably with those of savage nations. We cannot imagine an English swain calling his lady-love

[1] The obsolete *hay*, hedge, is also a common surname, *Hay*, *Haig*, *Haigh*, etc.

"Laughing Water." From Roman times onward,
European nicknames are in their general character
obvious and prosaic, and very many of them are
the reverse of complimentary. The most objection-
able have either disappeared,[1] or the original meaning has become so obscured as to cease to give
offence to the possessor. When a man had any
choice in the matter, he naturally preferred not
to perpetuate a grotesque name conferred on some
ancestor. Medieval names were conferred on the
individual, and did not become definitely hereditary
till the Reformation. In later times names could
only be changed by form of law. It is thus that
Bugg became *Norfolk Howard*, a considerable transformation inspired by a natural instinct to "avoid
the opinion of baseness," as Camden puts it. We
no longer connect *Gosse* with *goose*, nor *Pennefather*
with a miser. Cotgrave has *pinse-maille* (*pince-maille*),
"a pinch peny, scrape-good, nigard, miser, *penie-
father*." In *Purcell* we lose Old Fr. *pourcel* (*pourceau*),
little pig, *Fitch* no longer means a pole-cat, nor *Brock*
a badger. On the other hand, we generally regard
Gosling as a nickname, while it is more often a variant
of *Jocelyn*.

Names descriptive of appearance or habits often
correspond pretty closely with those that are found in
French. In some cases they are probably mere translations. Examples are: *Merryweather* (*Bontemps*),
Drinkwater (*Boileau*[2]), *Armstrong* (*Fortinbras*), *Lilywhite*

---

[1] The following occur in the index to Bardsley's *English Surnames*:—
Blackinthemouth, Blubber, Calvesmawe, Cleanhog, Crookbone, Damned-
Barebones, Drunkard, Felon, Greenhorn, Halfpenny, Hatechrist, Hogsflesh,
Killhog, Leper, Mad, Measle, Milksop, Outlaw, Peckcheese, Peppercorn,
Poorfish, Pudding, Ragman, Scorchbeef, Sourale, Sparewater, Sweatinbed,
Twopenny, Widehose. Some of these are still found.
[2] Cf. also Ital. *Bevilacqua*.

(*Blanchefleur*). Among colour names we have *Black,
Brown, White,* and *Grey,* but seem to miss *red.* The
explanation is that for this colour we have adopted
the Northern form *Reid* (*Read, Reed*), or such French
names as *Rudge* (*rouge*), *Rouse* (*roux*), *Russell* (*Rousseau*).
With the last of these, Old. Fr. *roussel,* cf. *Brunel* and
Morel. Fr. *blond* has given *Blount, Blunt,* and the
diminutive *Blundell,* which exist by the side of the fine
old English name *Fairfax,* from Mid. Eng. *fax,* hair.
Several other French adjectives has given us surnames,
e.g., *Boon* (*bon*), *Bonner* (*débonnaire*), *Grant* (*grand*),
Curtis (*courtois*), *Power* (*pauvre*), etc. *Payn* is the
French adjective *païen,* pagan, Lat. *paganus,* in early
use as a personal name.

But many apparent nicknames are products of folk-
etymology. *Coward* is for *cowherd, Salmon* for *Salomon,
Bone* for *Boon* (v.s.), *Dedman* is a corruption of *Deben-
ham. Playfair* means play-fellow, from an old word
connected with the verb to *fare,* to journey. *Patch* may
sometimes have meant a jester, from his parti-coloured
garments, but is more often a variant of *Pash, Pask,* a
baptismal name given to children christened at Easter,
Old Fr. *Pasque* (*Pâque*). Easter eggs are still called
pash, pace, or *paste* eggs in the north of England.
Blood is a Welsh name, son of *Lud ;* cf. *Bevan, Bowen,*
etc. *Coffin* is Fr. *Chauvin,* a derivative of Lat. *calvus,*
bald. It has a variant *Caffyn,* the name of a famous
cricketer. *Dance,* for Dans, is related to Daniel as Wills
is to William. In the same way *Pearce* comes from
Peter or Pierre. The older form of the name *Pearce*
was borne by the most famous of ploughmen, as it still
is by the most famous of soapmakers. Names such as
Bull, Peacock, Greenman, are sometimes from shop or
tavern signs. It is noteworthy that, as a surname, we
often find the old form *Pocock.* The *Green Man,* still

a common tavern sign, represented a kind of "wild man of the woods"; *cf.* the Ger. sign *Zum wilden Mann.*

In these remarks on surnames I have only tried to show in general terms how they come into existence, "hoping to incur no offence herein with any person, when I protest in all sincerity, that I purpose nothing less than to wrong any whosoever" (Camden). Many names are susceptible of alternative explanations, and it requires a genealogist, and generally some imagination, to decide to which particular source a given family can be traced. The two arguments sometimes drawn from armorial bearings and medieval Latin forms are worthless. Names existed before escutcheons and devices, and these are often mere puns, *e.g.*, the *Onslow* family, of local origin, from Onslow in Shropshire, has adopted the excellent motto *festina lente*, "on slow." The famous name *Sacheverell* is latinised as *De Saltu Capellæ*, of the kid's leap. This agrees with the oldest form *Sau-cheverell*, which is probably from a French place called Sault-Chevreuil du Tronchet (Manche). The fact that *Napier* of Merchiston had for his device *n'a pier*, no equal, does not make it any the less true that his ancestors were, like Perkin Warbeck's parents, "really, respectable people" (see p. 57).

Dr Brewer, in his *Dictionary of Phrase and Fable*, says of his own name—

"This name, which exists in France as Bruhière and Brugière, is not derived from the Saxon *briwan* (to brew), but the French *bruyère* (heath), and is about tantamount to the German *Plantagenet* (broom plant)."

A "German" Plantagenet should overawe even a Norfolk Howard. A more interesting identification, and a true one, is that of the name of the great engineer *Telford*, a corruption of *Telfer*, with *Taillefer*, the "iron cleaver."

A curious feature in nomenclature is the local character of some nicknames. We have an instance of this in the Notts name *Daft*[1]—

"A *Daft* might have played in the Notts County Eleven in 1273 as well as in 1886." (BARDSLEY.)

The only occurrence of the name in the Hundred Rolls for the year 1273 is in the county of Notts.

[1] This word has degenerated. It is a doublet of *deft*.

CHAPTER XIII

ETYMOLOGICAL FACT AND FICTION

ROMANCE and Germanic etymology dates from the middle of the 19th century, and is associated especially with the names of two great Germans, Friedrich Diez, who published his *Wörterbuch der romanischen Sprachen* in 1853, and Jakob Grimm, whose *Deutsches Wörterbuch* dates from 1852. These two men applied in their respective fields of investigation the principles of comparative philology, and reduced to a science what had previously been an amusement for the learned or the ignorant.

Men have always been fascinated by word-lore. The Greeks and Romans played with etymology in a somewhat metaphysical fashion, a famous example of which is the derivation of *lucus a non lucendo*. Medieval writers delight in giving amazing information as to the origin of the words they use. Their method, which may be called learned folk-etymology, consists in attempting to resolve an unfamiliar word into elements which give a possible interpretation of its meaning. Thus Philippe de Thaün, who wrote a kind of verse encyclopedia at the beginning of the 12th century, derives the French names of the days of the week as follows: *lundi*, day of light (*lumière*), *mardi*, day of toil or martyrdom (*martyre*), *mercredi*, day of market (*marché*), *jeudi*, day of joy (*joie*), *vendredi*, day of truth (*vérité*), *samedi*, day of sowing (*semence*). Here we perhaps have, not so much complete ignorance, as the desire to be edifying, which is characteristic of the medieval etymologists.

Playful or punning etymology also appears very early. Wace, whose *Roman de Rou* dates from about the middle of the 12th century, gives the correct origin of the word *Norman*—

> " Justez (*put*) ensemble *north* et *man*
> Et ensemble dites *northman*."

But he also records the libellous theory that *Normendie* comes from *north mendie* (begs). We cannot always say whether an early etymology is serious or not, but many theories which were undoubtedly meant for jokes have been quite innocently accepted by comparatively modern writers.[1]

The philologists of the Renaissance period were often very learned men, but they had no knowledge of the phonetic laws by which sound change is governed. Nor were they aware of the existence of Vulgar Latin, which is, to a much greater extent than classical Latin, the parent of the Romance languages. Sometimes a philologist had a pet theory which the facts were made to fit. Hellenists like Henri Estienne believed in the

---

[1] The following "etymologies" occur, in the same list with a number which are quite correct, in a 16th-century French author, Tabourot des Accords :—

Bonnet, de *bon* et *net*, pource que l'ornement de la teste doit estre tel.

Chapeau, quasi, *eschappe eau ;* aussi anciennement ne le souloit on porter que par les champs en temps de pluye.

Chemise, quasi, sur *chair mise*.

Velours, quasi, *velu ours*.

Galant, quasi, *gay allant*.

Menestrier, quasi, *meine estrier* des espousées.

Orgueil, quasi, *orde gueule*.

Noise, vient de *nois* (*noix*), qui font *noise* et bruit portées ensemble.

Parlement, pource qu'on y *parle et ment !*

Greek origin of the French language, and Périon even derived *maison* from the Gk. ὃικον (ὃικος, a house) by the simple method of prefixing an *m*. At other periods there have been Celtomaniacs, *i.e.*, scholars who insisted on the Celtic origin of French.

The first English etymological dictionary which aims at something like completeness is the *Guide into the Tongues* of John Minsheu, published in 1617. This attempts to deal not only with English, but with ten other languages. It contains a great deal of learning, much valuable information for the student of Tudor literature, and some amazing etymologies. "To *purloine*,[1] or get privily away," is, says Minsheu, "a metaphor from those that picke the fat of the *loines*." *Parmaceti*, a corruption of *spermaceti*—

> "And telling me, the sovereign'st thing on earth
> Was *parmaceti* for an inward bruise.
>
> (1 *Henry IV.*, i. 3.)

he derives from Parma, which has given its name to *parmesan* cheese. On the word *cockney*[2] he waxes anecdotic, always a fatal thing in an etymologist—

"*Cockney*, or *cockny*, applied only to one borne within the sound of Bow-bell, that is, within the City of London, which tearme came first out of this tale : That a cittizens sonne riding with his father out of London into the country, and being a novice and meerely ignorant how corne or cattell increased, asked, when he heard a horse *neigh*, what the horse did ; his father answered, the horse doth *neigh*; riding farther he heard a *cocke* crow, and said, doth the *cocke neigh* too ?"

Molière often makes fun of the etymologists of his time and has rather unfairly caricatured, as Vadius in

---

[1] Old Fr. *pourloignier*, to remove ; cf. *éloigner*.

[2] A very difficult word. Before it was applied to a Londoner it meant a milksop. It is thus used by Chaucer. Cooper renders *delicias facere*, "to play the wanton, to dally, to play the *cockney*." In this sense it corresponds to Fr. *acoquiné*, made into a *coquin*, "made tame, inward, familiar ; also, growne as lazy, sloathful, idle, as a beggar" (Cotgrave).

Les Femmes savantes, the great scholar Gilles Ménage, whose *Dictionnaire étymologique*, published in 1650, was long a standard work. Molière's mockery and the fantastic nature of some of Ménage's etymologies have combined to make him a butt for the ignorant, but it may be doubted whether any modern scholar, using the same implements, could have done better work. For Ménage the one source of the Romance languages was classical Latin, and every word had to be traced to a Latin word of suitable form or sense. Thus Fr. *haricot*[1] is connected by him with Lat. *faba*, a bean, *via* the conjectural " forms " **fabarius*, **fabaricus*, **fabaricotus*, **faricotus*, **haricotus*, a method to which no problem is insoluble.[2] He suggests that Fr. *geindre*, or *gindre*,[3] baker's man, comes from Lat. *gener*, son-in-law, because the baker's man always marries the baker's daughter ; but this practice, common though it may be, is not of sufficiently unfailing regularity to constitute a philological law. Perhaps his greatest achievement was the derivation of Span. *alfana*,[4] a mare, from Lat. *equus*, a horse, which inspired a well-known epigram—

> " *Alfana* vient d'*equus*, sans doute,
> Mais il faut avouer aussi
> Qu'en venant de là jusqu'ici
> Il a bien changé sur la route."

These examples show that respect for Ménage need not prevent his work from being a source of innocent merriment. But the above epigram loses some of

---

[1] Thought to be a Mexican word.

[2] " Sache que le mot *galant homme* vient d'*élégant ;* prenant le *g* et l'*a* de la dernière syllabe, cela fait *ga*, et puis prenant *l*, ajoutant un *a* et les deux dernières lettres, cela fait *galant*, et puis ajoutant *homme*, cela fait *galant homme*." (Molière, *Jalousie du Barbouillé*, scène 2.)

[3] Old Fr. *joindre*, Lat. *junior*.

[4] Of Arabic origin.

its point for modern philologists, to whom equations that look equally fantastic, *e.g.* Eng. *wheel* and Gk. κύκλος,[1] are matters of elementary knowledge. On the other hand, a close resemblance between words of languages that are not nearly related is proof presumptive, and almost positive, that the words are quite unconnected. The resemblance between Eng. *nut* and Ger. *Nuss* is the resemblance of first cousins, but the resemblance of both to Lat. *nux* is accidental. Even in the case of languages that are near akin, it is not safe to jump to conclusions. The Greek cousin of Lat. *deus* is not θεός, God, but Ζεύς, Jupiter.

An etymology that has anything to do with a person or an anecdote is to be regarded with suspicion. For both we want contemporary evidence, and, in the case of an anecdote, we never, to the best of my knowledge, get it. In Chapter III. are a number of instances of words formed according to authentic evidence from names of persons. But the old-fashioned etymologist will not be denied his little story. Thus, in explanation of *spencer* (p. 40), I find in a manual of popular information of the last century,[2] that—

" His Lordship, when Lord-lieutenant of Ireland, being out a-hunting, had, in the act of leaping a fence, the misfortune to have one of the skirts of his coat torn off ; upon which his lordship tore off the other, observing, that to have but one left was like a pig with one ear ! Some inventive genius took the hint, and having made some of these half-coats, out of compliment to his lordship, gave them the significant cognomen of *Spencer !*"

[1] That is, they are both descended from the same Indo-Germanic original. Voltaire was thus, superficially, right when he described etymology as a science in which the vowels do not count at all and the consonants very little.

[2] *Pulleyn's Etymological Compendium*, 3rd ed., revised and improved by M. A. Thoms (Tegg & Co., 1853).

This is what Pooh-Bah calls "corroborative detail intended to give artistic verisimilitude to a bald and unconvincing narrative." From the same authority we learn that—

"*Hurly-burly*[1] is said to owe its origin to Hurleigh and Burleigh, two neighbouring families, that filled the country around them with contest and violence."

and that—

"The word *boh !* used to frighten children, was the name of Boh, a great general, the son of Odin, whose very appellation struck immediate panic in his enemies."[2]

The history of *chouse* exemplifies the same tendency. There is no doubt that it comes from a Turkish word meaning interpreter, spelt *chaus* in Hakluyt and *chiaus* by Ben Jonson. The borrowing is parallel to that of *cozen* (p. 110), interpreters having a reputation little superior to that of horse-dealers. But a century and a half after the introduction of the word we come across a circumstantial story of a Turkish *chiaus* who swindled some London merchants of a large sum in 1609, the year before Jonson used the word in the *Alchemist.* "Corroborative detail" again. The story may be true, but there is not an atom of evidence for it, and Skinner, who suggests the correct derivation in his *Etymologicon* (1671), does not mention it. Until contemporary evidence is adduced, the story must be regarded as one of those fables which have been invented in dozens by early etymologists, and which are perpetuated in popular works of reference. It is an article of faith in Yorkshire that the coarse material

[1] *Cf.* Fr. *hurluberlu,* which occurs in Rabelais, and in Rostand's *Cyrano de Bergerac.*

[2] *Tit-Bits,* which honoured the *Romance of Words* with a notice (8th June 1912), approvingly quoted these three "etymologies" as being seriously propounded by the author. This is dramatic justice.

called *mungo* owes its name to the inventor of the machine used in its fabrication, who, when it stuck at a first trial, exclaimed with resolution, " It *mun go*."

Many stories have been composed *après coup* to explain the American *hoodlum* and the Australian *larrikin*, which are both older than our *hooligan* (see p. 12). The origin of *hoodlum* is quite obscure. The story believed in Australia with regard to *larrikin* is that an Irish policeman, giving evidence of the arrest of a rough, explained that the accused was *a - larrikin'* (larking) in the street, and this was misunderstood by a reporter. But there appears to be not the slightest foundation for this story. The word is perhaps a diminutive of the common Irish name *Larry*, also immortalised in the stirring ballad—

" The night before *Larry* was stretched."

As I write, there is a correspondence going on in the Nottingham papers as to the origin of the nickname *Bendigo*, borne by a local bruiser and evangelist. According to one account, he was one of triplets, whom a jocular friend of the family nicknamed Shadrach, Meschach, and *Abed-Nego*, the last of which was the future celebrity. It is at any rate certain that his first challenge (*Bell's Life*, 1835) was signed " Abed-Nego of Nottingham." The rival theory is that, when he was playing in the streets and his father appeared in the offing, his companions used to warn him by crying " *Bendy go !* " This theory disregards the assertion of the " oldest inhabitant " that the great man was never called *Bendy*, and the fact, familiar to any observer of the local dialect, that, even if he had been so called, the form of warning would have been, " Look aht, Bendy, yer daddy's a-coomen."

In the Supplement to Littré there is an article on

domino, in which he points out that investigation must start from the phrase *faire domino* (see p. 102). He also quotes an absurd anecdote from a local magazine, which professes to come from a "vieille chronique." Littré naturally wants to know what chronicle. In Scheler's *Dictionnaire étymologique* (Brussels, 1888), it is "proved," by means of the same story elaborated, "que c'est là la véritable origine du mot dont nous parlons."

In Brewer's *Dictionary of Phrase and Fable*, s.v. *sirloin*, we read that "it is generally said that James I. or Charles II. knighted the loin of beef, but Henry VIII. had done so already." This sounds like a determination to get at the root of things, but does not go far enough. The word is found in the 15th century, and Fr. *surlonge*, from which it comes, in the 14th. It is compounded of *sur*, over, and *longe*, a derivative of Lat. *lumbus*, loin. The belief in the knightly origin of the *sirloin* was so strong that we find it playfully called the *baronet* (*Tom Jones*, iv. 10). Hence, no doubt, the name *baron* of beef for the double sirloin. *Tram* is persistently connected with a Mr *Outram*, who flourished about 1800. This is another case of intelligent anticipation, for the word is found in 1555. It means log or beam, and was probably first applied to a log-road laid across bad ground, what is called in America a "corduroy" road. On the other hand, the obvious and simple derivation of *beef-eater*, *i.e.* a man who is in the enviable position of being sure of his daily allowance,[1] has been obscured by the invention of an

---

[1] The following explanation, given in Miège's *French Dictionary* (1688), is perhaps not far wrong: "C'est ainsi qu'on appelle par dérision les *Yeomen of the Guard* dans la cour d'Angleterre, qui sont des gardes à peu près comme les cent Suisses en France. Et on leur donne ce nom-là, parce qu' à la cour ils ne vivent que de bœuf : par opposition à ces collèges d'Angleterre, où les écoliers ne mangent que du mouton."

imaginary Fr. *beaufetier, waiter at the side-board. Professor Skeat attributes the success of this myth to its inclusion in Mrs Markham's *History of England.* But the most indestructible of all these superstitions is connected with the word *cabal*. It comes from a Hebrew word meaning hidden mystery, and is found in the chief Romance languages. The word is of frequent occurrence in English long before the date of Charles II.'s acrostic ministry,[1] though its modern meaning has naturally been affected by this historic connection.

Even anecdotic etymologies accepted by the most cautious modern authorities do not always inspire complete confidence. *Martinet* is supposed to come from the name of a well-known French officer who re-organised the French infantry about 1670. But we find it used by Wycherley in 1676, about forty years before Martinet's death. Moreover this application of the name is unknown in French, which has, however, a word *martinet* meaning a kind of cat-o'-nine-tails. In English *martinet* means the leech-line of a sail, hence, possibly, rope's end, and Wycherley applies the term to a brutal sea-captain. The most renowned of carriers is probably Hobson, of Cambridge. He was sung by Milton, and bequeathed to the town Hobson's conduit which cleanses the Cambridge gutters. To him is also ascribed the phrase *Hobson's choice*, from his custom of refusing to let out his horses except in strict rotation. But we find a merchant venturer, living in Japan, using "*Hodgson's* choice" fourteen years before the

[1] An acrostic of this kind would have no point if it resulted in a meaningless word. In the same way the Old Fr. *Fauvel*, whence our *curry favour* (see p. 131), has a medieval explanation of the acrostic kind. It is supposed to be formed from the initial letters of the vices *Flatterie, Avarice, Vilenie, Variété, Envie, Lâcheté.*

carrier left this world and became a legendary figure—

"We are put to *Hodgson's choise* to take such previlegese as they will geve us, or else goe without." (*Correspondence of Richard Cocks*, Oct. 1617.)

The most obvious etymology needs to be proved up to the hilt, and the process is rich in surprises. *Cambridge* appears to be the *bridge* over the *Cam*. But the river's older name, which it preserves above the town, is the *Granta*, and Bede calls the town itself *Grantacester*. Camden, in his *Britannia* (trad. Holland, 1637), notes that the county was called "in the English Saxon" *Grentbrigseyre*, and comments on the double name of the river. Nor can he "easily beleeve that *Grant* was turned into *Cam;* for this might seeme a deflexion some what too hardly streined, wherein all the letters but one are quite swallowed up." *Grantabrigge* became, by dissimilation (see p. 57), *Gantabrigge, Cantabrigge* (cf. *Cantab*), *Cantbrigge*, and, by assimilation (see p. 56), *Cambridge*, the river being rechristened from the name of the town.

A *beggar* is not etymologically one who *begs*, or a *cadger* one who *cadges*. In each case the verb is evolved from the noun. About the year 1200 Lambert le *Bègue*, the Stammerer, is said to have founded a religious order in Belgium. The monks were called after him in medieval Latin *beghardi* and the nuns *beghinæ*. The Old Fr. *begard* passed into Anglo-French with the meaning of mendicant and gave our *beggar*. From *béguine* we get *biggin*, a sort of cap—

> "Sleep with it (the crown) now!
> Yet not so sound, and half so deeply sweet,
> As he, whose brow with homely *biggin* bound,
> Snores out the watch of night."
>
> (2 *Henry IV.*, iv. 4.)

Cadger, or rather its Scottish form *cadgear*, a pedlar, occurs

N

about one hundred and fifty years earlier than the verb to *cadge*. We find, noted as foreign words, in 16th-century Dutch, the words *cagie*, a basket carried on the back, and *cagiaerd*, one who carries such a basket. These must be of French origin, and come, like the obsolete Eng. *cadge*,[1] a panier, from *cage*, for the history of which see p. 109. *Cadger* is used in Scottish of an itinerant fish merchant with his goods carried in paniers by a pony—

> " Or die a *cadger* pownie's death,
>   At some dyke-back."
>   (BURNS, *Epistle to J. Lapraik.*)

Tobacco does not take its name from the island of Tobago, but from the native name of the tube through which the Caribs smoked it.

The traditional derivation of *vaunt* is from Fr. *vanter*, and this from a late Lat. *vanitare*, to talk emptily, used by St Augustine. This looks very simple, but the real history of these words is most complicated. In Mid. English we regularly find *avaunt*, which comes from Old Fr. *avanter*, to put forward, from *avant*, before. This gets mixed up during the Tudor period with another *vaunt* from Fr. *vanter*, to extol, the derivation of which can only be settled when its earliest form is ascertained. At present we find *venter* as early as *vanter*, and this would represent Lat. *venditare* (frequentative of *vendere*, to sell), to push one's goods, " to do anything before men to set forth himselfe and have a prayse ; to *vaunt* ; to crake ; to brag " (Cooper).

---

[1] There is also a word *cadge*, explained in the glossary to a book on falconry (1615) as a kind of frame on which an itinerant vendor of hawks carried his birds. But it is unrecorded in literature and labours under the suspicion of being a ghost-word. Its first occurrence, outside the dictionaries, is, I believe, in Mr Maurice Hewlett's *Song of Renny*—"the nominal service of a pair of gerfalcons yearly, in golden hoods, upon a golden *cadge*" (Ch. 1).

A sound etymology must fulfil three conditions. It must not violate the recognised laws of sound change. The development of meaning must be clearly traced. This must start from the earliest or fundamental sense of the word. It goes without saying that in modern corruptions we are sometimes faced by cases which it would be difficult to explain phonetically (see p. 136). There are, in fact, besides the general phonetic and semantic laws, a number of obscure and accidental influences at work which are not yet codified. As we have seen (p. 188), complete apparent dissimilarity of sound and sense need not prevent two words from being originally one[1]; but we have to trace them both back until dissimilarity becomes first similarity and then identity.

The word *peruse* meant originally to wear out, Old Fr. *par-user*. In the 16th century it means to sort or sift, especially herbs, and hence to scrutinise a document, etc. But between the earliest meaning and that of sifting there is a gap which no ingenuity can bridge, and, until this is done, we are not justified in regarding the modern *peruse* as identical with the earlier.[2]

The maxim of Jakob Grimm, "von den Wörtern zu den Sachen," is too often neglected. In dealing with

---

[1] This seems to have been realised by the author of the *Etymological Compendium* (see p. 188, *n.* 2), who tells us that the "term *swallow* is derived from the French *hirondelle*, signifying indiscriminately voracious, literally a marshy place, that absorbs or *swallows* what comes within its vortex."

[2] It is much more likely that it originated as a misunderstanding of *pervise*, to survey, look through, earlier printed *peruise*. We have a similar misunderstanding in the name *Alured*, for *Alvred*, i.e. *Alfred*. The influence of spelling upon sound is, especially in the case of words which are more often read than heard, greater than is generally realized. Most English people pronounce a *z* in names like *Dalziel*, *Mackenzie*, *Menzies*, etc., whereas this *z* is really a modern printer's substitution for an old symbol which had nearly the sound of *y* (*Dalyell*, etc.).

the etymology of a word which is the name of an object or of an action, we must first find out exactly what the original object looked like or how the original action was performed. The etymologist must either be an antiquary or must know where to go for sound antiquarian information. I will illustrate this by three words denoting objects used by medieval or Elizabethan fighting men.

A fencing *foil* is sometimes vaguely referred to the verb *foil*, to baffle, with which it has no connection. The Fr. *feuille*, leaf, is also invoked, and compared with Fr. *fleuret*, a foil, the idea being that the name was given to the " button " at the point. Now the earliest *foils* and *fleurets* were not buttoned ; first, because they were pointless, and secondly, because the point was not used in early fencing. It was not until gunpowder began to bring about the disuse of heavy armour that anybody ever dreamt of thrusting. The earliest fencing was hacking with sword and buckler, and the early *foil* was a rough sword-blade quite unlike the implement we now use. *Fleuret* meant in Old French a sword-blade not yet polished and hilted, and we find it used, as we do Eng. *foil*, of an apology for a sword carried by a gallant very much down at heel. As late as Cotgrave we find *floret*, " a foile ; a sword with the *edge* rebated." Therefore *foil* is the same as Fr. *feuille*,[1] which in Old French meant sword-blade, and is still used for the blade of a saw; but the name has nothing to do with what did not adorn the tip. It is natural that Fr. *feuille* should be applied, like Eng. *leaf*, *blade*, to any-thing flat (*cf.* Ger. *Blatt*, leaf), and we find in 16th-century Dutch the borrowed word *folie*, used in the three senses of leaf, metal plate, broadsword, which is conclusive.

[1] And therefore identical with the *foil* of *tinfoil*, *counterfoil*, etc.

We find frequent allusions in the 16th and 17th centuries to a weapon called a *petronel*, a flint-lock fire-arm intermediate in size between an arquebus and a pistol. It occurs several times in Scott—

> "'Twas then I fired my *petronel*,
> And Mortham, steed and rider, fell."
>
> (*Rokeby*, i. 19.)

On the strength of a French form, *poitrinal*, it has been connected with Fr. *poitrine*, chest, and various explanations are given. The earliest is that of the famous Huguenot surgeon Ambroise Paré, who speaks of the "mousquets *poitrinals*, que l'on ne couche en joue, à cause de leur calibre gros et court, mais qui se tirent *de la poitrine*." I cannot help thinking that, if the learned author had attempted this method of discharging an early firearm, his anatomical experience, wide as it was, would have been considerably enlarged. Minsheu (1617) describes a *petronell* as "a horseman's peece first used in the Pyrenean mountaines, which hanged them alwayes *at their breast*, readie to shoote, as they doe now at the horse's breast." This information is derived from Claude Fauchet, whose interesting *Antiquités françoises et gauloises* was published in 1579. Phillips, in his *New World of Words* (1678) tells us that this "kind of harquebuse, or horseman's piece, is so called, because it is to aim *at a horse's brest*, as it were *poictronel*." When we turn from fiction to fact, we find that the oldest French name was *pétrinal*, explained by Cotgrave as "a *petronell*, or horse-man's peece." It was occasionally corrupted, perhaps owing to the way in which the weapon was slung, into *poitrinal*. This corruption would be facilitated by the 16th-century pronunciation of *oi* (*peitrine*). The French word is borrowed either from Ital. *petronello*, *pietronello*, "a petronell" (Florio), or from Span. *pedreñal*, "a

petronall, a horse-man's peece, ita dict. quod *silice petra*
incenditur" (Minsheu, *Spanish Dictionary*, 1623). Thus
Minsheu knew the origin of the word, though he had
put the fiction in his earlier work. We find other forms
in Italian and Spanish, but they all go back to Ital.
pietra, *petra*, or Span. *piedra*, *pedra*, stone, flint. The
usual Spanish word for flint is *pedernal*. Our word, as
its form shows, came direct from Italian.[1] The new
weapon was named from its chief feature; *cf.* Ger.
Flinte, "a light gun, a hand-gun, pop-gun, arquebuss,
fire-arm, fusil or fusee"[2] (Ludwig). The substitution
of the flint-lock for the old match-lock brought about a
re-naming of European fire-arms, and, as this substitution was first effected in the cavalry, *petronel* acquired
the special meaning of horse-pistol. It is curious that,
while we find practically all the French and Italian fire-
arm names in 17th-century German, a natural result of
the Thirty Years' War, *petronel* does not appear to be
recorded. The reason is probably that the Germans
had their own name, viz., *Schnapphahn*, snap-cock, the
English form of which, *snaphaunce*, seems also to have
prevailed over *petronel*. Cotgrave has *arquebuse à fusil*,
"a *snaphaunce*," and explains *fusil* as "a fire-steele for a
tinder-box." This is medieval Lat. *focile*, from *focus*,
fire, etc.

The most general name for a helmet up to about
1450 was *basnet*, or *bacinet*. This, as its name implies
(see p. 156), was a basin-shaped steel cap worn by fighting men of all ranks. The knights and nobles wore it

---

[1] It is a diminutive of some word which appears to be unrecorded (*cf.*
Fr. *pistolet* for the obsolete *pistole*). Charles Reade, whose archæology is
very sound, makes Denys of Burgundy say, "*Petrone* nor harquebuss shall
ever put down Sir Arbalest" (*Cloister and Hearth*, Ch. 24); but I can
find no other authority for the word.

[2] *Fusee*, in this sense, occurs in *Robinson Crusoe*.

under their great ornamental helms.[1]   The *basnet* itself
was perfectly plain.   About the end of the 16th century
the usual English helmets were the *burgonet* and
morion.[2]   These were often very decorative, as may be
seen by a visit to any collection of old armour.   Spenser
speaks of a "guilt engraven *morion*" (*Faerie Queene*, vii.
7).   Between the basnet and these reigned the *salet* or
salade, on which Jack Cade puns execrably—

"Wherefore, on a brick wall have I climbed into this garden,
to see if I can eat grass, or pick a *sallet* another while, which is
not amiss to cool a man's stomach this hot weather.   And I think
this word *sallet* was born to do me good, for many a time, but for
a *sallet*, my brain-pan had been cleft with a brown-bill."

(2 *Henry VI.*, iv. 10.)

It comes, through Fr. *salade*, from Ital. *celata*, "a scull, a
helmet, a morion, a *sallat*, a headpiece" (Florio).   The
etymologists of the 17th century, familiar with the
appearance of "guilt engraven morions," connected it
with Lat. *cælare*, to engrave, and this derivation has
been repeated ever since without examination.   Now
in the Tower of London Armoury is a large collection
of *salets*, and these, with the exception of one or two
late German specimens from the ornate period, are
plain steel caps of the simplest form and design.   The
salet was, in fact, the *basnet* slightly modified, worn by
the rank and file of 15th-century armies, and probably,

---

[1] Over the tomb of the Black Prince in Canterbury Cathedral hangs
his cumbrous tilting helmet.   But the magnificent recumbent bronze effigy
below represents him in his fighting kit, basnet on head.

[2] *Burgonet*, Fr. *bourguignotte*, is supposed to mean *Burgundian* helmet.
The origin of *morion* is unknown, but its use by Scott in *Ivanhoe*—"I have
twice or thrice noticed the glance of a *morrion* from amongst the green
leaves." (Ch. 40)—is an anachronism by four centuries.   Both words are
used vaguely as general names for helmet.

like the *basnet*, worn under the knight's tilting helm. There is no Italian verb *celare*, to engrave, but there is a very common verb *celare*, to conceal. A steel cap was also called in Italian *secreta*, " a thinne steele cap, or close skull, worne under a hat " (Florio), and in Old French *segrette*, " an yron skull, or cap of fence " (Cotgrave). Both words are confirmed by Duez, who, in his *Italian-French Dictionary* (1660), has *secreta*, " une secrette, ou segrette, un morion, une bourguignotte, armure de teste pour les picquiers." Ergo, the *salet* belongs to Lat. *celare*, to hide, secrete.

We now *caulk* a ship by forcing oakum into the seams. Hence the verb to *caulk* is explained as coming from Mid. Eng. *cauken*, to tread, Old Fr. *cauquer*, *caucher*, Lat. *calcare*, from *calx*, heel. This makes the process somewhat acrobatic, although this is not, philologically, a very serious objection. But we *caulk* the ship or the seams, not the oakum. Primitive *caulking* consisted in plastering a wicker coracle with clay. The earliest *caulker* on record is Noah, who pitched[1] his ark within and without with pitch. In the Vulgate (*Genesis*, vi. 14), the *pitch* is called *bitumen* and the verb is *linere*, " to daub, besmear, etc." Next in chronological order comes the mother of Moses, who " took for him an ark of bulrushes, and daubed it with slime and with pitch " (*Exodus*, ii. 3), *bitumine ac pice* in the Vulgate. Bitumen, or mineral pitch, was regularly applied to this purpose, even by Elizabethan seamen. Failing this, anything sticky and unctuous was used, *e.g.*, clay or lime. *Lime* now means usually calcium oxide, but its original sense is anything viscous; *cf.* Ger. *Leim*, glue, and our bird-*lime*. The oldest example of the verb to *caulk* is about 1500. In

---

[1] See *pay* (p. 160). It will be found that all verbs of this nature are formed from the name of the substance applied.

Mid. English we find to *lime* used instead, *e.g.*, in reference to the ark—

> "Set and *limed* agen the flood" (c. 1250),

and—

> "*Lyme* it with cleye and pitche within and without." (Caxton, 1483.)

Our *caulk* is in medieval Latin *calcare*, and this represents a rare Latin verb *calicare*, to plaster with lime, from *calx*, lime. Almost every language which has a nautical vocabulary uses for our *caulk* a verb related to Fr. *calfater*. This is of Spanish or Portuguese origin. The Portuguese word is *calafetar*, from *cal*, lime, and *afeitar*, to put in order, trim, etc.

The readiness of lexicographers to copy from each other sometimes leads to ludicrous results. The origin of the word *curmudgeon* is quite unknown; but, when Dr Johnson was at work on his dictionary, he received from an unknown correspondent the suggestion that it was a corruption of Fr. *cœur méchant*, wicked heart. Accordingly we find in his dictionary, "It is a vitious manner of pronouncing *cœur méchant*, Fr. an unknown correspondent." John Ash, LL.D., who published a very complete dictionary in 1775, gives the derivation "from the French *cœur*, unknown, and *méchant*, a correspondent," an achievement which, says Todd, "will always excite both in foreigners and natives a harmless smile!"

It is thus that "ghost-words" come into existence. Every considerable English dictionary, from Spelman's *Glossarium* (1664) onward, has the entry *abacot*, "a cap of state, wrought up into the shape of two crowns, worn formerly by English kings." This "word" will no longer appear in dictionaries, the editor of the *New English*

Dictionary having laid this particular ghost.[1] *Abacot*
seems to be a misprint or misunderstanding for a *bicocket*,
a kind of horned head-dress. It corresponds to an Old Fr.
bicoquet and Span. *bicoquete*, cap, the derivation of which
is uncertain. Of somewhat later date is *brooch*, "a
painting all in one colour," which likewise occurs in all
dictionaries of the 18th and 19th centuries. This is
due to Miège (*French Dict.* 1688) misunderstanding
Cotgrave. There is a Fr. *camaïeu*, a derivative of
cameo, which has two meanings, viz., a cameo *brooch*, and
a monochrome painting with a cameo effect. Miège
appears to have taken the second meaning to be
explanatory of the first, hence his entry—*brooch*,
"camayeu, ouvrage de peinture qui n'est que d'une
couleur." In Manwayring's *Seaman's Dictionary* (1644),
the old word *carvel*, applied to a special build of ship, is
misprinted *carnell*, and this we find persisting, not only
in the compilations of such writers as Bailey, Ash, etc.,
but even in technical dictionaries of the 18th century
"by officers who serv'd several years at sea and land."
The Anglo-Saxon name for the kestrel (see p. 100) was
stangella, stone-yeller (*cf.* nightin*gale*), which appears
later as *stonegall* and *staniel*. In the 16th century we
find the curious spelling *steingall*, *e.g.*, Cooper explains
tinnunculus as "a kistrel, or a kastrell; a *steyngall*."
In Cotgrave we find it printed *fleingall*, a form which
recurs in several later dictionaries of the 17th century.
Hence, somewhere between Cooper and Cotgrave, an
ornithologist or lexicographer must have misprinted
fleingall for *ſteingall* by the common mistake of *fl* for *ſt*,
and the ghost-word persists into the 18th century.

The difficulty of the etymologist's task is exemplified
by the complete mystery which often enshrouds a word

[1] See letter by Dr Murray, afterwards Sir James Murray, in the
Athenæum, Feb. 4, 1884.

of comparatively recent appearance. A well-known example is the word *Huguenot*, for which fifteen different etymologies have been proposed. We first find it used in 1550, and by 1572 the French word-hunter Tabourot, generally known as des Accords, has quite a number of theories on the subject. He is worth quoting in full—

" De nostre temps ce mot de *Huguenots,* ou *Hucnots* s'est ainsi intronisé : quelque chose qu'ayent escrit quelques-uns, que ce mot vient *Gnosticis hæreticis qui luminibus extinctis sacra faciebant,* selon Crinit : ou bien du Roy Hugues Capet, ou de la porte de Hugon à Tours par laquelle ils sortoient pour aller à leur presche. Lors que les pretendus Reformez implorerent l'ayde des voix des Allemans, aussi bien que de leurs armees : les Protestans estans venus parler en leur faveur, devant Monsieur le Chancelier, en grande assemblee, le premier mot que profera celuy qui portoit le propos, fut, *Huc nos venimus :* Et apres estant pressé d'un reuthme (*rhume*, cold) il ne peut passer outre ; tellement que le second dit le mesme, *Huc nos venimus.* Et les courtisans presents qui n'entendoient pas telle prolation ; car selon la nostre ils prononcent *Houc nos venimous,* estimerent que ce fussent quelques gens ainsi nommez : et depuis surnommerent ceux de la Religion pretenduë reformee, *Hucnos :* en apres changeant *C* en *G, Hugnots,* et avec le temps on a allongé ce mot, et dit *Huguenots.* Et voylà la vraye source du mot, s'il n'y en a autre meilleure." [1]

The only serious etymology is Ger. *Eidgenoss,* oath companion, which agrees pretty well with the earliest recorded Swiss - French form, *eiguenot,* in Bonivard's *Chronique de Genève.*

The engineering term *culvert* first appears about 1800, and there is not the slightest clue to its origin. The victorious march of the ugly word *swank* has been one of the linguistic phenomena of recent years. There is a dialect word *swank*, to strut, which may be related

[1] The *Encyclopædia Britannica* does not imitate the wise reticence of Tabourot's saving clause, but pronounces authoritatively for the *porte de Hugon* fable

to the common Scottish word *swankie*, a strapping youth—

"I am told, young *swankie*, that you are roaming the world to seek your fortune." (*Monastery*, Ch. 24.)

But, in spite of the many conjectures, plausible or otherwise, which have been made, neither the etymology of *swank* nor its sudden inroad into the modern language are at present explained. The word *ogre*, first used by Perrault in his *Contes de Fées* (1697), has occasioned much grave and learned speculation. Perhaps the philologists of the future may theorise as sapiently as to the origin of *jabberwock* and *bandersnatch*.

INDEX

205

bilbo, 50
billiments, 66
Billingsgate, 48
billy-cock, 40
binnacle, 63
bird-lime, 200
Bishop, 175
biz, 67
black art, 130
blackguard, 84
Blood, 181
Blount, 181
bluff, 94, *n.*
Blundell, 181
blunderbuss, 127
Blunt, 181
Bob, 172
bobby, 45
bodice, 118
Bodkin, 171
boer, 84, *n.* 1
boîte, 127
Boleyn, 173
bombasine, 96
bombast, 96
bona-fide, 4
Bone, 181
bonfire, 151
bonhomme, 80
bonne femme, 80
Bonner, 181
bonus, 4
boojum, 16
book, 86
Booker, 178
boom, 17
Boon, 170, 181
boor, 84
boot and saddle, 129
bordereau, 93
borel, 73
boss, 20
boudoir, 75
boulevard, 121
boussole, 127
boutique, 114
bouvreuil, 33
bovril, 16
bowdlerise, 41
bower, 160
Bowery, 160, *n.* 2
bowie, 39
Bowser, 85, *n.*

Bowyer, 176
boycott, 41
Boyer, 176
Brabazon, 173
brand new, 107
brandy, 68
branks, 8
brasse, 87
Brazil, 51
breeches, 117
breeks, 117
Brett, 173
Brewer, 182
briar, 165
bridal, 121
Bridges, 173
brig, 67
brigantine, 67
brisk, 63, *n.* 2
Bristow, 173
Britton, 173, *n.* 2
Brock, 180
broderer, 178
broker, 150
bronze, 48
brooch, 151, 202
brose, 118
brougham, 39
Bruin, 36
Brunel, 181
buccaneer, 63, *n.*
Büchse, 127
Buchstabe, 86
buck, 150
Buckhurst Holt, 135
budget, 88
bugle, 69
Bull, 181
Bullen, 173
bulwark, 121
buncombe, 48
bungalow, 94, *n.*
bunkum, 48
burden, 157
bureau, 73
burgonet, 199
Burgoyne, 173
burke, 41
Bursche, 94
bus, 69
bushes, 127
butcher, 150
buttery, 165

chase, 143, 157
Chater, 143
chaton, 33
chattel, 143
Chaucer, 175
chauvin, 13
chawbuck, 26
Chawner, 177
Chaworth, 173
cheat, 84
check, 87, 120
cheer, 135
chelidonium, 30
chenapan, 55
Chenevix, 174, *n.* 2
chenille, 33
cheptel, 143
cheque, 89
chequer, 87
chercher, 57
cherry, 116
Chesney, 174
chess, 120
chesterfield, 40
cheval-de-frise, 47, *n.* I
chevalet, 39
chevaucher, 66
chewet, 37
chieftain, 139
chime, 8
Chinee, 116
chippendale, 40
Chipping, 67, *n.*
chit, 96
chore, 2
chortle, 16
chou, 153
choucroute, 129
chouse, 189
chuet, 37
chum, 94
churl, 84
cinch, 24
cinematograph, 11
cipher, 147
cit, 66
citizen, 122
Clark, 145
Claude, 45
claymore, 132
Cleaver, 178
clerk, 145
clothes-horse, 39

clove, 91
club, 78
cobalt, 44
Cobbett, 171
cobra, 26
cockney, 186
cocoa, 23
cocoa-nut, 23
coffer, 140
Coffin, 181
coffin, 140
cognovit, 4
colander, 154
Colas, 45
cole, 153
Collet, 170
colon, 6
colonel, 58
Coltman, 177
colza, 153
comadreja, 92
comma, 6
commère, 94
companion, 93, 165
compassion, 2
compère, 94
complex, 4
compound, 157
comptroller, 88
comrade, 94
connect, 105
constable, 89
contrôle, 88
controller, 88
Conyers, 173
coon, 64
cooper, 81, *n.*
coopering, 67
cordonnier, 128
cordwainer, 128
corne, 117
Corner, 177
Cornwall, 151
Cornwallis, 174
corp, 116
corsair, 22
costermonger, 63, *n.* I
couleuvre, 7
counterpane, 137
counterpoint, 137
court-card, 129
Coward, 181
coward, 36

O

jackass, 37
jackdaw, 37
jacket, 44
Janaway, 174
jaquette, 37
jarvey, 41
jaunty, 127
jean, 47
jemmy, 42
Jenner, 176
jenneting, 121
Jenny wren, 37
jeopardy, 108
jesses, 120
Jessop, 171
jest, 74
jilt, 46
jingo, 13
jockey, 45, 111
Johannisapfel, 121
jolis fous, 129
Jönköping, 67, *n.*
jonquil, 153
joss, 27
journeyman, 106, 165
jovial, 106
jug, 43
Juggins, 43, *n.*
jumble, 144
junket, 153
Jütte, 42

KAFIR, 26, *n.* 1
kail, 153
Kanzel, 88
Kapelle, 152
Kemp, 176
kennel, 158
kerseymere, 47
kestrel, 100
kickshaws, 116
Kiddier, 176
kidnap, 110
kilderkin, 21
kilt, 19
kimmer, 95
King, 175
kirtle, 150
Kisser, 178
kit, 149
kitcat, 42
kite, 38
kittle, 59

Kjöbenhavn, 67, *n.*
kjönne, 92
Klaus, 42
kloof, 91
knapsack, 18
knave, 55
Knecht, 84
knickerbockers, 44
knight, 84
Knoblauch, 91
Kohl, 153
kooi, 109
kraal, 25

LAAGER, 18
label, 93
Labouchère, 178
lace, 24
lacrosse, 164
lady-bird, 35
lady's bedstraw, 35
lady's garter, 35
lady's slipper, 35
Lambert, 179
Lambertsnuss, 35
lampoon, 9
lancegay, 25
Lander, 178
landier, 115
landscape, 18
Langlois, 115
lanterloo, 69
larboard, 121
larder, 165
lariat, 24, 115
Larkin, 171
larkspur, 29
Lärm, 115
larrikin, 12, 190
larum, 115
lasso, 24
lateen, 51
Latimer, 177
Launay, 174
Launder, 178
lavandière, 34
lawn, 47
lay-figure, 18, 166
leaguer, 18
leech, 155
legend, 3
Leggatt, 171
lemon, 160

P

PRINTED IN GREAT BRITAIN BY
OLIVER AND BOYD, EDINBURGH

By ERNEST WEEKLEY, M.A.

WORDS
ANCIENT AND MODERN

Second Impression.   5s. net.

A collection of "short stories" illustrating word-history.   The author has taken a number of English words whose origin, mode of introduction or sense-development is unusually interesting, and has written the record of their lives from the time of their first appearance down to the present day.   An attempt is made to solve the etymology of many words described by the Oxford Dictionary as "of obscure origin."   In other cases, widely accepted etymological superstitions are shown to be untenable. The author has tried throughout to adopt a method which may appeal equally to the professional philologist and to the educated amateur with a taste for word-lore.

"We cordially recommend to the discriminating reader a book altogether fresh, amusing and delightful."—*Morning Post.*

"Professor Weekley is a lively and amusing writer, with an immense magazine of information ; he is both amusing and informing."—*Daily News.*

"But talking about this delightful book is too apt to take the form of comparing notes ; one should rather acknowledge the richness of its entertainment."—*The Spectator.*

"The book would be a most acceptable gift to lovers of English, and it should be placed in the hands of all whom we wish to inspire with that love, for assuredly not even the laziest or most indifferent could be bored or repelled."—*Journal of Education.*

"A new book by Professor Weekley stirs one more than a new romance by any living author."—*The Daily Graphic.*

JOHN MURRAY, Albemarle Street, London, W. 1

A CONCISE ETYMOLOGICAL DICTIONARY OF MODERN ENGLISH

By ERNEST WEEKLEY, M.A.   7s. 6d. net.

This is an abridgment of the author's *Etymological Dictionary of Modern English* published in 1921. The process of abridgment has been carried out, not by omitting the less common words (for it is usually the uncommon word or the neologism that excites legitimate curiosity), but by making the explanations as brief as possible and by abstaining from the discussion of unsatisfying conjectures. It contains the whole of our literary and colloquial vocabulary, together with sufficient indications to show the origin of modern scientific terms. Account has been taken of what has been done in etymology in the last few years, and some of the statements in the larger book are corrected or modified. A number of new words of quite recent introduction are here for the first time "booked" and explained—*copec, fascist, insulin, mah-jongh, rodeo,* etc.

ORIGINAL EDITION.   Crown 4to.   Pp. xx+852.
£2, 2s. net.

"An amazing curiosity shop of the English language. There is not one of his pages which does not contain something to fascinate. It is not a dictionary as the ordinary man understands the word. It does not tell us how words are pronounced, nor does it even tell us, except occasionally, what they mean. Professor Weekley's task is much more interesting. He sets out to tell us how words came to mean what they do mean, and how they came to have their present forms. . . . He is at once lively and learned—a specialist on the roots of ancient speech and on the artificial blooms of the latest slang."—ROBERT LYND in *The Daily News.*

"It is as really and truly a book, with personality in every line of it, as Johnson's Dictionary."—E. B. OSBORNE in *The Morning Post.*

JOHN MURRAY, Albemarle Street, London, W.1

By ERNEST WEEKLEY, M.A.

SURNAMES

Second Edition. **6s.** *net.*

PROFESSOR WEEKLEY, in his earlier books, *The Romance of Words* and *The Romance of Names*, set a new fashion in dealing with the fascinating subject of the history of words. Packed with curious information set forth in an interesting way, they are attractive alike to the ordinary reader and to the student. His new book, *Surnames*, is written in a style which will appeal more particularly to those readers who wish to go more deeply into this fascinating study.

" Mr Weekley's very able book on surnames . . . is assured of a welcome, because we all like to know what our names imply and how they came to be what they are. Mr Weekley inspires confidence by his scholarly method of handling a subject which has been left, for the most part, to the amateur or the crank."—*The Spectator.*

" In his *Romance of Names*, published more than two years ago, Mr Ernest Weekley chose an alluring title to awaken interest in his favourite subject, the origins and history of English surnames. Now that he is sure of his public, and has found how much people will put up with when they are caught by the interest of a new hobby, he is able to extract, from the great dictionary of surnames he is preparing, a still larger mass of learned information, with the assurance that it will all be welcomed. . . . Mr Weekley has so artfully sprinkled his pages with odd and impossible names . . . that we simply cannot help reading him, and before long we fall under the fascination of this new collector's mania, and are in danger of becoming ourselves surname enthusiasts."—*The Times.*

" Readers of Prof. Weekley's fascinating books entitled *The Romance of Words* and *The Romance of Names* will hasten to possess themselves of the more elaborate work which he has now given to the world on the subject of surnames."—*Journal of Education.*

" Professor Weekley is well known to our readers as the most entertaining of living word-mongers. He is a man who makes the wilderness of the dictionary blossom like the rose. . . . The present book is a mine of curiosities and interest—a delightful volume to dip into."—*Daily News.*

LONDON : JOHN MURRAY, ALBEMARLE STREET, W.

By ERNEST WEEKLEY, M.A.

THE
ROMANCE OF NAMES

Third Edition. **6s**. *net.*

"Professor Ernest Weekley has a singularly happy knack of combining entertainment with erudition in the production of a popular book. He did so in *The Romance of Words*, and he has now written an equally delightful volume. Under his guidance a study of the origin and significance of surnames becomes full of fascination for the general reader."—*Truth.*

"Professor Weekley is one of those rare teachers who know how to make learning interesting. We welcomed his book on *The Romance of Words*, and we are equally glad to have its companion, *The Romance of Names*, which is at once entertaining and scholarly. It does not make the mistake of giving us too much."—*Athenæum.*

"For a thoroughgoing essay in iconoclasm, for a really turbulent, topsy-turvy wrecker of snobbery and puttings down of the social mighty from their seats, commend us to this well-written, witty, and erudite work of Mr Weekley. . . . The exceedingly witty and readable style which Mr Weekley adopts confronts one with the temptation of enjoying his book too keenly to criticise it from a scientific point of view. It is really a well-conceived and concisely written work, which must rank henceforth as an authority on its subject. It is learned and full of information."—*Outlook.*

"Mr Weekley has succeeded in writing a book that is scholarly, vastly entertaining, and that 'steers a clear course between a too learned and a too superficial treatment of the subject.' It is a book delightful to dip into, and from which the ordinary man may extract much enjoyment and much curious information."—*Birmingham Post*

LONDON : JOHN MURRAY, ALBEMARLE STREET, W.

Medium 8vo.　　　viii + 532 pages.　　　18s. net.

THE PLACE-NAMES OF ENGLAND AND WALES

BY THE

REV. JAMES B. JOHNSTON, M.A., B.D.

———————

THOUGH various monographs have appeared on the Place-Names of particular portions of England and Wales, this is the first attempt, so far as the author is aware, to deal with the subject as a whole.

" The last word must be of congratulation to the author, whose leisure hours have been spent to such good purpose ; he will not miss the reward due to his industry and judgment. There are over 5000 place-names explained, and the carping philologist can challenge only a few dozen derivations."—*Athenæum.*

" He shows the soundness of judgment essential in a study so full of obscurity and pitfalls, and his book is the best general guide yet published." —*The Times.*

" Shows a marked advance on earlier works of a similar character. . . . With him, however, his work has been a labour of love, and as the fruit of twenty years' research, he has given us what is undoubtedly the most complete and reliable dictionary of English place-names that has yet been published."—*Connoisseur.*

" This really valuable volume, a competent conspectus of a vast subject, is one more instance of the truth that the gleanings of the time of a really busy man are of more value than the full work of a learned dilettante who dawdles for years over a subject without leaving the world the richer. . . . We heartily recommend this admirably printed and really learned book."— *Contemporary Review.*

" The work as a whole is of undoubted value. It furnishes a conspectus of the subject and an epitome of data which all investigators are bound to take into account, and for which the author ought to, and will, receive well-deserved thanks."—*Celtic Review.*

———————

LONDON : JOHN MURRAY, ALBEMARLE STREET, W.

By HENRY CECIL WYLD,

Baines Professor of English Language and Philology in the University of Liverpool.

A SHORT HISTORY OF ENGLISH

This work is intended for those who wish to make a serious scientific study of the subject upon the lines of modern philological method. It should be of use to students of English in the Universities, and to teachers elsewhere who desire to know the results of recent research. 9s. net.

THE HISTORICAL STUDY OF THE MOTHER TONGUE

An Introduction to Philological Method.

The object of this book is to give, not a history of our language, but some indications of the point of view from which the history of a language should be studied, and of the principal points of method in such a study, and to prepare the way for the beginner to the study of at least some of the great writers. 9s. net.

THE GROWTH OF ENGLISH

An Elementary Account of the Present Form of our Language and its Development.

This book is intended for students in Secondary Schools and Training Colleges. The ground covered is approximately that required by the Board of Education in their Regulations for the Training of Teachers. 5s. net.

THE TEACHING OF READING IN TRAINING COLLEGES

This book is intended as a practical guide for those who have to teach Primary Teachers in Training how to read their own language. It contains a collection of extracts in prose and verse, suitable for reading aloud, transcribed into a simple phonetic notation. 3s. net.

STUDIES IN ENGLISH RHYMES FROM SURREY TO POPE

A Chapter in the History of English. 5s. net.

THE PLACE OF THE MOTHER TONGUE IN NATIONAL EDUCATION 1s. net.

LONDON : JOHN MURRAY, ALBEMARLE STREET, W.

THIN PAPER EDITION OF THE WORKS OF
ARTHUR CONAN DOYLE

First 18 Volumes.   Cloth, 3s. 6d. net ;   Leather, 5s. net each.

ADVENTURES OF SHERLOCK HOLMES.   Keenest thrills and mysteries *de luxe*.

MEMOIRS OF SHERLOCK HOLMES.   Thousands of his admirers will revel in these memoirs of the famous sleuth.

THE RETURN OF SHERLOCK HOLMES.   Again is Sherlock . Holmes triumphant !

HIS LAST BOW.   Some reminiscences of Sherlock Holmes. 'They are of the first vintage, sparkling, rich and very palatable.'—*Daily Graphic*.

THE VALLEY OF FEAR.   ' One of the most fascinating stories unravelled by Holmes.'—*Daily Graphic*.

THE HOUND OF THE BASKERVILLES.—A Curse, a Mystery ; at last the solution by Sherlock Holmes.

THE SIGN OF FOUR.   Who murdered Sholto ? Sherlock Holmes was roused to solve that problem—and solved it.

THE WHITE COMPANY.   What of the men ?   The men were bred in England : The bowmen—the yeomen —the lads of dale and fell.

SIR NIGEL.   A prelude to ' The White Company,' wherein the gallant Sir Nigel wins his spurs and his lady.

EXPLOITS OF BRIGADIER GERARD.   Intrepid, witty and always gay is the hero of these amazing exploits.

ADVENTURES OF GERARD.   With sword, imagination and wit, he served Romance—and the reader—well.

RODNEY STONE.   A gallant, stirring story of sport and sportsmen in olden times.

MICAH CLARKE.   A moving romance of the Monmouth Rising—of stirring gallantry and of proved appeal.

THE TRAGEDY OF THE ' KOROSKO.'

THE RUFUGEES.

TALES OF THE RING AND CAMP.

TALES OF PIRATES AND BLUE WATER.

TALES OF ADVENTURE AND MEDICAL LIFE

THIN PAPER EDITION OF THE WORKS OF
HENRY SETON MERRIMAN

With a Biographical Note in Volume One. Cloth, 3/6 net ;
Leather, 5/- net each. Cloth Case to contain the 14
Volumes, 5/- net.

THE SLAVE OF THE LAMP	RODEN'S CORNER
THE SOWERS	THE ISLE OF UNREST
FROM ONE GENERATION TO ANOTHER	THE VELVET GLOVE
	THE VULTURES
WITH EDGED TOOLS	BARLASCH OF THE GUARD
THE GREY LADY	TOMASO'S FORTUNE AND OTHER STORIES
FLOTSAM	
IN KEDAR'S TENTS	THE LAST HOPE

THIN PAPER EDITION OF THE WORKS OF
CHARLOTTE BRONTË and her
SISTERS EMILY and ANNE BRONTË

HAWORTH EDITION.   7 Volumes.   Introductions by
Mrs. HUMPHRY WARD. Cloth, 3/6 net ; Leather, 5/- net each.

JANE EYRE.   By CHARLOTTE BRONTË.

SHIRLEY.   By CHARLOTTE BRONTË.

VILLETTE.   By CHARLOTTE BRONTË.

THE PROFESSOR.   By CHARLOTTE BRONTË.—POEMS
by CHARLOTTE, EMILY, ANNE and PATRICK BRONTË.

WUTHERING HEIGHTS. By EMILY BRONTË.—AGNES
GREY. By ANNE BRONTË. With a Preface and Biographical Notice of both Authors by CHARLOTTE BRONTË.

THE TENANT OF WILDFELL HALL.   By ANNE
BRONTË.

THE LIFE OF CHARLOTTE BRONTË.   By Mrs
GASKELL. Introduction and Notes by CLEMENT K
SHORTER.

POEMS : Selections from the Poetry of Charlotte, Emily,
Anne and Branwell Brontë.   Including some Poems
hitherto unprinted.   Edited by ARTHUR C. BENSON.
With Portraits of the Sisters and two Facsimile MSS.
F'cap 8vo. 3/6 net.